Dream Quest

THOSE WHO HAVE INSIGHT WILL SHINE BRIGHTLY LIKE
THE BRIGHTNESS OF THE EXPANSE OF HEAVEN, AND
THOSE WHO LEAD THE MANY TO RIGHTEOUSNESS, LIKE
THE STARS FOREVER AND EVER.
(DANIEL 12:3 NASB)

Dream Interpretation: 8 Easy Steps

By

Vonda Brewer

Dream Quest

Dream Interpretation: 8 Easy Steps

Scripture quotations marked (NLT) are taken from the *Holy Bible*, New Living Translation, copyright © 1996, 2004, 2007. Used by permission of Tyndale House Publishers Inc., Carol Stream, Illinois 60188. All rights reserved.

"Scripture quotations from *THE MESSAGE*. Copyright © by Eugene H. Peterson 1993, 1994, 1995, 1996, 2000, 2001, 2002. Used by permission of NavPress Publishing Group."

Scripture quotations marked "NKJV™" are taken from the New King James Version®. Copyright © 1982 by Thomas Nelson, Inc. Used by permission. All rights reserved.

Thomas Nelson Publishers
Attn: Bible Rights and Permissions, P.O. Box 141000
Nashville, TN 37214-1000

"Scripture quotations taken from the New American Standard Bible®, Copyright © 1960, 1962, 1963, 1968, 1971, 1972, 1973, 1975, 1977, 1995 by The Lockman Foundation
Used by permission." (www.Lockman.org)

Unless otherwise indicated, all Scripture quotations are taken THE HOLY BIBLE, NEW INTERNATIONAL VERSION® , NIV®. Copyright © 1973, 1978, 1984 by International Bible Society. Used by permission of Zondervan Publishing House. All Rights Reserved

Dedication:

With my deepest gratitude, I really want to dedicate this book to my heavenly Father. I thank and praise you Lord, for giving me wonderful and godly parents who showed me the way to Christ at an early age and raised me in a loving Christian home. Thank you Lord for using Ken and Sue Hansen as an expression of your unconditional love! I love you Lord and I love you Mom and Dad!

To Clae Brewer, my faithful and loving husband, I honor you and thank you for being a wonderful reflection of our heavenly Father. You reflect Him with the expression of your love and kindness towards me. You have blessed me with your patience, provision, support, and sacrifice, therefore enabling me to happily pursue my God given destiny in serving God, especially in writing this book. I love and cherish you dearly for being you; but better yet, you're a better husband then I could have ever dreamed of receiving! I love you baby, from the inside out! And **YES**, you can take care of the kids!

Last but not least, I also honor, Herman Riffle for mentoring me in the beginning stages of my dream journey. You welcomed me into your home and allowed me to sit in your personal dream group for almost a year. You helped me immensely in understanding my dreams and the roles they play in my walk with the Lord. Without you and your wonderful friend, Bruce Sanders, who by the way wowed me with his ability to break down a dream; I may still be in the dark today! I praise the Lord that you both made yourselves available to me, concerning dream interpretation. I sincerely admire and thank you both!

Preface

The reason I'm writing this book is for the passion I have to teach the body of Christ, in hearing from God through understanding their dreams. I zealously share these insights with you because in the beginning when God gave me my first prophetic dream, somehow by His grace I understood what God was saying to me. I received the hope of His word by the revelation He showed me about my life, through a dream! Shortly after, I started having dreams that I didn't understand what the Lord was trying to show me. As I searched and searched for dream information from many reputable Christian dream authors, I became bewildered and confused. I wondered how in the world, would I ever be able to successfully apply all of this unfamiliar dream information. I really tried to apply their wisdom, but I struggled with understanding how I was to implement all of their great information and be correct in my interpretations. How could I know if I had the right interpretation or not? For a little over a year, learning how to interpret my dreams was difficult and very confusing. However, like anything, you know how the old saying goes, "practice makes perfect." But, the previous statement is only true, if you're practicing correctly! I've heard many false dream interpretations over the years, from many people who genuinely love God and do the best they can with the information they have gathered. Yet, they seriously struggle within the area of procedure, process, and application of interpreting their dreams. Many times this leads them into false interpretations. So, my friends, this book is for all the dreamers who desire to understand their dreams more thoroughly. Please understand that my heart goes out to you as you learn to apply these steps in your dream interpretational walk with the Holy Spirit.

For several years the idea of a book has been in my spirit. Now in Gods timing, He has laid on my heart to write this book and share it with you. Like me, God desires to bring spiritual edification and encouragement to you through dreams. He wants to share with you the secrets of His heart, concerning your personal relationship, friendship and God given calling in Christ Jesus. God bless you!

Contents

Introduction:

Chapter 1: My Testimony...1

Chapter 2: My Marriage Promise.......................................13

Chapter 3: My Dream Quest 19

Chapter 4:10 Key Principles...25

Chapter 5: Dream Symbols: 53
    Symbolic Scenes Streets, Evolving Symbols,
    People, One Person Many Hats, Celebrities:

Chapter 6: Dreams – Lucid Dreams....................................91

Chapter 7: Reflection Dreams...97

Chapter 8: Prophetic Dreams (4 Types)...........................131
    Reflective & Prophetic Combination,
    Night Visions, Wisdom and Knowing
    General Prophetic dreams

Chapter 9: Time Frames...187

Chapter 10: Evangelism through Dream Interpretation......199

Chapter 11: The Action & Feeling of the Dream.................209

Chapter 12: 8 Easy Steps: Dream Interpretation...............219

Chapter 13: Misapplication & Misinterpreting Dreams......251

Chapter 14: Devil Dreams? Not!.......................................261
    Troubling Dreams

Chapter 15: Closing thoughts...287

Introduction:

All may learn from this book. and my purpose in writing *Dream Quest*, is to help anyone that is interested in dreams; but, even more the mature dream student who has been striving unsuccessfully to interpret their dreams, but just can't seem to get it! Meaning, I am not starting from square one. My book is more geared towards the mature dream student Just so you know, this book is not meant to be a foundational book that teaches about the historical origins of dreams. Christendom already has many books that commence with the definition of a dream and then teach in depth about Joseph and Daniel, while taking you step by step through almost every single dream in the bible. Many of these books emphasize why dreams are not respected in the western culture; moreover, teaching in depth on the meaning of symbols, expounding on many colors, animals, numbers, metaphors, metonymies, and similes. So, if you feel you need a good foundational book on dreams and dream inter-pretation, then I highly recommend a wonderful book called, *"Dream Dreams"* by authors, Steve and Diane Bydeley. *Dream Dreams*, is a well-rounded dream interpretation book and it will truly bless you as you begin your personal dream quest. If you would like to purchase, *Dream Dreams*, you can order their book online from www.Lapstoneministries.org

Unlike other books, with the help of my 8 easy step dream interpretation formula, the goal of this book is to help coach you into a more successful stage of interpreting your dreams. If you've been trying for years to piece your dreams together, I believe this book will help you take what you already know and just be that one extra resource that finally, enables you to score a concise and accurate dream interpretation! I believe you will truly be amazed and blessed as you apply the principals within this book, and may God be glorified!

My 8 easy step process will condense and guide your dream interpretation efforts into an easy and systematic process. These concise steps will trim all of the excess fat of information concerning dream interpretation, its confusion, and help the dreamer to stay on track while interpreting their dreams. So, Dreamers, I invite you to come and join in with me as I share my testimony, dream experience, and many insightful lessons I learned on my hard but very fruitful, **Dream Quest.**

Dreamers Endorsements:

Usually, at the beginning of every book, the author has some "big wig" give them kudos about how knowledgeable the author is on the books subject matter they're writing about. However, I did not choose to go that route. Instead I decided to share the many responses from the dreamers that I have successfully assisted on my radio show over the years, by using these same 8 dream interpretation steps.

Ann from United Kingdom says..............

Hello Vonda, I Love your program, Your Awesome, WOW ! WOW ! WOW ! THANKS!!! So much of what you said, straight away rings crystal clear to me. You couldn't have known..... AMAZING!!! Your interpretation is so accurate, and so meaningful and such a blessing to me. Thank you, thank you, and thank you so very much. I am awestruck. May the Lord Jesus reward you for taking time to interpret my dream so beautifully. Love in Jesus!

La Donna from New York says........

Vonda, Oh my goodness that is it! Oh my goodness; oh my goodness. Yes Yes Yes - that's it. Again I say you pressed in again, for someone else; this is rare in Christendom. Thank you for your time and patience. The fruit of the Spirit is operating in your life, which is evident in speaking with you the few times we have spoken. Continue submitting yourself to God. Blessings to you!

Gail from North Carolina says,................

Hi, Vonda, thank you, I enjoyed every aspect both talking to you and finding out about my dream. I have a new prospective and from now on will make God the guiding force in my life. I feel like God has been speaking to me but, I wasn't able or open to realize what he was trying to get me to understand, so HE sent you to me. You are truly a blessing to many.....Your goodness and God's love beams through you. God bless and keep you; continue to do His work and grow.

Gwendolyn from Virginia says......

Hi Vonda, I listened to the program today while at work, Oh my God! I felt the power of God while you were praying for me, I nearly shouted at my desk. :)

Matthew from Georgia says.............

I'm listening to you interpret this woman's dream, and I really like how you are NOT giving this woman what she wants to hear (she was hoping you would give her a way out of her marriage), but instead you are giving her the truth about her marriage and her covenant (till death do you part), and how she must endure and press in on God. Awesome!

I have heard sooooo many dream interpreters and prophets "tickle" the ears, and exaggerate or give people what they want to hear, and you aren't about that :)

Erin in Texas says..........

Hello Vonda, I want to tell you how much this radio talk show has been a blessing in my life. The dream interpretation you helped me with in December has been so liberating. I've found that since we last spoke I am even aware of what my purpose is in life. God is so awesome.

I think that the Lord is using you in a mightier way then you are even aware of. I've come to realize that when the Lord speaks to us in dreams or through visions there is a purpose behind His messages. Not only is it the message He sends, but the revelation within the message. This is what is so powerful. My eyes were opened to this for the first time. May God bless everything you put your hands to and may His name be glorified.

Suzanne, from Canada says......
Vonda, I listened to a few in your archives, and I really like your style and sensitivity when dealing with people's personal issues, and I like the fact that you feel led to pray for them at the end. WHAT A MINISTRY! Your, Sis in Christ Suzanne

Juanita Woodard of Ohio says.....
Vonda, it was so nice talking to you! After talking to you and reflecting on things you said, I have a whole new outlook on interpreting my dreams. Like so many others, I was patching my dreams together from symbols in a book. It becomes much more personable and understandable when you factor in what your thoughts and activities were before you had the dream. In the past, when I had a dream, I'd spend a few days looking in my dreams books trying to patch the dream together. Most of the time, I went a way very confused. I'm looking forward to the dream courses you might offer!

Corhi from Africa says.....
Vonda, I tuned into your Radio show last night through the internet. What can I say? But, for the first time I realized that God speaks to me through my dreams; not only to intercede for others but, to minister to me. Listening to the Spirit of Truth communicating through you, His love and compassion manifest in your ministry. May God increase your gift to heal the body.

Betty Ann, from Nova Scotia, Canada…..
Hi Vonda, I took the link from Mark Virkler's …. website to listen to your radio show. What a great radio show! Your radio broadcast is a great example of it - live and interactive. Hope to find more archived programs. I'm eating up the 4 shows that are on the web. God bless you.

Straud from Kansas City, MO ………
Hi Vonda, I just wanted to let you know that God and you did an awesome job revealing what my dream meant. It was humbling and empowering. Thank you for showing me what my heart has been trying to show me. I can truly see God working in, and through, my wife. It has given me renewed strength in spiritual warfare. Praise God forever!

Darcy from Missouri says,… I am grateful to GOD for our conversation!! Thank you so much for submitting yourself to GOD and clearly being obedient to how he wants to use you to minister and bring healing to others!!

Tracy from Washington State says…..
I listen to your interpretation regarding a woman that was having a reoccurring dream about a demon possessing her. You did an awesome job explaining what salvation is and what means to be a Christian. You-go-girl!

Kathryn from Virginia says…..
I'm so excited I actually understand something……

La Shema, from Florida says…..
Hey Vonda, I just wanted to thank you for taking the time to speak with me, and honestly when I got off the phone with u I felt so light, like a weight had been lifted. And I just thank God for allowing me to meet you, and to receive a revelation. May GOD continue to use you, be blessed :o)

Chapter 1
My Testimony

I was saved when I was ten years old. I don't remember the exact day on the calendar, however I do remember the exact moment that my father took me in the living room and led me to the Lord. I remember my father saying to me, "now sweetie, you know that Jesus is the Lord and our Savior don't you"? I said, yes daddy! And then he said would you like to invite Jesus into your heart so you can go to Heaven? I said yes daddy and then we proceeded to say a prayer inviting Christ to be my Lord and Savior. At that moment I believed and receive Christ as my Lord and Savior and I had been adopted into the Kingdom of God. As many of you may be able to relate, I had received and been introduced to Christ, but sadly enough, I'm sorry to say that this was the extent of my relationship with Him until the time I turned twenty seven.

In those days, I lived on 3711 Peterson Street in Norfolk Virginia and my dad was an ordained minister at a small local non-denominational church down the street. The church was literally two blocks away and we walked to church every Wednesday night and Sunday. This ritual went on for about ten years after I got saved. During those years, I learned all of the books in the bible, bible stories and I could even quote a few memory verses. As I grew in age, my parents had tight reigns on my life and in the name of religion I was not allowed to wear pants because they believed that only men wore pants, nor I could not wear shorts because a man might lust after my legs; I could not go to the beach, because it was wrong to swim with the opposite sex, nor could I listen to any rock and roll music because it was not of God. Through this experience, these rules kept me from socializing with the most of the kids I knew, who were my own age and most of the children I knew possessed more freedom than I was accustomed too.

Throughout my youth I thought I knew God as well as anyone, after all wasn't I in the right place doing the right things and believing in the right God? Jesus was His name and I believed in Him! But I want you to know, other than saying grace at the dinner table once in a while and occasionally singing a solo in church, I can never remember one time when I prayed to God or read my bible by myself on my own accord. Sure, others had prayed with me, for me and around me, but past the initial act of salvation I did not have relationship with Jesus or the Holy Spirit for myself! The fact that I did not know God for myself was not a revelation to me until much later in my life at the age of twenty seven and that was when I desperately called out to God and soon became aware of my spiritual ignorance. This was when I realized my lack of really knowing God and the absence of true fellowship with Christ had allowed the devil to kick my butt! Up until that point, I had been on a long hard road and I was also beginning to experience suicidal thoughts and totally unaware that I had inevitably and deceptively been lured down a long miserable road of sin and brokenness, since the ripe age of eighteen. At the age of eighteen I was now out on my own and little did I know, I was in for a deadly ride.

On my own

At the time I moved out on my own, I was seemingly a spiritual girl, healthy and physically speaking, I was not too bad to look at! On the contrary, I was an attractive, green eyed, blonde haired, young woman who was 5 ft 7 inches tall and slender, with the whole world before me. Also, I had just finished beauty school and I was ready to take the Virginia State Board Cosmetology exam. After graduation, I happily moved away from 3711 Peterson St. and I thought yes sir, I was finally out! I could do now my own thing! Less then a month after graduating, I started my first hairdressing job and with the help of my mother I was able to rent a small duplex and now all was well and I was finally on my own.

I remember when I first moved out and I went over to visit my parents. I wouldn't wear pants or shorts around them for quite some time. I did this out of respect and for fear of disappointing them or letting them down. Nevertheless, this behavior only lasted for about a year before my parents soon discovered my "worldly path".

My first hair salon job lasted for about two years. During this time, I'd made new friends and boyfriends came and went. I'd met a new boyfriend, I'll call him Eric; Eric is not his real name, but that's what we'll call him in this book. At this point, my life was full of dancing, drinking and fornication; these were the early days on my road to destruction. Near the two year mark, there was a misunderstanding on my job and I soon found myself relieved of my duties. Quickly, I found another stylist job and I stayed with Eric, in an on and off again, doormat type of relationship for ten years.

After I started my new hair job, I was not making the money I needed in order to pay my bills. A girlfriend of mine told me about this night club she'd started waitressing at, in order to make some extra money. I was easily influenced, so I soon started working alongside of her. And before I knew it, I was working for people that put me in sleazy clothes, serving sleazy drinks to sleazy people and before too long, I was sleazy! Me the innocent, protected and good little Christian girl was hanging out in satan's backyard and loving every minute of it, except for the clothes! But, there was that still small voice inside of me that knew it just wasn't right, but I believed that it was the "same voice" that my parents had listened to all of those years. But at that time, I believed it was the voice of religious rules and regulations and I felt that they were way off and that the things I was doing were normal, fun things and before I knew it, this life style consumed me for 10 long years. I'd only been a waitress for about 2 weeks and soon my boss noticed that I loved the music and loved to dance to the music they played; I liked the music so much that I use to dance in the waitress area, while waiting to serve the drinks to the customers.

3

My boss liked this about me and because of my enthusiasm and love for the clubs "worldly music", before I knew it, I was quickly promoted and trained to be the next up and coming D.J. in this bar. The money was good and steady. So, I quit my hair dressing job and I grew at my new found profession and this became my main source of income for the next 10 years.

During this time and line of work, several men came and went; men that I had relationships with and with whom I liked, until one night I met Eric. As far as Eric goes, I started the relationship with a lie and told him that I was married because I wasn't sure that I wanted him to think that I was available for the long haul. There were several reasons I felt this way, but I'll keep them private. Soon and very soon, I realized that Eric was the love of my life and that I did want him around forever. So, I told him the truth and uncovered the lie, but it was too late for us because the foundational stage of deceit had already been laid. I discovered later, Eric had done more than his fair share of lying as well; at that time I believed we were only seeing each other. Then the drama began, as Eric dropped in and out of my life for about 10 years. He was here one month and gone for 3-5 months and before I knew it, Eric had somehow turned into my part time lover/boyfriend. We'd become on and off, mostly off; but I didn't know we were on and off until 9-11 months later in our relationship, when I'd found out that he already had an actual real girlfriend and to my surprise, I was his side girl. I was so devastated to find out that He was cheating on me the whole time I thought we were together. I was naive, ignorant, gullible, vulnerable and inexperienced in relation-ships and most of all just plain stupid; but I was already deeply in love with this man, deeper than any words could describe.

Eric had become my idol and my god and I was beyond help. At that point all I could do was hope that, as I patiently waited he would return and that the endurance of my wait would eventually pay off for me. Don't get me

4

wrong, when I found out that he was cheating I decided that I should shop around also, but in my heart I knew that I would never love another like I had loved him. And all the time I was shopping around, I always remained true and available to him in my heart, while in the end it turned out that I got crushed beyond, what any words could express. After this life shattering experience and the piercing of my soul, I lived in the past; I stayed hurt, broken and stagnant. For years I pined away and longed over and for the few wholesome months that we'd initially once shared.

My soul was severely crushed, depressed, broken and wounded beyond all hope; I lived hopelessly devoted to him, as I squandered the precious moments, hours, days, nights and years on the painful memories of a mere short term romance. The spirit of death hovered over me and my mind, while the years passed I longed for the day that the phone would ring, and to my satisfaction I would finally hear him beg me for my forgiveness and announce to me his sorrow and stupidity for leaving me. As I waited, I continually talked of him to my friends as if he were still mine and as if it were just a matter of time before he would return unto me. Meanwhile, I was deceived by fantasy as I lived vicariously through soap operas, dreaming of the day he would come back to me. I kept thinking, finally he would come back to me and be with only me and finally we would reunite forever as married soul mates that had finally made their way back home together. So, I faked my way through life trying to remain strong and appear as though I was normal, but my heart broke with each day that passed, until one day I hysterically realized that this day would never come. Unaware, I'd replaced one dream with another, all while the thief called depression had stolen my life. Depression had arrested and killed the purposes for my youth; my life was over, it was finished and I felt as though I could not go on without him! My heart was crushed and beyond broken when I cried out to the Lord! Soon, I realized Jesus heard me, answered me and He'd healed my broke heart! And now I rejoice in Jesus, the healer of my heart, and because of His love for me and His healing power, my life has never been the same! Christ is wonderful! There are many disgusting details that I could tell about the one, seemingly love of my life; details of his adultery, betrayal, hurt, deception and lies, but we were both guilty of wrongdoing. We both sinned against ourselves and others, but most importantly we sinned against God. It's an ugly and closed chapter in my life, in which God has so graciously forgiven me and I'm forever grateful to God for His grace and mercy in my life; and as a result, soon after my repentance it was a "New Day" for me!

A New Day

On July 7th 1995 I was sitting on my bed living vicariously thru my soap operas and in my heart day after day I was waiting and hoping for the phone to ring. I remember that out of the bitterness in my heart, in my frustration I spoke these words, **"God life has got to be better than this**"! As I took the Lord's name in vain like that, it's as if a light bulb went off in my head. And I thought of the Lord for the first time, it was the first time I ever really thought of Him on my own. It was at that moment that I got on my knees beside my bed and said this prayer out loud; I said, "Lord if you're up there and you can help me, please help me, amen." And little did I know that it was a "New Day" for me! The Lord had heard my prayer and before I knew it, He sent one lady across my path to invite me to come to her church and I went. Also, my mom had been inviting me to go to church with her, and even though I didn't want to go with her, it was during that time I felt as if there were something on the inside that reasoned with me; a knowing that I should be in church on Sundays. So, as the Holy Spirit continued to prompt me on and off, I did go to Calvary Revival Church of Norfolk, with my mother. After a while, I ended up loving it and this was where the Lord established me to learn more about Him, until September of 2006. During this time I learned about God and His Word, while having a fervent relationship with Him. As I continued to serve Him I soon developed the overwhelming desire to be great for God and greatly anticipated the Holy Spirit's plans and will for my life!

6

I'm assuming that most who are reading this book have already received Christ into their heart, which in turn gives you, as a child of God, the perfect right to hear supernaturally from the Holy Spirit, in the form of a dream or a vision. However, if you have not confessed Christ as your Lord and Savior, you do not have this right. But I want to encourage you that you can, so easily become His child just by accepting Christ as your Lord and Savior and have every benefit that God has to offer! If, you would like the opportunity to accept Christ, please know that He loves you dearly and invites you to come in to the Kingdom of God to become a part of His family today! When you accept Christ into your heart, your confession of accepting Him as Lord and Savior will transfer you from being a creature that God created, into being a family member and a child of God!

When, Jesus gives you His gift of Salvation and Eternal Life with Him, you then become a child of God and are "born again" into His family by His Holy Spirit. This action gives the Holy Spirit your permission to take up residence in your heart and it invites Him to speak to your inner spirit man in many ways. Moreover, you especially open the door to Him, so He can talk to you in the form of dreams and visions. So, if you would like to give God an open door to supernaturally speak to you, like He often does with His own children, then please take Jesus up on His offer, by receiving from Him and His free gift of Salvation. How do I do this, you ask? Well you do it by confessing Christ Jesus as the one and only Savior and Lord of your life. If, His free gift of salvation appeals to your heart then please read below and believe and receive Jesus today through the light of His Word. Relationship with God, through His one and only son Jesus, is the first step to opening up intimate communication with the Heavenly Father, while having supernatural access to the Spirit of God. God has literally amazed me, by showing me wonderful insights for my life through dreams!

5 Steps to Salvation

God's Word says:

1. <u>Romans 3:10</u> As it is written: "There is no one righteous, not even one;

What this verse is saying, Is that we all have sin in our lives and we all have done things that were wrong. And no one can measure up to God's standards of goodness. We all come up short!

2. <u>Romans 3:23</u> for all have sinned and fall short of the glory of God,

This means, God's penalty for sin and for us coming up short, is death; but the gift of receiving God's gift, which is the sacrificial death of Jesus and His righteousness, is eternal life!

3. <u>Romans 6:23</u> For the wages of sin is death, but the gift of God is eternal life in Christ Jesus our Lord.

God loves people so much that he allowed his one and only son Jesus to die and pay our death penalty so we would not have to die for our own wrongdoings. So whoever believes in him will have eternal life with Jesus, forever in Heaven.

"For God so loved the world that he gave his one and only Son, that whoever believes in him shall not perish but have eternal life. John 3:16

4. <u>Romans 10:9</u> That if you confess with your mouth, "Jesus is Lord," and believe in your heart that God raised him from the dead, you will be saved.

So, of you confess verbally that Jesus is Lord of all and truly believe it in your heart then you will be saved. It's that easy! Come on and say this small but life changing prayer! God's been waiting for you.

5. <u>Please pray (say) this prayer</u> out loud or quietly to receive salvation:

Dear Father: I realize that I was born into sin and therefore I am a sinner, so please forgive me. I know I should have died for my own wrong doings, but I choose to accept your free gift of Salvation by declaring that "Jesus is Lord". I believe in my heart that God has raised Him from the dead and I thank you that your Holy Word says I will be saved! Amen.

My friends, now that you're saved you are a temple of the Holy Spirit; God can now, by adopting you into the Kingdom of God, share with you the secret things He has in store for you. Isn't this so exciting? I'm excited for you! Because you are now His child and He longs to share His Word with you and reveal to you the secrets of His heart concerning your life. So, if you just accepted Christ as your Savior, look me up on Face book. Go to "**IN YOUR DREAMS**" dream posting page and share the good news with me. I would love to hear from you! So, now that you're saved, I highly recommended that you go to church! Take my word for it, you need to learn God's Word, it's a necessity! Learning His word is your first priority and it's of the utmost importance, because the Bible or the Word of God is infallible and it's always dependable! You need the Word of God as your guideline for truth, and you can never, go wrong by following His Word.

Finally, now that you are forgiven, saved and born again with His Holy Spirit living and breathing in you; you can now EXPECT the Holy Spirit to speak to you through this very important vein of dreams and visions! This is one of the many parts of your God given inheritance through Jesus Christ, our Lord!

Great for God

Like me, do you desire to hear from God supernaturally in the night; do you desire to be great for God? Well, if you do then you have the right book. This book is not to imply in any way, shape or form that I have arrived at my final destination. This is just a pit stop, so I can share with you how great God is and how great His desire is for us to know Him and be great for Him, in our lives! The intent of this book is to share a glimpse into the secret truths that God revealed to me, through dreams and visions about His desires, promises and will for my life. And if, He showed me things in a dream, He can and will show you His will for your life in a dream too. God loves you so dearly and He is no respecter of persons!

Just as God has shown me about His divine plans for my life, you can rest assured that there is a divine, wonderful and specific plan and purpose for your life. Choose to believe God when He says that we are made in the image of God, and because we are made like Him we have the potential to be GREAT! There is greatness in every person! God's word says that before the foundation of the world was laid that He formed us and knew us, while we were in our mother's womb.

So, it's through your salvation, obedience to God, and because of His agape love and wonderful faithfulness to His children, that we can be great for Him! Isn't it exciting to know that He can produce unlimited possibilities for His glory in our lives? For with man it is impossible, but with God all things are possible!

Please hear me when I say that greatness in God is not determined by jobs, money, status, educational degrees or by the outward appearance of a man. But, it is determined by our relationship with the Heavenly Father purchased by the blood of Jesus; as well as through our expressions of faith, hope and love towards the heart of God and man.

For Jesus said, "if you love me you will keep my command-ments" and believe me as you "love the Lord and follow God with all of your heart and with all of your soul" you will surely prosper and have good success!

Where ever you are and whatever you are doing, whether it's in your job, school, ministry, or family life, do it as if you were doing it unto the Lord! Meanwhile, as you continue to display your faith in action with a spirit of excellence, God will see you and show you His favor! Whether it is throughout the encouragement and praise of friends, family, co-workers, promotions, wealth, wisdom, influence, or fame; somehow, God will promote and use you for His sovereign plan. Only God knows why, and for what purpose we were created, so stay with Him and watch Him blow your mind! Believe and know that if you will humble yourself under His mighty hand that He will exalt you and reveal His plan to you in due time. Continue to trust God, and know that He will give to you, according to His will, your hearts greatest desires! God is very faithful to fulfill His word and He is no respecter of persons. So, hold on and get ready for the ride, because God is great and He has great things in store for you!

I would now like to share with you my first personal example, of a promise dream God gave me concerning my life. After a very long wait of asking and praying to the Lord about "when was my husband coming"? The Spirit of God finally revealed to me the time frame of when my husband would finally come. This prophetic dream encouraged me and revealed the will of God for my life, concerning marriage. Please know I wish you nothing but the best and I have great hope for you; moreover, I'm praying that God will reveal His desires for you to you.

Chapter 2
My Marriage Dream

A little history

After my recommitment to Christ in July of 1995, I continued to love God and grow in Him at Calvary Revival Church of Norfolk from 1996-2006. During my Christian growth at CRC, I learned that God, actually had prophets and that God could and would supernaturally speak through visions to guide His people. I'm telling you, when I learned that, I was wowed! By learning this, I had discovered some wonderful hope and became ignited to know the Lord God, in this new and fabulous way; but up until that point in my life, I had never heard that God <u>still</u> communicated to His people through dreams and especially visions. This new found revelation was very appealing to me because, in my past as an ignorant and underdeveloped Christian, I had started going to physics and mediums as a source of hope concerning my future. So, this was a very exciting revelation for me concerning God's ability and willingness to speak to His children in this way; and understanding God's ability to speak to me in this manner, brought great expectation, excitement, anticipation and comfort into my spiritual life!

In 1997, I became came a member of CRC and during this time, I willingly submitted myself to their leadership and served God with all of my heart, while I grew in the understanding of His love, faithfulness and purposes for my life. In addition to this, I also took many college courses in different topical areas of Christianity because I was very hungry to learn about God. Moreover, in those years of my spiritual walk at CRC, I had hoped and prayed that God would give me dreams and visions, just like He did with the prophets who had prophesied in my church.

Oh, how I longed to hear from God, because I really wanted to be married. So, I hoped, yearned, confessed and prayed so hard to hear from God in a dream or vision about my husband and with much faith, I patiently waited for a dream or vision; better yet I waited for my husband, by hoping he would soon come to me! However, the years came and went and I never received a vision much less a dream until eight years later.

Finally, the long awaited day had come, just when I was about to keel over from husband starvation, the message had finally arrived in a dream. On June 8, 2003, the Spirit of God within me gave me a dream of His plan and will for my life concerning my marriage! Finally, finally and did I say finally? God had spoken to me in a dream and I was wowed! This dream was the beginning of many other prophetic message dreams. But, for example I would now like to share with you my first prophetic **message dream**. And I pray that God will reveal His wonderful and blessed desires for you in dreams and visions as well! I remember this dream so clearly, just like it was yesterday. God imparted revelation, insight and hope when He revealed His perfect plan for my future through this dream in the night!

Dream 1- June 8, 2003: My Marriage Promise
A Prophetic Message Dream (see chapter 8)

In my dream, I was sitting on the front row at my church, just like I normally did in real life. In the dream a Prophet named Bobby Hill came up to me and laid his hands on my forehead and he spoke this prophetic message to me.

Bobby said, " For the Lord would say to you, that it will not be 10 years and it will not be 5 years, but I was in the final stretch of the race and that I should hold on, because I was almost there. And then he said, God wanted me to look around because I was not running this race by myself, but others were running the race with me.

14

Then I woke up and I said "wow Lord, I had a dream from you and that's great"! I was in awe and I then started to think about the wonderful dream God had finally given me! I finally had a BIG breakthrough and I knew exactly, what race the Lord was referring to in the dream. He was referring to the race that I was running in my single life, it was the race of holiness. I was just trying to remain holy and faithful to God in my singlehood walk and I wanted to make it to the finish line without messing up!

So, as I prayed about the dream, I said OK Lord you're telling me that it will not be 10 years and that it will not be 5 years, but that I would be married before or within 5 years. So, I started counting and it was almost June 10th which would have been my 37th birthday, and I thought "OK.... that puts me at about the age of 42, when I will get married. Then I said to myself, 42? "My Lord that's a long time and then I said to the Lord, well at least you finally told me something". I continued to talk to the Lord and said that I can't believe that I have to wait that long, but, if that's what you think is best then, I guess I don't really have a choice. So, I then prayed for the Lord to help me to be good for that long, because I was already struggling with the flesh. At the time there are 2 married men that I think I could have had some fun with and no one would have known. I'm sorry to say that my flesh and my mind contemplated, what if? Not in the sense that I wanted to sin against God or be a home wrecker, but if I'm honest I did think to myself that maybe, I could have my cake and eat it too and no one would ever know. You know the way we can think sometimes! Now, whether that was the enemy or just my flesh, I'll never quite know for sure, because in my heart I didn't really want to go against God. It's just that I was told, if I did things God's way that life would be better and He would bring me the husband that He had planned for me and that I would be better off for waiting. But, it never occurred to me that the wait would have been a total of **15 years**. After all, I had prayed my initial **"please help me"** prayer on July 7, 1995.

15

So, then I said "OK God, I guess I have to trust your judgment and whatever you have for me, you know best; but God, "just please help me to stay focused for the next 5 years." I prayed this, because I had already begun to lose sight, and I'd lost most of my vision for the future. I was beginning to cast off restraint and no longer were the old prophecies, which I had received through my church confirmation grounding me. After many years of serving God I'd seen no tangible or sexual evidence in reference to a spouse, of God's promises concerning His plan of greatness concerning my life. At this point, I was searching for direction and I had lost most of my zeal for the call of God. I thought to myself, that this Christian walk is not as good as the people of God had promised me that it would be; it was extremely hard and I was in a drought!

So this Word from the Lord encouraged me to press on and it gave me new hope. God had let me know that He had not forgotten about me and that all of this, as far as the timing of my marriage in my life was not an accident. He reminded me that before the foundation of the earth He had spoken plans concerning my life and that He was in control and that it was He who had written the script to my life and not me. Below are the symbols with their meanings to my dream.

The Symbolism: My Meanings

Bobby Hill: symbolic of a literal **TRUE** prophet.
Prophesying: Specific revelation, concerning a **time** from the Lord about the unknown future.
My church: was a literal place that I expected to hear God speak to me.
Running a race: A biblical metaphor.
Time: not 10 years and not 5: A literal promise of God's timing.

Do you see? The pastor in the dream was a person in real life, which I recognized as a prophet and he was a person who had the gifting and ability to speak a true Word from the Lord? That is why God chose him to present the Word of the Lord to me, in the dream.

When I had the dream I had a wonderful pastor, but my pastor did not believe in speaking a lot of personal prophecies into the audience, unless it was a corporate confirmation ceremony or something of that nature. He believed and taught us that usually when God prophesied in His Word, it was usually to a nation or to a leader of nation. So, that was why the Lord didn't use my pastor as the deliverer of His word to me, in my dream; because, my heart did not recognize my pastor as a prophet who would prophecy a personal prophecy to me in a crowd. So the Lord used Bobby, a person that I knew in real life, would present a personal Word from the Lord to an individual by the leading and prompting of the Holy Spirit.

So, in the dream Bobby Hill was symbolic, to me as someone who would give me a Spirit led Word from the Lord. The message in the dream was a Rhema Word, because it was a revelation from the Holy Spirit within me and it was prophetic in its nature, because it made me a prediction. Before the dream in my real waking daily life, my mind, when I was awake in the natural had no idea as to the time frame that the Lord would be sending my husband to me. So the dream revealed that it would not be 10 years and not 5 years, but that I was in the final stretch of the race and I would meet my husband to marry within five or less years.

My marriage dream was a prophetic message dream that brought me much hope, as well as correction. Hope, because it gave me a sure word to depend on, involving my future marriage and correction because it caused me to change my focus, of me constantly looking for my husband around every corner during that time. So, when I see what emotions the dream produced, I am confident that the Holy Spirit revealed His truth to me because the Holy Spirit does offer hope and correction to those who desire to hear the whole truth from Him.

Marriage Promised Fulfilled!

Today, as I'm writing this book, I'm extremely happy to tell you that I won the race and maintained a holy life unto the Lord and the Word of the Lord did come to pass **EXACTLY** when the Spirit of God said it would. I met my husband, Clae Brewer in the second week of March 2008, which was the fourth year; and we were happily married on August 8, 2008, which was 2 months into the fifth year. What a blessing from the Lord, for Him to share with me the divine timing, I would meet and marry my God fearing, anointed, amazing, generous, faith filled, strong, kind, loving, faithful, loyal, handsome and very wonderful husband!

Chapter 3
My Dream Quest

After receiving God's revelation in my "marriage dream," my dream quest had begun and I had many of what I like to call "**Reflection dreams**", in which we will explore in depth, later in chapter seven. The second major dream I had, was what I call a "**Night Vision**" dream. Night vision dreams are prophetic dreams in the night, while you are sleeping. And it's usually a glimpse of some picture or scene where you're looking at something that is playing out before you. When your night vision involves people, I have found that within a night vision dream, you can be watching the actual person in the dream or this person can be playing a part of yourself; meaning, you are watching someone that is symbolic of you, who is playing a part of who you are in real life. Or the dreams scene can be about other people, places or things. But, nevertheless night visions are usually shorter, simplified and more straight foreword then a reflection dream. Let me share with you a night vision dream, where I saw a young boy romping around in his wheel chair.

Dream 2: The boy and his wheel chair (Night vision dream)

In this dream I saw a young 6 or 7 year old boy wearing black rimmed glasses, and he was playfully thronging himself in and out of his wheel chair. Onetime he threw himself in the wheel chair so hard that he tumbled over in the chair. It was clear that he was playing and having fun at the wheel chairs expense!

The reason God showed me this night vision dream was because, the Sunday before as I was leaving church to go to my car, I noticed a handicapped boy in a wheel chair who was lethargic and disabled. So, led by the Spirit of God I asked the mother if I could pray for her son. She joyfully welcomed the prayer and joined in with me as we intensely prayed for him to be healed!

I'm telling you that this prayer was so intense that the earth could of shook! God was in it and it was powerful!

Boy and his wheel chair: (night visions, see pages 150 and 236)
NOTE: It's very important to know what is going on in your life at the time of a dream. This is a key factor and it will help you, in understanding the meaning of the dreams inter-pretation.

Dream Type: Night vision: I was not active in this night vision dream; I was just watching a little boy playing as he thronged himself in and out of a wheel chair.

My Interpretation: God was showing me that this little boy would overcome his handicap and at some point now or in the future he would no longer need the wheel chair as a crutch/vehicle to carry him from place to place; but that he had received his **healing** and was no longer bound and that he had turned or would turn his wheel chair into a toy!

So, when I saw this night vision dream, I recognized the boy as the boy I had just prayed for, the previous Sunday. So, God was showing me that the boy was or would become normal and that this boy had the victory over that wheel chair. God was confirming to me that the boy was, or would walk in his healing! The dream showed, God had healed the boy!

A little history
In my life, when I had this dream I had been taking some Christian college classes at a local Christian institution. It was a time in my life, when I was very new in learning about dreams. And even though I had a heart to learn and understand my dreams, I wasn't very knowledgeable in this area. The day after I had this dream, I interpreted it to the best of my ability and I was very excited about what God had showed me concerning this boy. But, because I was new at interpreting dreams, I decided to run this dream by one of my Christian college professors.

20

This professor operated in the prophetic and had been a pastor for many years. I knew he had experienced many visions in his walk with the Lord and that he had much wisdom, in several different areas of Christendom. So, during our class break, I spoke with him about the dream because I wanted to know what he thought about the dream, and see if he could confirm my interpretation. But, on the contrary to my surprise and bewilderment, I gasped as he shared with me his negative comments concerning my dream.

After I told him the dream, he commented this exact phrase. His exact words were, "Vonda, I think since you are a hairdresser, you have a very creative mind and this dream is just your creative mind working overtime." Can you believe that? I could hardly believe, he was actually saying that to me! I mean this was a well seasoned man of God! When I heard those words come out of his mouth, I was truly appalled and I know he had to of seen the look of utter horror and disbelief on my face, as he uttered those useless words to me. So, I walked away from him, extremely appalled and went back to my seat and from that moment on, I determined in my heart to learn all I could within the area of dream interpretation. I don't tell you this story to make him look bad, but it is what it is!

However, I do share this story with you to show you how God used this incident to spur me on, in my quest to understand dreams and their interpretations. It's amazing to me that most Christians can be so close to God in so many ways and yet miss God when He attempts to communicate with us through a dream. I mean biblically speaking it was one of His major methods of communicating with His people. It's a fact, time after time from Genesis to the testimony of Matthew, God communicated to His people in dreams, and our God is the same yesterday today and forever!

21

The bible says in Acts 2:17.

> "it shall come to pass in the last days, says God. That I will pour out of My Spirit on all flesh; Your sons and your daughters shall prophesy. Your young men shall see visions, Your old men shall dream dreams. Amen.

You know, each day that goes by, is the last day of the moment we are living in, so these are "The Last Days". So, knowing the truth of God's word that He still gives us dreams and visions, I know beyond a shadow of a doubt that God was showing me that the boy was healed or would be healed and live a normal life. And by our belief, faith, intercession and the blood of Jesus, this boy had the victory over that wheel chair! Sometimes it's just a matter of God's timing, but God was confirming to me that the boy was, or would walk in his divine healing! Jesus Christ still heals today by His blood that was shed for us, well over 2,000 years ago; praise God, what a night vision!

After the incident with my professor, God laid on my heart to go to the local Christian book store and purchase a book on dream interpretation. And to my surprise there was only one book on the shelf concerning dream interpretation; the book was called Dream Interpretation: A Biblical Understanding by Herman Riffel. So, I bought the book, read it and gained some valuable insight on dreams and interpretation. This was a good start, but it still felt like I needed more. I noticed in the back of his book that he had some other teaching resources available. So, I called the number in the back of the book and I really expected to get some big organization on the other end of the phone. But, I'm happy to say that this was not the case and to my surprise, I actually spoke with, in person Mr. Herman Riffel himself! We conversed for a few minutes and I ordered his work book and audio tapes on dream interpretation and as we spoke I asked him about the possibility of me attending one of his dream group workshops. He let me know that at 90 years of age, he rarely did them; but, if he was led to do a workshop, I would need to bring a group of 5-10 people. So, throughout my e-mails and conversations with him, he was led by God to make himself available to me and he invited me and my friends into his home to conduct a dream group workshop. This was amazing in itself, that 89-90 year old man, whose wife was bed ridden with Alzheimer's would open up his home to me, so I could learn about dream interpretation. Right away, I realized that this was a God thing and I jumped at the chance to seize this kairos moment!

Herman was not right around the corner; he lived four long hours away in Maryland. And after my first initial visit with him I asked him if he would consider mentoring me. He agreed and he opened up his door to me, for me to come and learn from him more often. So, throughout the next eight to nine months I drove from Virginia, up to Maryland and visited him about 2 to 3 times a month. He was a blessing to me and I learned much from him. I cannot express enough gratitude to him and his group for the "hands on help," given to me in the realm of dream interpretation from a biblical perspective. Regularly sitting in his personal dream group was the main equipping that I needed to be able to understand symbolism and how symbolism in a dream can parallel the activities of our daily lives. His group helped me immensely in my dream interpretation development. And even though later I learned some things on my own and from others, I do not believe that I would have mastered the area of understanding my dreams as well as I did, if I did not have his one on one personal training. So, I thank God for him! After my training with Herman, I came across some other Christian authors of dream interpretation and over time, I have discovered many key principles that I've incorporated into my interpretation skills. So, I thank God for them and for the additional principles God taught me, because learning and implementing these ten key principles will definitely make all the difference when you are trying to understand your dreams.

Chapter 4
10 KEY PRINCIPLES

When it comes to key principles of dream interpretation, in my own heart, I already believed and expected that God could and would speak to His children through a dream; and some things concerning dreams, I already knew just by reading and studying the Word of God. After all, it was by the enlightenment of the Holy Spirit that I'd already received a profound dream from God, and interpreted it correctly! However, like many I was under the understanding that in order for a person to be used in the realm of interpreting dreams, like Joseph and Daniel, I thought that they needed to walk in a "**Special Gifting**" from God. But, the Lord showed me in His word that it wasn't so much, about someone having the gifting; but that it was about His Spirit who gave them the gifting or the ability! So, in this chapter I will point out some key principles I learned from others, on my personal dream quest; and I will also share a few key principles the Holy Spirit impressed on my heart, along the way! Here are ten key principles every Christian dreamer should know.

Principle 1: All Christians Have "The Gift"

Daniel 1:3-6 (NKJV)
3. Then the king instructed Ashpenaz, the master of his eunuchs, to bring some of the children of Israel and some of the king's descendants and some of the nobles, 4 young men in whom there was no blemish, but good-looking, **gifted in all wisdom,** possessing knowledge and quick to understand, who had ability to serve in the king's palace, and whom they might teach the language and literature of the Chaldeans. 5 And the king appointed for them a daily provision of the king's delicacies and of the wine which he drank, and three years of training for them, so that at the end of that time they might serve before the king. 6 Now from among those of the sons of Judah were Daniel, Hananiah, Mishael, and Azariah.

Daniel 1:17 (NKJV)
As for these four young men, <u>God gave them knowledge</u>
<u>and skill</u> in all literature and wisdom; and <u>Daniel had under-</u>
<u>standing in all visions and dreams.</u>

Daniel 5:12 (NKJV)
"Inasmuch as an **excellent spirit**, knowledge, understanding,
interpreting dreams, solving riddles, and explaining enigmas
were found in this Daniel, whom the king named Belteshazzar, now let Daniel be called, and he will give the interpretation."

As I looked at these scriptures more closely, I could
see that two of the scriptures stated, these four young men
were gifted in all wisdom and Daniel was singled out as being
gifted in the area of understanding all visions and dreams.
However, the text shares that God was the One who gave
him the wisdom to do these things. So, I believe anyone who
is saved and filled with the Holy Spirit can walk in the same
wisdom of God and interpret dreams just like Daniel. Now,
I'm not saying that everyone is called into the governmental
office of dream interpretation like Daniel was, but I am saying
as the children of God who are now under a new and better
covenant, that we too can understand our dreams with the
help of the Holy Spirit, because He is the gifted one that lives
inside of us!

I will now share with you some of the "Key Principles" I
gleaned from sitting and learning under other reputable
Christian teachers within the Body of Christ. And since I am
NOT at liberty, to re-teach their copyrighted material, you
would need to purchase their books for their in depth
teaching, because I'm definitely not trying to re-invent the
wheel! ha ha… So, please feel free to be a blessing to them.

Principle 2: Dream Interpretation Can Be Learned

Shortly after my dream quest began, I learned from Herman Riffel that dream interpretation could be learned. He learned this, when he attended the Carl Jung Institution. And at the time I didn't know what he had scripturally to support his findings, but after learning this it became more and more evident in my life, the more I practiced with my dreams, I knew I didn't need this so called one of a kind "**special gifting.**" When Herman taught me dream interpretation could be learned, even though I didn't understand how? I just knew that what he taught me was working and it was true, just like he said! And before too long this principle, became a reality in my life and I'd learned to interpret some of my dreams.

Meanwhile, as I studied dream related scriptures for myself, I was thrilled to see that the Holy Spirit brought some things to my attention and showed me in and through His Word, that this principle was true! God showed me that it was not so much as about a person having the so called "gifting" to be able to interpret dreams; but, it was really about the **"ONE" who is the GIFT**, which is the Holy Spirit that was living in me, who gives me the ability to interpret the dreams! I praise God for that revelation from the Holy Spirit! God is good! Also, God showed me that many biblical patriarchs were able to interpret dreams. For example, in the book of Genesis, Abraham dreamt and understood what God said to him. Then Jacob had the dream of heavenly angels descending and ascending. And by this he understood that the place he laid his head and struggled with the Angel of the Lord, was as a portal in and out of Heaven and that the God of his forefathers was his source in life! Then most people are familiar with Joseph "The Dream Interpreter"; he was Jacob's eleventh son. Usually, Jacob doesn't really come to our minds when thinking of dream interpreters, but he too had a great understanding of dreams. If you read the scriptures closely you will see that not only did Jacob know what Joseph's dreams meant, but so did his brothers! They all knew how to interpret dreams. Check this out!

27

Genesis 37:5-8 (NKJV)

Now Joseph had a dream, and he told it to his brothers; and they hated him even more. So he said to them, "Please hear this dream which I have dreamed: There we were, binding sheaves in the field. Then behold, my sheaf arose and also stood upright; and indeed your sheaves stood all around and bowed down to my sheaf." And **his brothers** said to him, **"Shall you indeed reign over us? Or shall you indeed have dominion over us?"**

So, as you can see they hated him even more for his dreams and for his words because they knew what he was saying. They could definitely read a dream! Here is how his father responded when he heard and interpreted Joseph's dream.

Genesis 37:9-11 (NKJV) Then he dreamed still another dream and told it to his brothers, and said, "Look, I have dreamed another dream. And this time, the sun, the moon, and the eleven stars bowed down to me." So he told it to his father and his brothers; and **his father rebuked him and said to him, "What is this dream that you have dreamed? Shall your mother and I and your brothers indeed come to bow down to the earth before you?"** And his brothers envied him, **but his father kept the matter in mind.**

Once again, all twelve of them knew what Joseph was saying and it's obvious that they could definitely read and interpret his dream! Okay, continuing on with more of our patriarchal dream interpreters. Most Christians are familiar with Joseph "The Dream Interpreter," but later in the book of Judges we have Gideon who was from the tribe of **MANASSAH**. It just so happens that the tribes of Manasseh were descendants from Joseph's son Manasseh, and I don't believe this was a coincidence! I believe Joseph passed down a fear, reverence and a great respect for dreams and their interpretations. Scripture reveals that Gideon had a great understanding and respect, for the dream interpretation of the Midianite man, so much that he staked his life and the lives of others on that dream interpretation, as confirmation! Then as time progresses God raises up the prophet Daniel; he is one of the two major dream interpreters. Like Joseph, who learned from his forefathers, Daniel also learned the skill of dream interpretation. I hear your brain ticking, but yes it's true!

Daniel 1:3-6 (NKJV) Then the king instructed Ashpenaz, the master of his eunuchs, to bring some of the children of Israel and some of the king's descendants and some of the nobles, 4 young men in whom there was no blemish, but good-looking, gifted in all wisdom, possessing knowledge and quick to understand, who had ability to serve in the king's palace, **and whom they might teach the language and literature of the Chaldeans**. 5 And the king appointed for them a daily provision of the king's delicacies and of the wine which he drank, **and three years of training for them**, so that at the end of that time they might serve before the king. 6 Now from among those of the sons of Judah were Daniel, Hananiah, Mishael, and Azariah.

So, we can see that Daniel was schooled in Babylon by the Chaldeans for 3 years and he was trained in their language and literature, because he was being preparing for the King's service. But, please take note that we have no scriptural record of Daniel operating in any dream gifting or interpretation services, prior to Daniel 1:17. Actually, the text implies that the special insight came, while his schooling took place. The word says.

Daniel 1:17 (NLT); God gave these four young men an unusual aptitude for understanding every aspect of literature and wisdom. And God gave Daniel the **special ability** to interpret **the meanings of visions and dreams**.

The text implies, interpretation as something he became good at and known for, with the aid of Gods Spirit. Daniel became so, trusted at dream interpretation that he out ranked all of them! Before too long, he was known as the "**Chief Magician**."

How did Daniel learn? Well, he's in there learning everything the Babylonians were about and held dear to their hearts. He was learning things like, their culture, literature, symbols, astrology, sun gods and moon gods. Daniel, was right in the mix of all the magicians, soothsayers, diviners, sorcerers, and enchanters. But, the difference was, he did not operate out of a spirit of witchcraft; he operated by the Holy Spirit of God!

Daniel 5:11 (NKJV)
There is a man in your kingdom in whom [is] **the Spirit of the Holy God**. And in the days of your father, light and understanding and wisdom, like the wisdom of the gods, were found in him; and King Nebuchadnezzar your father—your father the king—made him **chief of the magicians**, astrologers, Chaldeans, [and] soothsayers.

So, we can see throughout the biblical ages that dream interpretation was highly regarded and passed down from parent to child and person to person. We can see that they desired, learned and maintained the ability to hear from God through their dreams. So, just like Daniel had the help of the Holy Spirit, the Holy Spirit lives in me to give me help and wisdom, in all things. Today, I am a gifted dream interpreter, because I have the Holy Spirit working in and through me. And like Daniel, I'm also skilled in knowledge and under-standing, simply because I searched out knowledge and understanding from other reputable dream interpreters and the Word of God. Over time, like Daniel in the school of Babylon, in my own culture I have developed skills that go hand and hand with the "Holy Spirits gifting". As I've proven from the Word of God, this qualifies me to be a modern day dream interpreter. So hopefully you can see that it's because of the anointing of the Holy Spirit that lives in me, as well as the knowledge and insight, I have gained throughout my personal "Dream Quest" that enables me to walk in the calling of a "Dream Interpreter." Today, because of this equipping, I as well as many others are enjoying and benefitting, from the fruit of my labors!

So, like Joseph, Daniel and many others who are a type of them, we as Christians have "The Gift", of the Holy Spirit and can learn the skills necessary, by those who have gone on before us. Yes, it's true, like me you too can learn to interpret dreams! Believe me it's true; you can!

Principle 3: Symbolism is personal to the dreamer.

Herman Riffel, passionately taught me that in order to arrive at an accurate interpretation, it is critical to search our own hearts to understand the meanings of our own personal symbolism. Symbolic meanings are personal to each and every dreamer and they should not be generalized. It was through his heart probing dream techniques, that I understood the importance of going to the heart of the dreamer to obtain their personal meaning, concerning the symbolism in their dream. He desperately **warned** me not to look to the dream dictionaries for generic dream symbolic meanings to apply to the interpretation of my dreams, but in doing so, would lead me to an inaccurate interpretation.

Principle 4: Male and Female counterparts in your dreams.

Herman's book, Dream Interpretation: A Biblical Understanding" emphasized and elaborated, on the meaning of Genesis 1:27.

> **So God created man in his own image, in the image of God he created him; male and female he created them.**
> (Genesis 1:27 NKJV)

While sitting under Herman, I learned firsthand that his interpretation of this scripture was, since God created men and women in His image that God has male/masculine characteristics, as well as female/feminine characteristics. Thus, both genders and their traits come from, within HIS IMAGE. God's image is **masculine** and **feminine** and this was an eye opener to me. So, I understood Herman, to say that since we are made in the image of God we are like God In the sense that, like God we can have male and female characteristics or traits in each of us.

31

For his teaching on these three principles and more, please get his book "Dream Interpretation: A Biblical Understanding", by Herman Riffel. I highly recommended him and you may buy his book online at www.cgllcmedia.com

So, learning that women, who are feminine in gender, can at the same time carry some masculine traits; likewise men who are masculine in gender can display or carry some feminine traits. This key principle really helped me to understand why, as a female, these unknown male figures were showing up in my dreams. And now these unknown men figures have meaning and it's all because they can represent a part of me, wow what a revelation in the area of dream interpretation!

For Example:

I'm a woman in gender and very feminine, however, in certain situations and times, I can be domineering, tom-boyish, competitive, determined, tough, and very headstrong which to many, would be considered masculine traits. I was raised with four brothers, and because I was the only girl sibling in the family, I took on boyish behaviors at times. For instance, I would be the first to join in with all the boys in football and many times I would wrestle, throw mud balls, and play basket ball with my brothers and their friends in the neighborhood. Now, don't get me wrong, there were times, I would play with the baby dolls too, but most of my interaction in my youth was with males. So this definitely played a part in the way I was shaped, as an individual concerning the area of my masculinity. Sometimes my husband and I wrestle around a bit and he tells me, oh my Lord, "YOU'RE STRONG" and then he says to me that he doesn't need to worry about anyone trying to take advantage of me, because I'm so strong! Now Clae my husband, he's 6ft 3 inches tall, all muscle and extremely strong. So, when he says I'm strong you can bet that this is an accurate assessment! It's true and I know it! I am very strong for a woman and again, this would be commonly known as a masculine trait as well! So, you ask, how this applies in dream interpretation. Well, once I learned this principle from Herman, more of the male figures in my dreams started making sense to me. Below are three examples of male figures that have shown up in my dreams to represent a masculine part of me.

Male figure 1: Infant Boy

Dream Example: In the dream I saw a 1 month old infant wearing diapers; instantly the infant went from laying down to springing up on his feet and then he was off and running !

My Interpretation (see chapter 12) I asked myself, what is one month old and off and running? The answer was my marriage and this made perfect sense! At the time of my dream my husband and I had been married for one month. And spiritually and emotionally we were, doing extremely well in our relationship! This dream was showing me that even though we had only been married a short time, that our marriage was off and running! God was causing us to grow leaps and bounds, beyond the normal rate. So, this dream was very encouraging to me. God was showing me the infant boy, totally skipped the crawling and walking stage, and went straight into the running stage. This revelation en-couraged me. I believe because we allowed God to rule and reign in our whole marriage, God was giving us supernatural growth. God made it evident to me in this dream that our marriage growth was a God thing!

So, because there is nothing girly about Clae and I'm a masculine woman the Holy Spirit picked a boy baby to represent the area of our marriage. But, now we have been married **three** years, so the **one month** infant boy, who was symbolic of our marriage union, will **change in age**. Since time has **evolved**, the next time (if this year) God chooses to address an area of my marriage to me in a dream, this time the boy figure will show up as a **three** year old boy. He will no longer be an infant, because some symbols do **evolve** as time changes; we will discuss that in detail, in chapter five.

33

Male figure 2: Several times I've had dreams and visions with a 7 year old boy in them.

This boy represents my dream interpretation ministry that was started or "birthed" in my life, seven years ago. When this seven year old boy is in my dreams and visions, God is using him as a symbol that represents my dream ministry. Most of the time, he's with me like he's my child. However, this is only symbolic in the sense, like in real life, if I had a child it would be an area of responsibility to me. So, like a child, seven years ago, God birthed the dream ministry in my life and it has been and is still an area that I'm responsible, for stewarding in. So, when he shows up I know exactly what he represents based on his age within the dream or vision.

Male figure 3: At times I have dreams with a teenage boy; age 17

When I have dreams with a 17 year old male figure, I know that God is referring to the part of me that has been whole heartily committed to Him. I was saved younger, but I have been intensely serving God and growing in Him since 1995. So he would represent my 17 years of strong relationship in God. It's the part of me that's in love with God and that's fully committed to serving Him.

So, don't consider it strange when your dream reveals and unknown boy or girl baby, toddler, child, teen, or adult. Just consider the age of the figure and see if you can go back to the time and age of what the figure may be trying to represent. It could be a particular masculine or feminine part of you, which birthed something specific in your life. This symbolic gender principle applies to males who dream of female symbols as well as females who dream of male symbolic figures. Like God, we are made in His Image, male and female. So, remember, the people in your dreams can be playing a part of you or they could literally be playing themselves. (see page, 79)

For Example:

Let's say you're a very masculine man, but there is a part of you that just loves to knit, sew or has a natural flare for interior design. Everyone knows, these skills are commonly believed to be "something that a woman would do". However, if in real life you operate in these skills; then when you dream, the dream may pick a female, which is a feminine gender part of you to symbolize this so called "girly" part of you. It could be a symbolic figure such as Martha Stewart. If so, she can represent the homemaker part of you, which likes to express your creativity, by knitting, sewing or home decorating.

Even though on HGTV, we have many men who are making a living at interior design. I believe this male representation of decorating is mainly predominate in the entertainment industry. It's my opinion, in most circles interior design is normally considered to be an area that females dominate! So, this is why the dream may choose a female figure to symbolize a specific girlish area of your life. However, just because society views this line of work as a woman's job, it doesn't mean a man should be ashamed or hide his love for any type of domestic design. After all, our Heavenly Father is the greatest creator, artist, and designer of all! And there's nothing "girly" about Him! He is the Creator of Heaven and Earth and the great "I Am"; King David praises God for his heavenly designs!

Psalms 8:3
When I consider your heavens, the work of your fingers, the moon and the stars, which you have set in place.

Principle 5: Everyone Dreams

With the exception of brain injuries, everyone dreams. Mark and Patty Virkler write in their book "Hearing God through your dreams" that "sleep laboratories have proven that everyone dreams one to two hours each night during a certain period of sleep known as the alpha level, which is a light sleep. Every 90 minute cycle of sleep begins with alpha, then goes into deeper sleep which is called theta, and finally deepest sleep which is called delta.

At the close of the first 90-minute cycle each night, the individual returns to alpha level sleep, where he has a short, five minute dream period. The next time he cycles up to alpha, he has a ten-minute dream period. The third time in alpha, the dream period is about 15 minutes, and so on. If one sleeps a full 8 hours the entire last hour is essentially spent in alpha level sleep. Thus, the average person sleeping for eight hours a night will dream about one to two hours of that time.

Alpha level sleep is where one has what is called Rapid Eye Movement (REM). Rapid Eye Movement is exactly what it sounds like: the eyes of the dreamer begin moving rapidly. He is actually watching the scenes in the dream, and thus his eyes are literally moving back and forth, observing the action.

By observing the alpha level sleep when Rapid Eye Movement occurs, researchers in sleep laboratories have determined when a person is dreaming and how much time is spent dreaming in the average night. They have discovered that if they awaken a person every time REM begins, preventing him from dreaming, after about three nights the individual will begin to show signs of having a nervous breakdown."

Clearly dreams are an inner release mechanism which helps provide us with emotional balance and maintain our sanity. Dreams can be considered guardians for our mental and emotional well being." To purchase **"Hearing God through your dreams,"** go to www.cwgministries.org

It's funny to me when I hear people say, "Oh, I don't sleep deep enough to dream." When I hear this, I never miss an opportunity to jump in and reply. Well, did you know that you don't have to sleep deep in order to have a dream? Then I tell them, you actually dream in the lightest sleep state, which is the REM state. They're usually very surprised to hear me relay this little fact to them. So, remember you don't have to sleep long and hard to have a short little dream! God often speaks to me in a dream, within the narrow moments of a short little nap. Exciting!

Ps. If you have Netflix you should watch "What Are Dreams"? by Nova.

Principle 6: Feeling in the dream (Mark and Patty Virkler)

Finally, the key principle I gleaned from the Virklers was that the feelings and thoughts you have, while in the dream or while dreaming the dream are of the utmost importance. Meaning, it is vitally important to consider your line of thinking in the dream or the feelings you're having in the dream, as a key factor to arriving at the correct dream interpretation. When I started to apply this principle, while interpreting my dreams, it became the final key to unlocking the dreams <u>true</u> interpretation. To purchase **"Hearing God through your dreams,"** go to http://www.cwgministries.org

Principle 7: Look for Metaphors, Similes and Metonymies!

In the book, "Dream Dreams by Steve and Diane Bydeley" they pointed out two very insightful nuggets of knowledge to me concerning understanding my dreams. One nugget of truth was that, during the age of enlightenment, America was negatively influenced by philosophers and science concerning dreams and the things of the spirit realm. Secondly, this married couple brought much light to the importance of considering metaphors, metonymies, and similes when interpreting your dreams. So, for in depth teaching on this and more, make sure you get their book called Dream Dreams, at http://www.lapstoneministries.org

B. Metaphors, Metonymies, and Similes: Merriam -Webster online dictionary states.

Metaphors: (met·a·phor: noun)
A figure of speech in which a word or phrase literally denoting one kind of object or idea is used in place of another to suggest a likeness or analogy between them (as in drowning in money); broadly : figurative language

Metaphor examples:

A Walk in the Clouds
All the world's a stage (Shakespeare)
A Sleeping Giant
A new lease on life
Beyond the horizon
New frontier
Stone Cold
Food For Thought
A City that Never Sleeps

House of Glass
A sea of troubles
A Leap of Faith
Playing with Fire
Gone in a Flash
A Birds Eye View
Hold your Horses
Out of the Blue
Old flame

38

For Example: "Old Flame"

Maybe, in your dream your trying to blow out a candle and for some reason the candle is old and you can tell, by looking at the candle that it's been used over and over, before on previous cakes. And when you wake up you're thinking, what is going on? Why on earth am I trying to blow out an old raggedy candle?

Well, you should consider the events of your waking life. Maybe, just maybe, recently you'd run into an old boyfriend or girlfriend somewhere. And when they showed up in your life they started chasing after you again. But, unlike them you're NOT interested! So, metaphorically speaking the dream may have you trying to blow out or blow off and "Old Flame" tee hee hee, Get it? Can you see it?

Or, maybe your dream has you in a house made of glass; this could be the dreams way of representing you. If the house is symbolic of you, then it could mean that you're a very transparent person or that you're so touchy that you are fragile and will break easily. BUT, it could mean that you live in a glass house; meaning your world is perfect or ideal.

Metonymies: (me·ton·y·my: noun)
A figure of speech, consisting of the use of the name of one thing for that of another of which it is an attribute or with which it is associated (as "crown" in "lands belonging to the crown")

Bible = Sword	Car = wheels
Hands = Paws	Christian = Lamb
House = Crib	Woman = Skirt
Sweat = Hard Labor	Man = Cat
Alcohol = The Bottle	Teeth = Grill
USA government = Washington	Feet = Dogs

Similes (sim·i·le: noun)
A figure of speech comparing two unlike things that is often introduced by like or as (as in cheeks like roses)

Quick as lightening	As cold as ice
Growing like weeds	Working like a slave
Fit as a fiddle,	Right as rain,
Snug as a bug in a rug	Like a shooting star
Sharp as a tack.	Flat as a pancake
Poor as dirt	Straight as an arrow
Like a bad dream	Cheeks like roses
Thick as mud	Thick as thieves
Cute as a button	Light as a feather
Stiff as a board	Old as the hills
Phony as a three-dollar bill	White as a ghost,
As dark as the moonless night	Dead as a door nail

Idioms; (id·i·om : noun)
A: the language peculiar to a people or to a district, community, or class.

A chip on your shoulder	A dime a dozen
A piece of cake	A shot in the dark
A wolf in sheep's clothing	A slap on the wrist
Beat a dead horse	As high as a kite
Birds of a feather flock together	Don't burn your bridges
Cry over spilt milk	Cold turkey
In over your head	In the dog house
Nose out of joint	Pulling your leg
Out of the woods	Off the hook
The writing on the wall	Rock the boat
Third wheel	Tie the knot
Under the weather	When pigs fly
When it rains it pours	A bull in a china shop

Dream: Idiom, Example: "Small Pants"

Once I had a dream that I was in a bathroom and I was trying to pull up my pants. I really struggled with getting these jeans on and finally, I barely got them pulled up and then I couldn't zip them up.

Dream Interpretation:

Now some of you may be thinking, well, that's easy enough! The dream is showing you that you need to go on a diet, ha ha! Well, if that's what you're thinking, I forgive you! tee hee, ha, ha!

Well dreamers, this may be an accurate and true assessment, if I was overweight at the time and it would be something for me to seriously consider. But, that is not what the dream was saying at all! The dream was using a figure of speech called an idiom. The dream was really showing me, at the time I had the dream, "I was too big for my britches"! Isn't that hilarious? It's funny to me now, however at the time of the dream it wasn't too funny, because I didn't consciously know I was in spiritual error, at the time of the dream. When I had the dream, God was showing me the truth about myself; He was correcting me and showing me through a dream that I had some pride issues. And I'm happy to say that because of the dream, I did heed God's correction and I tried very hard to make some adjustments to my self-righteous attitude. So, it was definitely a correction dream, and I'm thankful for it!

So dreamers, metaphorically speaking, sometimes were not able to see the "forest for the trees." So, when interpreting, it's extremely important to look at your dreams metaphorically to see if a bigger picture can apply to your dream's meaning!

Principle 8: Colors, Numbers and Deliverance

Later, I bought and read Ira Milligan's book called "Understanding The Dreams you Dream." His book showed me the importance of understanding, how certain colors and color combinations in our dreams can play a very important role in us getting the most out of the meanings in our dreams. When I read his book, I was already accurately embracing and identifying my personal colors and numbers, within my dreams. But, when I came across a number, in my dream that was not a personal number to me and was a number that I was not familiar with, his biblical numerology study became very beneficial to me. Moreover, as I read through some of the dream interpretation skills he used in ministering to others, I noticed that he occasionally used the dream's interpretation to share God's heart in their situation to minister healing and deliverance to some of the dreamers. I find this principle to be of the utmost importance and Jesus does too. It's the call of the believer, in the Great Commission to bring deliverance and salvation. For his teaching on the importance of colors and numbers in your dreams, check out "Understanding The Dreams You Dream" volume 2. And for in depth teaching on deliverance, I recommend "The Anatomy of A Scorpion" both are by Ira Milligan and you may buy them online at, **http://servant-ministries.org**

Mark 16:15-20 (NKJV)

15 And He said to them, "Go into all the world and preach the gospel to every creature. 16 He who believes and is baptized will be saved; but he who does not believe will be condemned. 17 And these signs will follow those who believe: <u>In My name they will cast out demons</u>; they will speak with new tongues; 18 they will take up serpents; and if they drink anything deadly, it will by no means hurt them; <u>they will lay hands on the sick, and they will recover.</u>"

Principle 9: Stick to the Storyline (Vonda's principle)

As I practiced using the skills I learned in Herman's group, God impressed in my heart, that it's very important to walk through the storyline of the dream, from beginning to end without adding or taking away from it.

For example, let's say you have a dream that you're drifting uncontrollably in a small boat that you know is heading for a dangerous, cliff type of waterfall. And your dream ends with you fearing you will go over the edge and being killed, but in the dream you did not actually go over the edge, you just feared it.

Well, the dream is what it is! In order to arrive at an accurate interpretation, you cannot add to the storyline or take away from it. You can't say, I'm dead; I'm going to get killed! This would NOT be true!!!! The dream just gave you a symbolic picture of you about to go over the edge. So this may be a warning dream.

So, if it were my dream I would ask myself, where at in my life, am I in an uncontrollable situation and **about to go over the edge**? It may be symbolic of some type of addiction or a situation at work, church or anger problem, within a personal relationship that paints the symbolic picture that you are "**on the edge**" or you're about to "**go over/off the deep end**" and you need to try and reel yourself back in, or you need someone to help reel you back in!!

So, please take note that you cannot say that the dream showed you going over the waterfall and dying, if the dream never showed that. You have to stay within the story line of the dream. The dream shows what the dream shows and you are in error if you add or take away from the storyline of the dream. So, be sure to stick to the storyline of the dream!

Principle 10: Give Godly Counsel (Vonda's principle)

I love and desire to please the Lord, so I have embraced the Great Commission and Gods calling in my life, especially as I minister to others in the area of dream interpretation. It's like I always say, when I'm teaching a class on dream interpretation; I can interpret dreams until I'm blue in the face, but the real work is done when one applies the wisdom of God's word and His power into their life, concerning their dream and its interpretation. To back this up with scripture, walk with me as I share the insight God showed me, about Joseph and Daniel. In the word of God we can see that they both operated in this same counseling principle during their dream sessions, it was the heart of God in them to enlighten and offer advice to these two kings. Below are two scriptural examples, I would like to share with you concerning the application of God's word through counseling, after understanding the revelation of the dream and its interpretation.

Josephs Interpretation and counsel: Genesis 41:28-37(NKJV)

28. "It is just as I said to Pharaoh: God has shown Pharaoh what he is about to do. 29. Seven years of great abundance are coming throughout the land of Egypt, but seven years of famine will follow them. 31.Then all the abundance in Egypt will be forgotten, and the famine will ravage the land. 32.The abundance in the land will not be remembered, because the famine that follows it will be so severe. 33."And now let Pharaoh look for a discerning and wise man and put him in charge of the land of Egypt. 34 <u>Let Pharaoh appoint commissioners over the land to take a fifth of the harvest of Egypt during the seven years of abundance. 35.They should collect all the food of these good years that are coming and store up the grain under the authority of Pharaoh, to be kept in the cities for food. 36.This food should be held in reserve for the country, to be used during the seven years of famine that will come upon Egypt, so that the country may not be ruined by the famine.</u>" 37. The plan seemed good to Pharaoh and to all his officials.

44

I want to point out that after Joseph gave Pharaoh the interpretation to his dream, it was immediately after the interpretation that he offered a **wise solution** to aid Egypt during the time of their natural disaster. Notice that the pharaoh never asked Joseph for his advice, but Joseph was right there ready and willing to step out and minister the wisdom of the Lord to him. And in turn, Joseph's godly counseling, wisdom and plan brought a type of salvation to Egypt, even though the earth would still need to go through the famine season. It was the sovereign plan from a loving God to spare the lives of the Egyptians and all those who would be affected by this famine.

So, Pharaoh recognized that Joseph walked in the true wisdom of God and Pharaoh the dreamer and leader, chose to apply the wisdom of the Lord and heed the dreams warning. And as a result, all of Egypt was spared the consequences of a very harsh famine because God is very loving and good, and He desires to be merciful. Also, in the passages below we can see that Daniel operated in this same principle. He offered God's wisdom after the interpretation of Nebuchadnezzar's "tree dream." After Daniel finished his interpretation of Nebuchadnezzar being the great tree; he also relayed to the King the angel's message of the King's heavenly judgment. Let's read the scriptures below and review the interpretation and Daniel's godly counsel.

Daniels counsel: Daniel Explains the Dream
Daniel 4:19-28 (NLT)
19. "Upon hearing this, Daniel (also known as Belteshazzar) was overcome for a time, frightened by the meaning of the dream. Then the king said to him, 'Belteshazzar, don't be alarmed by the dream and what it means.' "Belteshazzar replied, 'I wish the events foreshadowed in this dream would happen to your enemies, my lord, and not to you! The tree you saw was growing very tall and strong, reaching high into the heavens for all the world to see. It had fresh green leaves and was loaded with fruit for all to eat. Wild animals lived in its shade, and birds nested in its branches.

That tree, Your Majesty, is you. For you have grown strong and great; your greatness reaches up to heaven, and your rule to the ends of the earth. "Then you saw a messenger, a holy one, coming down from heaven and saying, "Cut down the tree and destroy it. But leave the stump and the roots in the ground, bound with a band of iron and bronze and surrounded by tender grass. Let him be drenched with the dew of heaven. Let him live with the animals of the field for seven periods of time. "This is what the dream means, Your Majesty, and what the Most High has declared will happen to my lord the king. You will be driven from human society, and you will live in the fields with the wild animals. You will eat grass like a cow, and you will be drenched with the dew of heaven. Seven periods of time will pass while you live this way, until you learn that the Most High rules over the kingdoms of the world and gives them to anyone he chooses. But the stump and roots of the tree were left in the ground. This means that you will receive your kingdom back again when you have learned that heaven rules. <u>"King Nebuchadnezzar, please accept my advice. Stop sinning and do what is right. Break from your wicked past and be merciful to the poor. Perhaps then you will continue to prosper."</u>

Please take notice that in Daniel's counseling session with King Nebuchadnezzar, we can see that he did not apply the wisdom of the Lord, concerning his dream. And as a result God's judgment of King Nebuchadnezzar was administered to him quickly! God gave the King a dream and a full year to repent, but we can see through the scriptures, Nebuchadnezzar believed that he was "the man" who made things happen. So, just like the dream showed and predicted, he suffered the terrible consequences of his prideful heart. So, like Daniel, if God gives you a dream or and open door to help someone with their dream, please do not hold back in sharing the wisdom of the Lord for their situation. Take delight in knowing that you are God's representative, entrusted with the wisdom of His Word for the current opportunity!

So, my friends, as we interpret our dreams let's choose to be wise and apply Gods wisdom to our lives. Let's bring deliverance to those in need, whether it's preaching the gospel to every creature, casting out demons to those who have strong holds, laying hands on the sick and ushering in the manifestation of their healing, or by raising the dead, if the Lord wills it for that individual. With God nothing is impossible to him who believes!

For example, recently I interpreted a night vision dream for a Christian woman named Evelyn; below is her dream, dream interpretation, and counseling. And because of her receptive heart towards the dream and its counsel, she is now walking in a greater awareness of her divine calling as a prophet of the Lord; moreover, she experienced some inner healing and outward deliverance.

For Example: James is agitated and waiting
(Evelyn's dream and its symbolism.) Night visions see pages 150 & 236

In the dream, I saw myself (__night vision__) walking from a building and entering the crowded parking lot, where old and outdated vehicles were parked. It's as if, I had just come out of some type of conference (__inward spiritual discussion__). My brother James (__a loving prophet__) was sitting in a very nice 300 luxury car (__attractive and present tense ministry__); in real life he really has one, but this car was newer. He was sitting in the passenger seat (__he the prophetic part of her is waiting to be transported__) and he was wearing a dark blue suit (__Holy Spirit power__) and tie with a silver shirt (__refinement__). In the dream, James was somewhat agitated because I was taking too long (__dilly, dallying slow and poky__) and as I got ready to lean in the window he said "let's JUST GO"(__he's tired of waiting on her and it's time for her to get moving__) . So, I smiled and jumped in to drive and I saw that he had taken off his suit coat (__getting comfortable and ready for the ride__) because he was looking like he did not want to play around anymore or waste anymore time (__no time to waste__).

47

The Interpretation: This was a "Night Vision Dream"
(Interpretation steps in Chapter 12)

1. In the dream the dreamer is watching herself; she sees herself in this night vision. God uses night visions to reveal His revelations to us. A revelation is something He knows but we are not aware of until He chooses to make it known to us.

2. The conference building, to her symbolizes a Christian place, where she's learned areas of equipping, and where spiritual **discussion** usually takes place. Spiritually meaning, Evelyn is learned in the things of God and has been having a **discussion** within herself about her calling and when it would manifest.

3. James is symbolic for a part of Evelyn. James is representing the prophetic part of Evelyn that God wants to use in this area of ministry. In the dream, the "prophetic part" of Evelyn is waiting on the slow poke part of Evelyn to get in and get in the driver's seat and get him moving down the road and in the things of God! James, who is symbolic for Evelyn, wants her to transport him, so she can take her prophetic calling where it needs to be. So God has picked her brother James to represent a prophetic ministry area "part of her" that needs to stop poking around and GET MOVING in her prophetic calling of God.

4. All of the cars are old and out dated, except for her brothers. His car is symbolic for his ministry or the way God uses him in current prophetic revelation. His car represents a style of ministry is new, powerful, current and high end; this updated car is symbolic for an attractive and CURRENT ministry.

5. The night vision shows, when she realizes how James wants to go now, it will take her (Evelyn in real life) to get in the car and start driving. She will go nowhere, in her prophetic calling until she takes control and starts to drive the prophetic part of her where she needs to go.

48

INTERPRETATIONS, BOTTOM LINE: The calling is waiting on her.

God was showing her that her "prophetic calling" is waiting on her to get in and take control and that she is to get the prophet part of herself, ministering within her calling. Meaning, get into gear! The dream showed that, when in real life she realizes this she will happily answer the call.

I'm delighted to say that after I helped her with the interpretation she did respond just as the night vision dream predicted. She got into gear and started ministering prophetically, as God opened up doors of opportunity. Although, she was not aware of it at the time of her dream interpretation, it was a short time later Evelyn's new prophetic role and integrity were tested! All of the sudden a good looking man came knocking on the door of her heart, to try and get her to go back into the same old place of dilly dallying, she just came out from. Let me share with you how this all leads to dream interpretation and deliverance!

Long story short, Evelyn was married to a man in whom she married in spite of God's direction. God had warned her that her fiancé was not the one that God had for her. Overtime, they divorced and as a divorced woman she had promised her life to God, by vowing not to marry again until she knew it was Gods choice mate for her, as well as His ordained timing. During our counseling, Evelyn confessed some of the issues that have been holding her up in her life. She shared that she has struggles with, wanting men to be emotionally connected to her. She always struggled with and wanted their hearts to hold her as the dearest and most sexually meaningful woman they had ever encountered. So even though Evelyn answered the prophetic calling she still maintained a stronghold that needed to be severed. So, within a week of me interpreting her dream and with her heartfelt response of saying YES to God in the area of her prophetic calling, it was very soon that temptation came knocking on her door.

49

<u>Deliverance Prayer</u>: Bottom line, even though the enemy came knocking, Evelyn eagerly desired to be set free from her carnal mindset and whole heartedly agreed with me and the Holy Spirit in prayer that she would now lay this weakness down at the feet of Jesus. In the spirit realm we took authority over different types of Spirits and we cut all soul ties to the men in her past; we prayed a release and a blessing on all her former men friends. She was now freed, because of her transparency, obedience, and willingness to apply the truth of God's word, which enabled the Holy Spirit to minister His healing power to the void areas that once held her hostage. God delivered her right then and there, at our request and healed her, by His blood.

Sometimes, even though we have said the prayer in faith, we still wonder if anything has really changed. But, you must know that the Word of God does not return void. It does and will perform what it was sent to do! The next day I was praying and talking with God about her deliverance and the Lord was kind enough to give me a vision for confirmation. But, I want you to remember that whether or not we ever get a vision, that His Word always works in any given situation and God word is still true!

The Mud Pit: Vision

This was a "day vision" the Holy Spirit gave me in order to minister to her further; I was awake, so it was not a Night vision, while sleeping. But, I would like to share it with you to show the heart of God, concerning His heart to deliver her, from where she was at in her walk with the Lord.

In this vision, Jesus and I (Vonda) walked up to a large square mud pit. I saw Evelyn and she'd sunk and was stuck in the far corner of the mud pit. Then together Jesus and I walked across on top of this pit, without sinking and went over to her. At this time, I reached down and grabbed Evelyn from underneath her arms and lifted her up and out of the mud pit and put her feet back on solid ground.

My Interpretation: The Jesus in me and with me was walking beside me, in my (Vonda's) life and was the strength of me in the spirit realm to be able to reach down and pick up my sister, meanwhile enabling me to help her out of the miry clay type of mud pit. The mud pit represented the snares of the world and how easy it is, to get trapped in the areas of flesh and worldliness.

So, because we understood what God was saying to her in her dream and to me in this vision, she willingly answered the call. Through the counseling, after her dream interpretation, she humbly confessed and committed her areas of weakness to the Lord. And as a result of our faith in Christ, and prayer, He showed us this mud pit vision with the revelation that she had been set free and was on solid ground!

This mud pit vision confirmed our prayer and the vision is in line with His Word, by showing me that I am the hands and feet of Jesus; and that He is empowering me to do His will on this earth. But, as we know it's Christ that has delivered us by His blood, and He is the deliverer!!! So, as you can see, God gives direction and deliverance through dream interpretation.

So, if she stays the course she will reap the benefits of "blessings for obedience"! Our God is a good God! If, He did it for her, He can and is willing to do it for you!

Deliverance: Example 2

One Christian woman from Kentucky had an encouragement dream; and as we talked about her dream and its interpretation, she revealed that she had been considering quitting her teaching job as a public school teacher. But, this would have been a huge mistake because her dream interpretation showed her that she was really amazing at her job. Also she admitted that she really didn't have any type of

51

a godly leading to quit her job at that time in her life. So, I reminded her that she was not there by accident, but that she was divinely appointed by God. I encouraged her to realign her thinking and stay the course. And below is her response to the dream interpretation and counseling.

A lady from Kentucky says.....

"I just wanted to let you know how great it was to talk to you. I really got a lot out of the interpretation and I feel like that it was something that God wanted me to hear and just at the right time"!

So, she was encouraged, when she understood her dream and said "yes to God"! And because of her response she has kept herself, from getting out of the will of God concerning her purpose in life, during the time of the dream.

Example 3
One woman from Pennsylvania said after her dream interpretation ..."I know that you helped to bring a lot of **peace** to my mind through interpreting my dream."

As we know, the Holy Spirit is our teacher, guide, counselor, comforter and encourager, and Jesus is the peace giver. So, be receptive to the dream and its interpretation, by willfully choosing to listen and apply the wisdom of God in your life. You will be, so very blessed as you yield and apply God's word and wisdom into your own personal situation, concerning your dream. Finally, like Joseph and Daniel please know the people you are ministering to will benefit greatly as you allow the Holy Spirit to speak through you to guide them in their dreams revelation! So, never be afraid to humbly offer godly wisdom and advice to the dreamer God has put in your pathway because God is right there with you!

Chapter 5
Dream Symbols

When a person is awake they are conscious and the majority of us have the wonderful ability to talk, by using words in sentences, with emotions and facial expressions to convey our hearts inner thoughts into the ear, mind and heart of the receptive individual, they're choosing to communicate to. As people we are able express our heart and the voice of our inner man to others by talking. But in addition to our normal speaking voice, the dreams we have are a voice too, except the dream is communicating to us instead of another person. When we are a sleep, our mind is shut down and it's through the dream that our soul chooses to speak. Instead of our heart and soul expressing its feelings to us in words, it uses symbols, that make up pictures and scenes, which make up the dream. Your dream is the voice of your heart and this voice is expressing itself to you, while you are sleeping. Most of the time, your dream is showing you reflective images of your feelings that you're previously aware of or that are in your conscious thoughts. However, as Christians God will periodically interject His revelation into our dreams as insight from Him, into the dreams subject matter; if not give you the entire dream as well! He does this to speak His insight into our waking life, concerning the current or forthcoming issues in our hearts. So, can you see how it would be very advantageous, for you to learn how to interpret your personal dream symbols? Let's review the meaning of a symbol

Definition: [1] sym·bol (Merriam-Webster online dictionary)

2: something that stands for or suggests something else by reason of relationship, association, convention, or accidental resemblance; *especially*: a visible sign of something invisible <the lion is a *symbol* of courage

Learning your own symbolic language and interpreting your dreams is just like when you were younger and you learned the alphabet. In the beginning, while learning A, B, C, D, E, F, G, H, it was all foreign to you, but the more you heard, saw, and recited them, the more familiar the letters became and before you knew it you were writing letters, spelling words, reading sentences, paragraphs, and reading paragraphs then became reading books ! And since you stuck with it, now being literate is second nature to you and it's not a big deal, because you have learned to recognize the letters and words you needed to learn in order to read and write. Well, it's the same with dreams. You just have to spend some time and effort to become "dream literate" by learning your personal symbolic meanings as well as applying the information in this book to become a dream interpreter. Yes, it will take learning, persistence, time, practice, and endurance along with the Holy Spirit to become a skilled dream interpreter. But, just like me you can do it too! In this chapter we will cover, Revelatory symbols, Universal symbols, Personal symbols, and Evolving symbols.

1. Revelatory Symbols: Are unrecognizable and unknown symbols contained within a vision or prophetic dream, which are made known to the person having the dream, from the Spirit of God to receive revelation concerning a certain issue.

For example: Let's say God gives you a dream and in this dream you're standing in the middle of an African village, with an unknown man and some tribal people from that area. And in the dream the man looks at you and says, "I'm from Dinka." And upon awakening from the dream, you know that you knew the name Dinka from the dream, but in real life you have never heard nor have you known of the word Dinka?

God may give this type of prophetic dream to a person who has been passionately seeking God about their intense desire to go a mission's trip, to share the love of Christ!

This can be God's way of showing you things that are to come that are unknown to you and He is choosing to make known to you through a dream in the night. And the man from Dinka is a revelatory symbol because the Holy Spirit is revealing to you a people, place, and language that you had NO previous knowledge of, in your natural mind as well as showing you there standing among them. So, God may be saying, hey my child, I'm answering your prayers and in due time you'll be in Dinka sharing the love of Christ on a missions trip!

2. Universal Symbols: Are symbols that everyone in the whole universe identifies with, no matter their culture or geographical location on planet earth.

For Example: Land, water, sky, sun, moon and the stars are all universal entities, that no matter where a person lives in the world, they recognize and know of these things.

In scripture, when God promised Abram he would have an heir, this is what God spoke to him and the universal symbol He used to make Abram a wonderful promise. Let's read.

God took Abram outside and said, "Look up at the heavens and count the stars—if indeed you can count them." Then he said to him, "So shall your offspring be." (Gen 15:5)

"I will surely bless you and make your descendants as numerous as the stars in the sky and as the sand on the seashore. Your descendants will take possession the cities of their enemies." (Gen 22:17)

"I will make your descendants as numerous as the stars in the sky and will give them all these lands, and through your offspring all nations on earth will be blessed." (Gen 26:4)

55

As, we can see in these scriptures, God used the universal stars in the sky to be symbols of Abram's descendants and once God did this, the stars in the sky now held a new and more personal meaning to Abram. Originally they may have represented lights for the night time, directions for the astronomer or simply something very pretty to look at but, now their meaning had **evolved** into representing his personal children, heirs, and the descendants of his future family. (see pg 88, Evolving Symbols)

I'm sure that Abram shared his encounters and promises from God, with his son Isaac. And Isaac shared them with Esau and Jacob and I'm positive Jacob shared them with his children. Hence, three generations later, God gives Joseph this incredible dream in Genesis 37:9.

Then he had another dream, and he told it to his brothers. "Listen," he said, "I had another dream, and this time the sun and moon and eleven stars were bowing down to me." (Gen 37:9)

Can you see it? Joseph had learned and knew these **eleven stars** represented his brothers as the descendants of Abraham; even more, the whole family knew it! The eleven stars were a specific yet, personal symbol to Joseph that unmistakably represented his eleven brothers, while the sun and the moon represented his mother and father. So, God was speaking through symbols that were personal to Joseph the dreamer and God still uses this method with us, in our dreams today. Remember, **God works with what you know**!

3. **Personal Symbols**: Are symbols that only the individual can interpret based on their personal impression, opinion, knowledge, background and experience concerning the symbol in their dream that needs to be evaluated.

For **Example**: Personal symbols can be your car, a favorite cup, plate, chair, shirt, hat, ring, notebook, pen or a pet. It can be anything that is personal to you, with personal meaning.

For Example, let's say you have a dog and because you know your dog's nature very well, you're the only one that knows that your dog only freaks out when someone suddenly raises their hand near him. In real life you know that he freaks out like this because he was an abused dog (hit by his master) you rescued from the animal shelter.

So, now you just so happen to be praying for a girlfriend of yours because you're concerned about her and even though you can't put your finger on it, you sense something is just not right in her life. So, after praying for her a couple of days, God gives you a vision or night vision dream and in the vision he shows you <u>**your dog freaking out**</u>. Well this symbolic picture has personal meaning to you and it's personally symbolic to you for physical abuse. So, God is trying to reveal the message to you, that the person you have been concerned for and praying about, is or has suffered from physical abuse.

Only you would know this about your dog and only you know the extent of the things you have been praying for; so you are the only one who can interpret this "<u>**dog freaking out scene**</u>" correctly and this is because of your personal knowledge and experience concerning your dog. Others may say that the dog is acting like that in the dream, because it's going to rain and that the dog is obviously afraid of thunder and lighting. But, that's an inaccurate assessment and interpretation, because you know that your dog acts this way, because of his previous experiences in being physically abused. This is why it is so very important to go within your own heart and ask yourself what does this symbol, scene or picture mean to you?

God Works With What You Know

My personal "Dream Quest" began 8 years ago and to this day and I've literally interpreted hundreds of dreams for other people, and one of the major things I have learned, when it comes to symbolism, is 99% of the time **God works with what you know**! I've learned, it doesn't matter in the least, if a person understands scriptural symbolic meanings, within the pages of a dream dictionary. But, the only thing that truly matters is, the opinion of the individual dreamer and what the person knows, feels and thinks in their heart about a specific symbol. Whether positive or negative, it's their personal impression of what that symbol means to them that truly matters, when interpreting their dream, because God works with what we know!

You may not realize it, but since you were a child you have seen many things with your eyes and throughout your lifetime, each time you see a person place or thing with your eyes, these images are stored into your internal memory bank. Each of us have our own personal and unique memory bank of the thoughts and feelings we have experienced, based on the images that we have seen and processed over the many years of our lifespan. I call mine, my own internal, personal symbolic dictionary. Every person has a personal symbolic dictionary in their heart, whether they realize it or not. These memory banks differ from person to person but, the memory bank you posses, is where God will often select a specific picture or image that you have seen in your past, in order to relay a current thought or message to you, in your visions and dreams. **No book** on symbolism can give you the specific answers you need to know, in order to interpret your dream correctly. In my opinion, the worst thing one can do is, go to a dream dictionary to get the meanings for their dream symbols, and as Herman Riffle taught me, symbols are personal to the dreamer and they can and usually do contain different meanings for each individual dreamer.

When you as a dreamer rely on a dream dictionary to interpret your personal dream symbols in your dream, I can guarantee you that this is a **sure** way to receive an inaccurate interpretation! God speaks to you in your own picture language. He knows, what you know and how you feel about the things you've seen and experienced in your life and within the heart of every person, you have your own library of pictures or images that the Holy Spirit will choose from, in order to relay a current message to you. He chooses symbols from within your own heart and with some diligent practice, **not overnight**, but in time if you're persistent in your dream pursuit, you will learn what your personal symbols and your personal symbolic scenes mean to you; this principle works with visions also.

Personal Symbolic Scenes

Specific scenes and settings are personal to the dreamer and the dreams interpretation will vary depending on the dreamers' life and past experiences. So, if your dream has you in a past or present scene, be sure to ask yourself, what that scene or setting means to you, so you may apply the proper meaning and context, when interpreting the dream.

For Example:
Sometimes, your dreams may have you in the setting of a specific scene; it could be a **symbolic scene,** like the place or time…..

1. When you were picked on, in the school yard.
   (Fearful Environment)

2. Or a time when you won your first award.
   (Feeling Special)

3. It could be the day you drove a car for the first time.
   (Felt grown up)

4. The day you got that starting position on the basket ball team. (Felt like a Big Shot)

5. The day you got your first eagle on the golf course.
    (Feeling like you're the Man)

6. The place where you worked your first job.
    (Feeling of Acceptance)

7. The day you got fired. (Vulnerable)

8. The restaurant where your girlfriend or boyfriend dumped you. (Rejection)

9. A specific road you traveled on to start a new job.
    (New beginning)

For Example,

Let's say, you're a guy and back in the day when you were in high school, there were some guys that would bully or pick on you outside during your break time. In the past, this was a time, when you felt unaccepted, fearful or threatened. Now, let's say twenty years have gone by and now you're at your workplace and just like back in high school, you're not in the cool group.

Maybe there is a small group at your job that picks on you and makes you feel unaccepted and threatened. And even though it's twenty years later, you're experiencing that same feeling today, as you did when you were in back high school. So, this is the reason why you are currently having a dream of being in that same school yard; it's because the old school yard is symbolic of your current work environment. Get it?

Specific Symbols are Personal in Meaning.

Who the dreamer is and the context of their life is very important when it comes to evaluating the symbols in your dream. Let me share the following example of a bridge, an excerpt from the book "Dream Dreams" by authors Steve and Diane Bydeley.

The Bridge:

For example, "what do you think of when you hear the word bridge? Do you think of a steel structure that forms an arch over a river or maybe a pattern of ropes and boards swaying as it spans over the sides of a canyon? A banker may think of a type of financial transaction, and a dentist may think of one or more replacement teeth held in place by natural teeth. An optometrist pictures the bridge of a nose supporting corrective lenses, while the violinist thinks of a bridge that holds the strings taught and high above the soundboard. The thoughts of a Star Trek fan will be transported to the bridge of the USS Enterprise. For others, it could be the bridge of a cruise ship, a card game, a narrow strip of land between two continents, or a rest used to support the pool cue in a difficult shot. To the engineer type it might be a special type of engineer circuit, the connection between atoms or molecules, or it could be some other entity or concept in a field we have not yet bridged. This is only one example, of how important the background of the dreamer is to the dream." (Steve and Diane Bydeley "Dream Dreams" pg 137.)

So, as the previous example has demonstrated, a bridge does not mean the same thing to everyone. It's not "one shoe fits all," when interpreting symbols and their meanings.

Animals can be Symbolic of People or Entities

For Example, A Rooster: Recently, I was trying to explain this principle to a friend of mine and I told her that animals in our visions and dreams can often represent people; then as an example, I asked her what did a rooster mean to her? She quickly responded because she grew up on a farm, she sees a rooster as a fighter because they were very aggressive towards her and would always come after her fighting. So, I told her to consider that same meaning if, God ever showed her a rooster in a vision or dream. Then, I said to her, let's say that one day you're praying for someone or ministering to someone who complains that they just can't seem to keep a job. Then as your praying for them, God shows you a rooster in a vision or in a night vision dream. I then told her at that point, instead of saying, Lord, what in the heck does a rooster mean? She now knows that a rooster is personally symbolic to her for a fighter and through the imagery of a rooster, God is trying to show her that this person she's praying for can't keep a job because their always fighting against people. So, then she can minister to them through the Word of God based on the revelation the Holy Spirit just showed her.

Speaking for myself, since I did not grow up on a farm, when I think of a rooster I think of an alarm clock because their always waking people up early in the morning with their loud mouths! Maybe, when you think of a rooster, you associate them, with the time when Christ was denied.

Jesus said to him, "Assuredly, I say to you that today, even this night, before the rooster crows twice, you will deny Me three times." Mark 14:30 (NKJV)

If this is your association with a rooster then God could be using it as a symbol to show you that the person you have been seeking God about has **denied,** or is now **denying** him as their Savior and Lord. These are just a few examples of how symbolism is personal to the dreamer and how God can use animals to relay a personal message to you.

Many times, God has used animals to represent people to me, to relay a revelatory message about them. Below I will share some of my personal examples.

1. To me kangaroos can represent fighters because they are great boxers!

2. To me a fox can represent a beautiful woman because of the 1980's saying that "she's a fox or she's a foxy lady!

3. Donkey's can represent a stubborn person.

4. To me a buffalo can represent someone that is unmovable; because in my mind, moving a buffalo would be nearly impossible, thus it being un-movable!

5. To me an ox can represent strength, but to another it could represent a big person because you know the old saying, that he's as big as an Ox.

6. To me a bull dog represents someone that is bull headed.

7. Blue birds are known to be highly intelligent; so, sometimes they will represent an intelligent person or a spirit filled believer because their blue.

8. To me an eagle represents a prophet of the Lord.

9. A bull may represent a person who acts like a big bully.

10. A hippo has a very big mouth; so, to me it represents a person who is a "big mouth"!

11. To me a lamb can represent a Christian.

12. To me a hyena can represent a heckler or a person who laughs a lot; you know the term "the laughing hyena".

13. Bears are mean and can represent someone mean as a bear.

14. To me an <u>ant</u> can represent an <u>aunt</u>.

15. To me a <u>rat</u> can represent a person who <u>rats</u> someone out.

16. To me, <u>flies</u> are symbolic of small <u>demonic spirits</u> that keep pestering me.

17. To me, a <u>roach</u> represents an <u>unclean spirit</u> or demonic spirit.

18. To me, a <u>wolf</u> will represent a <u>false preacher</u> or <u>satan</u> himself.

19. To me, a <u>shark</u> represents a <u>creditor</u> with an extremely high percentage rate!

20. A long time ago, I read a book by Kenneth Hagin and he shared that God had shown him visions of demonic imps that looked like monkeys. This information has managed to stick with me; so, to me, monkeys in my dreams usually represent demonic imps!

21. Too me most birds can represent Christians and a flock of birds can represent a flock of Christians; like a church flock! One time I dreamed I flew through a flock of birds and God's hand placed me on a piece of prime beach front real-estate. So, God was showing me that He's going to move me right through the flock of other Christians at my church to put me in a desired spot that many would love to acquire.

22. Have you heard the saying he's or she's a tiger? This can mean he or she is someone you don't want to tangle with! One time I had a "reflection dream" of a big tiger who playfully loved on me, by lying on top of me across my upper chest. The heavy tiger didn't know it, but as it lovingly laid on me its big white furry neck was in my mouth. And the weight of the tiger on me, along with the hair that was in my mouth was suffocating me!

This tiger was symbolic of a person in my real life who loved me and I did not want to tangle with them. They suffocated me, by calling me on the phone all the time and it got to the point, where I felt suffocated by their love; just like, I was being suffocated by the playful and loving tiger in the dream.

Please remember, that I did not share these examples with you, so you will take on my meanings and turn them into your meanings, but I'm just sharing these examples with you that you can see how people differ in their thinking when it comes to symbolism. Who the dreamer is and **their opinions** about the animal in question, along with the context of their life are very important, when it comes to evaluating the symbols in your dream. Also, when you have a dream with an animal, it's important to consider our cultural phrases and terminology, as well as some of the everyday sayings we have become accustom to speaking. Please seriously consider the associations we make with animals, when trying to understand their significance within your dream; here are some examples.

Wise as an owl	Busy as a beaver
Sly as a fox	Mean as a snake
Strong as an ox	Slow as a turtle
Hungry as a lion	Lazy as a pig
He drinks like a fish	She swims like a fish
Eats like a pig	Mad as a hornet

Have you heard the metaphor, he or she is, in **Hog Heaven?** Well, recently God showed me a hog's head lying slanted on the arm of the couch. The hog is symbolic of me and lying slanted on the arm of the couch is usually where I spend time with God in the Spirit, which is a heavenly realm. So, God is showing me, since He called me out of my job and allowed my hubby to take the full responsibility of the bills, I've been in **"hog heaven"** and enjoying my time with God in the heavenly realm and things of the Spirit!

65

God is too funny and believe me, God knows all of our figures of speech! He knows everything! So, considering specific phrases like these will help you, immensely, as you ponder the meaning of the specific animal in your dream.

Symbols Vary : For example: Cake

Let's say you have a dream with cake in it. In the dream, the cake is being used as a symbol, with the intent of trying to relay a personal message to you as the dreamer. So, let's explore different symbolic meanings, for the symbol of a cake. Because cakes are for bridal showers, weddings, retirement, anniversary and birthday parties, often cakes can represent some type of celebration! In most cases a cake is usually thought of as a wonderful symbol. Some other ideas are, maybe the cake in the dream is in reference to someone who "wants their cake and wants to be able to eat it too." This would speak of selfishness.

I have one friend who doesn't eat cake with the icing on it because she says its way too sweet. So, for her if she found herself dreaming of eating cake it would most likely mean to her "something that is too sweet or something she won't eat."

I have read over the internet, that some people have mentioned that cake might represent a false doctrine that would be "fed" to the church. And I, Vonda say amen; yes to that person, because it may be their meaning and they should interpret it that way if, that is what they believe it to mean in their heart. However, for myself as far as the church and cake are concerned. In my foundational years as a Christian, I learned from my pastor, metaphorically speaking, that Jesus Christ is like the cake (**bread of life**) and the Holy Spirit is like the **icing** on the cake!

So, if it were my dream and I was dreaming of cake in reference to the church; then the false doctrine meaning would not apply to my dream because I have wonderful

66

thoughts of cake and the church! Because, if Jesus and the Holy Spirit are spiritually symbolic of cake and icing, then I believe we should freely indulge every day!

It is possible that if a cake shows up in your dream, at times the "celebration" meaning may be a true and accurate meaning for your dream symbol. But, before you can say "FOR SURE" it really depends on YOU and what is going on in your life in the PRESENT, at the time of the dream! When you interpret a dream you must consider the symbols and your personal feelings towards that particular symbol, during the time of the dream.

For example, maybe you're dreaming of cake and it's true that in many instances maybe the "celebration" meaning could apply. But, let's consider this, maybe you're going through a phase in your life when you're trying to lose weight. Ordinarily, the cake symbol might mean celebration, but now in the present tense meaning, because of your diet it would mean "something that is fattening" or something that you need to refrain from. Then it would be specifically symbolic to the dreamer of "something they're trying to stay away from" or something that they need to refrain from. Are you following me?

Cake: Literal or a spiritual parallel?

Dream example, let's say God gave you a dream of you eating a sweet piece of birthday cake, and in the dream you're eating it but you know you should not be eating it. If, in real life you truly are on a diet, then the dream could be showing you that you are literally eating from things that you should be staying away from. Then the cake in the dream would just be symbolic of "fattening foods". Receiving this message would help you see yourself in your weakness and then you could pray to God that he would help you to stay the course. You could even do some warfare with the word of God and say "man shall not live by cake (bread) alone but, by every word that proceeded out of the mouth of

67

God." In addition, you could ask God to anoint you and your thinking so you will be able to see your commitment though, until the end of your weight loss goal.

But, let's say in real life you're on a diet but you're not eating any sweets and you're being good in the area of self discipline. Then the cake dream could take on a spiritual meaning and God is using the cake symbol in the dream to correct you. He's correcting you by showing you the truth about you! If, the cake represents "something you need to refrain from," then He could be trying to show you that you're eating of "something that you should be refraining from". If, in real life cake is not something you are presently trying to restrain yourself from then it could represent an area of self indulgence. The cake may be a spiritual parallel of some type of junk you are indulging in; like, some known or unknown sin in your life that God is trying to address.

For example, maybe you've intended to refrain yourself from indulging in too much computer time, video gaming or too much television because like the cake it represents something unhealthy for your natural man. In a spiritual parallel the cake can be junk food for your spirit man. God could be using the imagery of you eating a bunch of cake in the dream, to show you that your spirit man is eating or consuming to much junk (T.V. and computer)! But, regardless of its meaning it's just a symbolic parallel to relay a specific meaning to the one who's had the dream. And only you, the dreamer can know what the symbol means to you based on the current events of your life at the time you had the dream. This is why it is extremely important to ask your heart, what this symbol means to you and then apply the meaning into the interpretation of your dream.

Speaking of cakes, this morning upon waking I had a "Night Vision Dream" of the "Cake Boss." It's a TV show where this guy named Buddy makes very elaborate, decorative cakes for all types of events that are extremely large and on his show he's called the Cake Boss.

68

Dream: Cake Boss

I Vonda dreamt, I saw the "Cake Boss" standing behind his bakery counter and as he looked over to the other side of the store, there were about 15-20 people sitting and patiently waiting in a darkened candlelit room, for him to be done with the cake he was currently working on. And as he looked over he told someone at the counter to tell them to move on, because it was going to be awhile before the cake was done. He really didn't like all those people waiting on him, while he was trying to work because it was a lot of pressure.

Below, is the dream with my personal symbol interpretations, within the parentheses.

My Interpretation:

I (Vonda) dreamt, I saw the "Cake Boss" standing behind his bakery counter and as he looked over to the other side of the store, there were about 15-20 people (symbolic of readers) sitting and waiting patiently in a darkened candlelit room, (Christians that have the light of Jesus' but are in the dark concerning dream interpretation) for him to be done with the cake (Holy Spirit and Word of God, concerning dream interpretation, revelation) he was currently working on. And as he looked over he told someone at the counter to tell them to move along and wait somewhere else, because it was going to be awhile before the cake (finished dream book/ big project) was done. He really didn't like all those people waiting on him, while he was trying to work. It was a lot of pressure (me feeling the pressure of Christians waiting for the book.)

It's extremely important to know what is going on in your life, when God gives you revelation from His Spirit because this will help you to know where to apply the insight He gives you. Since, I've been writing this book, for a while God has shown me that I only have a narrow window of time to get this book completed. So, last night before I went to bed, I was thinking of what I needed to do tomorrow and that's when God gave me this dream. God is letting me know that I need to finish up with this book because there are a lot of people who are waiting to eat from the elaborate spiritual food contained, within the pages of this book. So yes, like the job of the Cake Boss, writing this book is a big job, but people are waiting on the finished product. And just like the scene of the dream reveals, God wants me to know that there is pressure on me to hurry up and finish! So, I responded to the wisdom and direction of the Holy Spirit and got busy writing!

Synonyms: Will Vary

In dreams or visions, symbols can have several synonyms. It's important to note that their meanings will vary, depending on the person who has the dream/vision and depending on the thought process, of the person who receives the image in their spirit man. If you're having a hard time trying to understand what God is saying, it's extremely important to try several different words that represent the specific image the Holy Spirit is trying to relay to you in the dream or vision.

For example, let's explore the synonyms and interpretations of a toilet. Let's say, that for awhile now, you have been praying about something specific and God shows you an image of a toilet in a night vision. Here are some ways the toilet can vary depending on the dreamers' terminology of a toilet and their dilemma or prayer concern.

70

Synonyms: TOILET

Can, Commode, Pot, Potty, John, Latrine, Outhouse, Privy, or Throne.

1. Let's say that you are a person who has been praying about leaving your job and then the Holy Spirit shows you a **toilet**. God may very well be using this symbol in a night vision because He's confirming to you that the job is in the **toilet**, thus saying you are free to leave the job.

2. Maybe you've been praying to God about your teenage child and asking the Lord to reveal to you what's the deal with them because they have been acting different lately. Then God shows you the **toilet**. God could be saying, they're on "**pot**" or the pot is the problem!

3. Maybe you're a woman who has been praying for a husband and you keep asking God what is your husband's name? Then you have a night vision dream of the "**toilet**." God could be trying to show you that your husband's name is "**John**"!

4. Maybe you're a boss and you have a lazy employee and for some time now, it's been on your heart to fire them, but you've been asking God for guidance to do His will and not your will. Then you have a night vision of the **toilet** and your thinking, oh man, what in the world does that mean? Well, God is trying to show you that you're free to "**Can**" them! These are just some of the ways that God speaks to us through symbolism, depending on the person and their own symbolic terminology.

On a more personal note, I usually seek God and ask God's permission before I do something big in my life. For example, I've known for a very long time that I would be on TV, but I did not want to get ahead of God's timing. So, one day I felt God leading me to start making some videos on dream interpretation and to put them up on You Tube. So, I prayed and asked God, if it was okay with Him and if I could

71

do this at this particular season of my life? And this is when, God gave me a vision of a toilet and I then knew for sure that He was saying YES and that I was released to do it. Why, you ask? Well, this is because, when I see a toilet and the door is not closed or locked, to me it means that I'm free to go and release everything that is within me, whenever I feel the need too. Meaning, I'm free to go to the potty anytime I want, as long as someone else is not in there already. So, in the case of me wanting to make videos, instead of the toilet being a symbol for me to release my internal waste, I knew God was saying that I was free to "**release**" the things that were stored up inside me, spiritually! There have been many times that I have prayed to God, and I ask him if I have His consent, green light, permission, ok, or go ahead to do something and He shows me a vision of a toilet. And now I have learned that this means **yes**; I'm free to do it or I'm released to go! So, when the Lord uses a symbol, to relay a message it is very important to consider exactly what it is that you have been asking God about, as well as all the possible synonyms that can apply to your situation. And it's extremely important to apply the revelation to the specific concern of your heart God is referring too.

Streets Can Have Meanings

In the past I have helped dreamers with their dreams and in the dream they were driving or walking on a certain street. And I would ask them, what does that street mean to you?

One man told me a dream, of how he was walking across a street together, with his son in their hometown. Slightly separated as they walked, the father saw his son get slammed and run over by a truck. Then after a bit, his boy got right back up! So, I said to this man what does that street mean to you? And he said, oh, it's the street we would walk across to go to the football field. And as I continued to help him with the interpretation to his dream, it turned out that the whole dream was about his son and what was going on in his football interest. In the dream, on the way to the football field his son got hit and run over by a truck. In the dream He suffered a major blow! But after a bit, he got back up.

Well, just like in the dream, in real life this boy did suffer a major emotional blow, because originally, he did not make the line up in football tryouts; but, later the coach called him and told him that he could be on the team. Therefore, as the dream showed in reality the boy did suffer a major blow of rejection, but then was resurrected by the coaches re-assessment concerning the boy's placement on the team. Thus relaying, acceptance!

The son's father knew all the facts, of what had happened in his son's life. So, his son's major blow and his resurrection victory, was on the heart of this father. If this dream would have been dreamt before the actual event in his son's life then this dream would have been considered a "**prophetic dream**" foretelling what was to come. However, this dream was showing this after all of this had already happened in his son's life. So, this dream was a symbolic picture to the father, of what his son suffered by the devastating news that he didn't make the team, but then later was on the team.

So, this is an example of a "**reflection dream**" where his father's thoughts, feelings and emotions were processed as symbolic dream pictures, paralleling this particular event in his son's life. Like, this father there have been many times I have had dreams or visions that have emphasized a particular street that I'm familiar with, in my life. So, it is very important to consider every symbol in the dream or vision, to glean as much insight as possible. For example, I will now share with you some of my symbols and their interpretations concerning my life. However, **please remember** that these symbols are my personal examples and you will have your own personal meanings to relate to your symbols in your dreams. It's all about asking yourself; **what does this street, person, place, color, or setting mean to me**? Be sure to draw the answers out of your own heart and then you will have your meaning!

73

Specific Streets: My Personal Symbols and Meanings

1. Independence Boulevard = A Road of Independence
Independence Blvd is a road in my town and recently God showed me, I was driving on this road. God was letting me know that I would soon be on **a road of "independence"**; meaning, I would be independent with some more freedom in my life.

It was about 5 months after this heavenly revelation that my husband was offered the opportunity to go out of town. And now for a short time, I'm living a life of independence and freedom! Currently, as I'm writing this section of the book, my husband is not here with me, and even though I love him so much, now I'm in a season of independence, like when I was single. I'm enjoying the freedom of not having to cook for us, excessive laundry piles or go to the gym! I can just be free to lie around and listen to God, work on my TV show or write this book at my sole convenience. Life is good!

2. Military Highway = Straight shot
Military Highway is a road in my home town it doesn't have many lights. So, when I drive down this road, I can go 50 miles an hour and get where I'm going. So, when I'm dreaming that I'm on this road, it's God's way of showing me that I'm going to get where **I need to go, fast and without a bunch of hindrances!**

3. Poplar Hall Ave. = Good Bible teaching
I associate Poplar Hall Ave. with a street I went to church at for 11- 12 years. This street represents a **Bible School St.**

4. Elbow Road = Dangerous road
Elbow Road is a road that goes straight for some ways and then has a very sharp right turn that is in the shape of an elbow. If, I'm remembering correctly, several people have been killed on this road and so, in my mind I see this as a very **dangerous road**.

74

So, if God gives me a dream and I'm walking or driving on this particular road. He is using this road as a parallel to send me the message that, I'm on a very dangerous road! You know the old saying "you're on a dangerous road buddy"! If and when someone says this to a person in real life, it means that they are trying to warn you that whatever it is that you're doing that you should tread very lightly or get off it!

For Example, and only as an example:

Maybe in real life, at the time of my dream, I was toying with the idea of sinning against God or, doing something that would be a major offense to God. Symbolically, God could be using the picture of me being on this road to get a message to me, like "hey Vonda, you're on a dangerous road here". The picture or dream of me being on this road could relate to, bringing in some type of spiritual death into my life. And God is using the dream to show me a warning that this is not a road I should want or need to be on.

5. Gravenhurst Street = Death Road

Gravenhurst St. is in my neighborhood and because of its name, I associate it with death. It reminds me of a funeral car or in other words "**a death hurst.**" One time God gave me vision of 3 black cars on this street that were all involved in a really bad and messy accident.

At the time of the vision, I'm about to share with you, I'd received some encouraging revelations from the Lord to minister to a friend of mine who operates in the prophetic. One revelation God gave me for her showed me that God would be bringing a new man into her life; I believed based on the visions that God was showing me that he would be her new husband. But, because I knew her and some things concerning her past loves; I was thinking about how, and when I presented this word of hope and promise to her, that I needed to counsel her in "BALANCE" based on what God had prepared for her in the future, combined with what I knew about her past love relationships. So, as I thought of her I was thinking about how she had been married 3 times and I was wondering if, I should counsel her by digging up the past reasons of why her other 3 marriages ended up in divorce.

And it was at that time, as I was seeking the Holy Spirit that He showed me the following vision and I automatically knew what He was saying. In the vision below, God was showing me that HE, God is the cop/authority and the 3 black cars that have been in a collision, represent her 3 bad marriages that all ended up in a wreck on "death hurst st"; thus meaning divorce. I will elaborate more after sharing the vision with you. Below is the vision god gave me.

Vision: Police Car lights on Gravenhurst St.
In the vision I was looking from a bird's eye view over and down the street from the Lynnhaven road direction. I saw one of my neighborhood streets, called Graven Hurst Street. In the vision, the street looked very congested; it was as if there was some type of traffic hold up on that street. As I looked, I saw a police car with flashing red and blue lights and a police man that was evaluating the accident. There were 3 black cars that were involved in the accident on the very congested street and by the revelation of the Lord, I knew that it was a street that I didn't need to try and go down.

My Interpretation:
So, through this vision and its symbolic meaning, I see the police authority (God who upholds the law) is assessing the three car accident situation and that God (law authority) is taking care to administer the fault in this bad situation. I can see that the authorities (God) has it all under control and since Gravenhurst, to me is a street name that means death; God is showing me that it's not for me to go down that road with her, concerning her dead marriages.

76

It's a road where her bad marriages have been put to death and I'm not to go down that road and add to the confusion. In the vision, God makes it clear to me that He is the one who has the authority to access the situation and He has got everything under control!

So, when I shared with her the great news of a new love interest coming her way, it was by the leading of the Holy Spirit that I encouraged her only in the information concerning the new man and I left the old mistakes under the blood of Jesus. So, by the Holy Spirit showing me this, I felt that God was saying, Vonda, "it's been handled"; and it was His way of letting me know that she had learned what she needed to learn from these past marriages and that I was not to try and figure out, why her past marriages did not work out and bring them up to her now. So, I heeded the wisdom of the Holy Spirit and I'm so glad that God's mercy endures forever and His mercy is new every morning in each of our lives. So, the specific feelings the dreamer has towards cake, streets or any other personal symbol at the time of the dream is the only meaning or interpretation that counts!

Arriving at an accurate dream interpretation depends on the context of the dream, the individual dreamer and what you have or you are currently experiencing in your life. No dream dictionary book has the answers you need, for the correct interpretation of your dream. Only you possess the answers to the symbols you need to know about in your dreams and the answers are in your heart! So, before going to a dream dictionary I challenge you to go straight to your heart and ask yourself, self........ what does this cake, street or symbol mean to me? And there you will have the only answer that may apply and be able to aid you, in receiving your **ACCURATE** dream interpretation.

As I stated earlier, most symbols in dreams will be **personal** to the dreamer, because we each have our own symbolic dictionary encoded in our mind, thoughts, emotions, and heart concerning our life's experiences.

77

However, sometimes there is an exception to the rule and you will not understand your dream. The **exception to this rule** is, if the Holy Spirit is giving you a message with some type of foreknowledge; something that is yet to come like a person, place, thing, time, or circumstance in which your natural mind has yet to experience. Something like the name of a city, a scene that is specific, but you've never been there. You may investigate the word or symbol and get understanding, but sometimes, it will take hindsight to know or understand the reason God showed it to you as foreknowledge. Then as time goes on and the night vision comes to pass, there will be a clearer understanding. The only **exception to this rule** of you **NOT** knowing is, of course if, the dream's information is revealed to you by the Spirit of God in you or an angel shows up in your dream and explains it to you, like in the book of Daniel.

Finally, I have a dream **"warning"** for you. I learned it as I sat under Herman Riffle and I have found it to be great wisdom! The warning is, a person should **"NEVER force or insist your symbolic meanings to apply in the interpretation of someone else's dream."** You may suggest your meanings as an option for them to consider, but insisting it or forcing your meanings on to other dreamers and their dream interpretation will take you into error. I hope you can see the point I'm trying to relay too you. The point being that there is **NO, ONE** single symbol interpretation for every dream; but, on the other hand for "balance," there may be similar symbolic meanings that can apply to your dreams as well as other people's dreams. But, you will not be successful in dream interpretation if you use the **"one shoe fits all"** mentality. So, I passionately urge you to search your own heart for your meanings. And when helping others with their dream, you should pose the question them, **what does that symbol mean to you**? Be sure to draw their symbolic meanings out of their own heart to apply to their dream and never force your meanings onto some one else's dream.

One Person, "Many Hats"
(The People in our dreams)

There are three important keys to apply when learning how to understand and interpret the people symbols in your dreams. Shortly after my "Dream Quest" began, I soon found out that the people in my dreams could literally play themselves, another person entirely or they could be symbolically playing a part of me. When people actually represent themselves and who they really are in the dream, these types of dreams can be much easier to understand, because the person's role in the dream is the same role as they walk out in their real life and this is the most **simplistic** way to understand the people in your dreams. However, when the person and who they are in real life does **NOT** fit in your dream and he or she makes **NO** sense to you, within the context of the dreams theme, lesson, message, or interpretation, then there is **one very important principle** to consider and this principle is that the people in your dreams can represent a **part of you**! This is a very important key I learned while sitting in Herman Riffles dream group and in turn he learned this principle from his studies at the Carl Jung institution. Wow, isn't that amazing that the people that you know or just see in life at the mall, on the street, at church, Face book or on TV, whether good or bad can actually represent you? Yes, you heard me correctly. Isn't that weird? And I do have to admit, that weird is what I originally thought, when I first heard this principle and to tell the truth, before I met Herman, I'm not sure if the people in my dreams were playing parts of me or not? But, soon after learning this principle from him, I did start to see that the application of this principle was really beginning to help me. I soon began to have more successful dream interpretations, especially, when it came to uncovering the meanings of why certain people were showing up in my dreams. However, don't forget that the people in your dreams can represent some one else entirely; but here is an example of how another person can represent the dreamer.

For example, let's say in real life your husband has a very foul mouth, and for some reason Howard Stern keeps showing up in your dreams. Well, if you don't have a foul mouth then most likely he's not playing a part of you or himself, but it's very likely that Howard's playing the role of your hubby! Walk with me as I share some information and examples of these three key principles, with you in further detail.

Have you heard the saying, "she wears a lot of hats"? This is a metaphor for a person that plays a lot of different roles in her life. I will use myself as an example. Below I will show you all the different parts of me or roles I play, so you can relate to the message that one person can be divided into other symbolic people.

Vonda: One Person Who Wears Many Hats......... I AM

1. Daughter of my parents
2. Daughter of the Lord
3. Wife
4. Aunt
5. Sister
6. Prayer
7. Worshiper
8. Church member
9. Dream Interpreter
10. Counselor
11. Radio host
12. TV host
13. Producer
14. Teacher
15. Seer/Prophet
16. Writer and Author
17. Editor
18. Student
19. Hairdresser
20. Niece to others
21. Friend
22. Exerciser
23. Maid
24. Cook
25. Baby sitter
26. Health Nut
27. Servant
28. Clothes shopper
29. Ex disc Jockey
30. Scribe

So, because as an individual we can wear many different hats in our lives, when we are dreaming God will pick a person we've observed in our life time to symbolically play a part of us. Because when we see someone we form an opinion about them and we associate certain people with certain meanings. Let me give you some examples.

80

People Symbolic of you - some celebrities
Symbolic Examples: Oprah (symbolic of TV Voice)
For example, often Oprah Winfrey will show up in my dreams and this is because, Oprah has a very strong influence as a television host. So, when she shows up in my dreams, I know that this dream will have something to do with the influential part of me, which is a television host on "Heart Hope". God is symbolically using Oprah in my dream, to represent the part of me that is a TV Host (most certainly not the same religious beliefs) with a strong influence! Makes perfect sense, doesn't it?

Barbra Stanwick: Victoria Barkley: (wisdom and nobility)
There are times when Barbra Stanwick will show up in my dreams as Victoria Barkley. I've always loved the Big Valley, I used to watch this western as a kid and now, whenever I watch it online, I'm enamored at the wisdom of Victoria Barkley and her noble character. So, when Victoria Barkley shows up in my dreams I know she's representing the part of me that walks in God's wisdom and nobility!

Joyce Meyers: (Bible Teacher)
On occasion, Joyce Meyers will show up in my dreams because she is a wonderful bible teacher; so, God will use her to play a symbolic role in my dream that represents the part of me that is a good bible teacher.

Ira Milligan: (dream interpreter)
On occasion, Ira Milligan will show up in my dreams because he is a good and Christian dream interpreter. So, when he is in my dream I know that the dream will have to do with the "Dream Interpreter" part of me. This is part of me that likes to help others understand their dreams.

Dolly Parton: (Large Breast/ Nurturer)
To me, breasts were created to nurture babies, so large breasts mean the ability to nurture a lot. Since, Dolly has large breast, in my dreams she is symbolic for the part of me that nurtures a lot of people in the spirit realm. The women I mentor are nurtured and the radio and TV show are both a form of spiritual nurturing.

81

Eathel Martin: (prophet)

Often, I have dreams, with a woman I know and her name is Eathel. In real life she's a very seasoned prophet who mentors me. Since she's a prophet, **sometimes** when she shows up in my dreams she will be playing the prophet role of me, because like her I'm a prophet too.

Selina: (Hair Salon Owner)

Like Selina, I used to own a hair salon, so she will often play the hair salon owner, part of me in my dreams.

Hopefully, you can get the gist of what I'm saying from the prior examples. And in addition to people playing parts of me, there are also times where people **don't or cannot** play a part of you. But will literally play themselves a PART of THEMSELVES, or they can play someone else entirely different that you may know in your life.

People, literally playing themselves:

My Earthly Father: Sometimes my earthly father will be in my dream and he will literally be playing himself. A dream with him in it will most likely be a dream concerning something that is going on in my family with my mom, brothers, nieces, or nephews.

Literal Examples: Eathel Martin (prophet of the Lord)

Sometimes, I have dreams and a friend of mine will be in the dream, her name is Eathel; in real life she is a prophet who mentors me. And when she shows up in my dreams, she will usually speak a message in my dream and when I wake up, I think about what she said in the dream; because I know God is most likely using her to give me a prophecy in my dream, while I'm sleeping! I love it when she shows up in my dreams, because usually it's a prophetic message dream and she is speaking to me "something," that obviously God thinks I need to know, concerning my life!

Benny Hinn: Once, I had a dream with Benny Hinn in it, and I was playfully rubbing the top of his hand, because I was trying to get some of his healing anointing. And as I rubbed his hand he looked me in my eyes and said, <u>**you're anointed**</u>"! So, the Holy Spirit was using Benny Hinn to play himself and to give and remind me of an important message concerning my Christ like ability to heal the sick. Just like Benny, I'm anointed. So, in this dream Benny, was not symbolic, for anyone else, but he was literally playing the role of himself. Understanding this dream was a piece of cake!

<u>People playing the role of another:</u>

For Example: Barak Obama (President of USA 2008-2012)

Often in my dreams, Obama will symbolically represent or play the role of the Lord Jesus. **Not** because of who he is or who he is not, morally, but, because in real life Obama is the "Commander in Chief" of our U.S. Military forces, which is similar to the role of Jesus as the "Commander in Chief" of the Lords Army!

George W. Bush

The same thing used to happen in my dreams, when George W. Bush was in office. God would use him to symbolically represent or to play the role of Jesus Christ in my dream. And most likely, new and future presidents will show up in my dreams to represent Christ as they're voted into the office of "Commander in Chief"; thus making these dreams extremely exciting and 99% of the time prophetic in nature!

Hercules

Periodically, Hercules will show up in my dreams as a symbolic representation of Jesus. (see page 245)

Morgan Freeman

Recently, God gave me message about something I was praying about and in the vision I saw Morgan Freeman talking to a group of people as if he was organizing something.

God is using Morgan Freeman to play the role of God in the vision, because in the movies Bruce Almighty, and Evan Almighty, it was Morgan Freeman who played the part of God. And in my opinion he did it very well!

My Earthly Father:
Sometimes, in my dreams my earthly father will symbolically play the role of my heavenly Father. In the dream, when this happens, I'm never allowed to see his face. In the dreams that my father is playing my heavenly Father, his face is either, blurry, invisible or sometimes I can't even see him, but I just know he is there or sense His presence.

My Mother
As we know, in my life my mother birthed me and was the source for me having life; and two of her strongest character traits are a wonderful reflection of our Heavenly Father. How, you ask? Well, like God, she is very merciful and giving. So, there are times when God will use her in my visions and dreams to parallel or play the role of Him. Because, He is the one who truly "birthed" me (**gave me life**) and He is the "Source" of my life. So, at times He will use her to relay a message to me concerning these same specific character traits of Himself that He is trying to emphasize in the dreams message. He uses her when He wants me to remember that He's a God who gives and that He is a God of mercy. So, when she plays the role of God in my dreams, He's most likely highlighting or emphasizing the giving and merciful characteristics of His nature.

Hopefully, you can get the gist of what I'm saying, in the prior examples and see how people in your dreams can be symbolic of you, someone you know, or like "Barak Obama" he can literally play a part of himself, yet still represent another, like Jesus Christ. Keep practicing and you will get it!

84

Colors

There are so many dream books that give "reasonable definitions" to the colors that can show up in your dreams. However, in order to arrive at a concise and accurate interpretation, concerning the colors in your dream, it is critical to express your personal feelings of the color in reference to the particular item in question, when interpreting your dreams. For example, you may not like to wear a white shirt, but you may prefer to own a white car. When identifying your colors you will have different feelings about certain colors depending on the symbol. I would never buy a green car, but I love the way a green shirt looks on me! Also, please note that colors will contain "special significance" in their meanings, when the item in the dream is a different color then it normally would be in real life.

For example, a blue tree, green elephant or a black and white purple polka dotted airplane. When symbolic colors are extreme or abnormal in color, the colors, patterns, textures or color combinations are trying to make a specific point! So, be sure to pay extra consideration when people, places, things, or items are unnatural and abnormal colors in your dream. When this happens the dream is trying relay a specific message to you about the color. So, be sure to ask yourself how you feel about the color, concerning the specific symbol and don't accept someone else's definition of what that color means to them. If, you do take on their answer, then this will turn your dream into their dream and God is not trying to relay a message to them, but He's speaking to you and using a specific color that holds a specific meaning to you as the dreamer. However, if the answer from your heart is truly the same as theirs, then that's fine as long as it's your true meaning too. Let me give you a few examples.

White Shirt:

Let's say that in my dream I'm wearing a white shirt. If I looked this up in a dream dictionary it would most likely tell me that this represents purity or righteousness and this would be fine, if that was truly my opinion of a white shirt. However, in real life I don't really like white shirts because they make me look "washed out." I much prefer a shirt with some color. So, I need to assign my meaning to the shirt and not the meaning in the dream dictionary. My answer is the only answer that counts because it's my dream and my dream or vision symbols are "**personal**" to me and my feelings.

Lavender Dress Shirt:

One time I had a night vision dream and in it I saw a beautiful, fitted, long-sleeved, lavender shirt with ruffles going down the button area. It was my mom's shirt and it looked very professional. The tag on the shirt sleeve had been marked down to a sale price of $18.37.

My interpretation could not be found in a dream dictionary, but its interpretation could only be determined by me taking the proper steps of me seeking my own heart.

I love the <u>color lavender and I like the way it looks on me</u>. This shirt was a <u>professional shirt</u>, like something a trendy teacher would wear. In the night vision, <u>I knew it belonged to my mom,</u> but I wanted it for myself and the price was $<u>18.37</u>

Often my mom is symbolic for the **giving** or **merciful** part of God and in the dream the storyline shows that it's Gods (mom's) shirt to give or keep. Since, the professional shirt looks like a teacher's shirt and I'm a dream interpretation teacher, who in real life desires to teach again, then this is symbolic for the part of me that wants to wear that dream teacher's shirt (**position**) again. Just like, I desire the shirt in the dream.

The numbers that make up the markdown price were $18.37. Eighteen is symbolic for the 18 years, I've been saved and 37 is how old I was, when I had my first prophetic dream. So, God put two of my personal numbers on the shirt.

These numbers represent the saved part (<u>18</u>) of me and my personal number of <u>37,</u> which represents the prophetic dreamer part of me. God is saying, He has a shirt with my "number" on it! It's as if He is saying, I can have the shirt for the price of my own spiritual D.N.A. The numbers on the ticket represent the saved (18) dream (37) teacher (style of shirt) part of me and the fact that my personal numbers are on the tag, means that God has a NEW SHIRT for me to wear. Meaning, teaching on dreams again is in my future! Because, I have what it takes to wear the shirt! It's gonna cost me $18.37 and in real life, I "<u>**fit the bill**</u>" or <u>I can</u> pay the price of $18.37. Do you get it? So, as you can see my mom's meaning and the color lavender as well as the numbers eighteen and thirty seven are all personal symbols to me and only I would know those answers. God showed me this shirt because I have been praying and hoping for another teaching opportunity.

Salmon Peach Shirt

Recently, I had a night vision dream where I looked down at my own stomach and saw that my stomach was big and it was obvious that I was pregnant; I was wearing a salmon peach colored shirt. When I woke up I knew the interpretation was that God was telling me, I would be pregnant one day. The reason God had me in a salmon peach colored shirt was because in real life I would never wear this color. I don't like this color on me. So, because I know when I finally do get pregnant, I'm not going to like being big, plump and nauseated. God was using the unattractive color of the shirt to get the message to me that I will one day, literally wear the unattractive look of pregnancy. It's not merely symbolic of something I'm birthing in the Spirit realm, but it's representing a literal pregnancy. Get it?

The Black and White striped shirt:

First, let me give you a little background. The night of this dream, before I went to sleep my mentor and I had just ministered prophetically to several people on my radio show. Usually she did all the prophetic ministry, while I hosted, but this time God had given me some visions to share with a couple of the callers and it was that same night after ministering, I had the following dream.

In this "<u>Night Vision Dream</u>," as I looked at myself, I saw I was wearing a black and white striped shirt; the stripes were very thick in diameter and went horizontally across my body. In real life, I don't wear shirts like this, because I think that they make me look fatter or really big and most of us women, like to look as small as possible!

So, when I awoke and remembered what I'd seen in my dream, I instantly knew what God was trying to tell me. He was showing me that I was really BIG! Meaning, I looked like a BIG person in the realm of the spirit. So, the Holy Spirit was paying me a compliment and He was encouraging me, concerning my recent prophetic service to others on the radio show. I don't know about you, but I'll take as much encouragement from the Holy Spirit as He wants to give me! I mean after all, isn't that one of His functions, to encourage us. I can never get enough of that! God telling me that I'm really big in the things of the Spirit? I'll take that!

In this chapter, up until this point we have thoroughly covered revelatory, universal, and personal symbols. Finally, in closing we will cover evolving symbols.

Evolving Symbols

4. <u>Evolving Symbols:</u> Some symbols can change and will evolve over time. Things that once meant something specific to you, can as time passes become to mean something new and different to you, depending on your current view of that symbol. Let me give you some examples.

88

Remember earlier when I shared the meaning George W. Bush and how at one time, while he was in office he was symbolic in my dreams for Jesus the "Commander and Chief"?

Well, this is a perfect example of how symbols can **evolve**. At this particular time, when he was in my dream, this was an accurate symbolic interpretation, because at that time he was the president of the U.S.A. But as soon as he left the presidential office he no longer represented Jesus nor, kept his meaning of "Commander in Chief" because in real life things changed, therefore his symbolic meaning evolved.

Now, Barak Obama is the Commander in Chief and because of his current presidential status, he now represents Jesus in my dreams. So, now when Bush shows up in my dreams, because it is my opinion that Bush took us very deep into debt when he declared "The War on Terror;" he and his symbolic meaning has evolved and he currently represents a part of me that was responsible for going into some much needed business debt.

Another Example: Ryan, my best friend.
I used to have a friend name Ryan, he helped me renovate my hair salon, which entailed tons of work. He never complained and was such an amazing blessing to me, we hung out all the time and this man was so good to me that he was my like my best friend! So, back then, when I dreamt, God would use Ryan to symbolically play the part of the "Holy Spirit," because in real life the Holy Spirit was my best friend! Do you get my drift?

But, now things have changed and Ryan has moved on and I'm married to a wonderful man that is my new best friend who treats me like a queen. So, because symbols do evolve and change, according to the events in our lives, my friend Ryan, no longer plays the role of the Holy Spirit in my dreams. Now, he is simply symbolic of someone who was a huge blessing to me!

Finally, I will share this last example with you, concerning evolving symbols. When I was young I loved to go horseback riding. One year at the age of ten, I was at summer camp and during that time, I won a certificate for being the "best rider." I was so honored I felt ten feet tall, when I won this award. But, later when I was in my twenties, I went riding, and the horse I was on ran wild and took off. Finally, the horse came to a sudden halt as he found himself face to face with a barbed wire fence in front of him and it was at this screeching halt that he almost threw me. So, now I don't like horseback riding that much! I shared this with you so, you can see how specific scenes, or symbols can evolve, over time. In the past, I loved riding horses, but since this occurrence in my life, my feelings have evolved or changed and I'm now, more fearful of riding.

So, if God had me on a horse, in my dream, back when I loved riding them, it would mean something that **I loved to do**! But, today if I dream of riding, it would mean something totally different. Meaning, it would symbolize a scene or setting, **I'm leery, fearful and don't fully trust**!

So, when you are evaluating your symbols please keep in mind that your dream symbols can vary and will evolve so make sure that you keep your answers current and relative to the events that are occurring in your life presently and not for who or what they used to mean to you. Just because they meant something specific to you, yesterday doesn't mean they still fit that way in your dream interpretation today. So, stick with it and don't give up! It took me about a year or two of daily practice, with my dream partner to understand the mysteries of my soul. And I've learned that God has much to say to me and my ability to interpret my dreams is extremely beneficial in my walk with Him. Like anything, some people will catch on sooner than others, but nevertheless "with God all things are possible"!

Chapter 6
Dreams

Nelson's New Illustrated Dictionary/ Encyclopedia, defines the word "<u>Dream</u>": as a state of mind in which images, thoughts, and impressions pass through the mind of a person who is sleeping, and dreams have had a prominent place in the religious literature of ancient peoples."

"St. Jerome's mistranslation of certain key biblical passages led Medieval Christians to fear their dreams and to view them as the devil's invitation to sin (RandomHouse.com)." Today, for this reason many Christians within their church circles have thought it very taboo to dabble in dream interpretation. However, some Christians do appreciate its scriptural validity and long to understand the wonderful things God may be trying to say to them through their dreams. Often, I hear believers brag about how God speaks to them through their dreams, as if they are "someone special." This is a real pet peeve of mine because God longs to speak to each one of His children and every child of God is "special", whether they hear from God in their dreams or not! It has been my experience that many of what my brother and sisters call prophetic God dreams, are in fact **NOT** God dreams at all, but are reflection dreams expressing the desires of their own heart and in their naivety they have jumped to false conclusions, concerning the dreams interpretation. But, what people fail to understand, is just like breathing, seeing, thinking, talking, walking, and sleeping, one's ability to "DREAM" is a natural function of the human body. And "aside from those who experience certain kinds of injury, it's a biological fact that everyone dreams" (RandomHouse.com). Dreams are literal or symbolic pictures that surface in your being, while you are sleeping and Mark and Patty Virkler teach in their book *Hear God through your Dreams*, "it has been proven and is a scientific fact that we dream every night," but, whether or not you remember your dream is a different story all together!

Just because you're not remembering your dream doesn't mean you're not dreaming. The truth is you're just **NOT** remembering your dream. So my friends, if this is you and you're not remembering your dream, ask God to help you to remember and He will help you to remember them. It's my belief that learning how to interpret your dreams will revolutionize your walk with God. Just like understanding and applying God's Word to your life, interpreting your dreams <u>correctly</u> can be a critical tool to maintaining a godly walk. Does God still speak through dreams today? The answer is yes and He will continue to speak to us in the future through dreams and visions. Below are 8 scriptural reasons, why we should expect to hear from God today in the present as well as in our future dreams.

God Has Spoken: (Past Tense)
1. God declared that He <u>has or did speak</u> through dreams and visions (**Visions in the night**) and used similitude's in the Old Testament.

HOSEA 12:10 "I have also spoken by the prophets, and I <u>have</u> multiplied visions, and used similitude's, by the ministries of the prophets

God Will Speak: (Future tense)
2. God declared, in the Old Testament; He <u>will speak</u> and make himself known through dreams and visions.

NUMBERS 12:6 And He said, "Hear now my words: If there be any prophet among you, I the Lord will make myself known to him in a vision, and <u>will speak</u> to him in a dream.

3. **David** declared, God <u>counsel's</u> in the night and most likely it was through his dreams he was counseled.

Psalms 16:7 (NASB) I will bless the Lord who <u>has counseled</u> me: Indeed, my mind (inner man) <u>instructs me in the night.</u>

4. Even in the New Testament, God declared He <u>will communicate</u> through dreams and visions in the last days and this means TODAY, because we are definitely in the last days!

ACTS 2:17. "'In the last days, God says, I will pour out my Spirit on all people. Your sons and daughters will prophesy, your young men <u>will see visions,</u> your old men <u>will dream dreams.</u>'"

5. Dreams are calling us <u>to change</u> so we will not perish

<u>JOB 33: 14-18,</u> For God does speak—now one way, now another—though man may not perceive it. **In a dream, in a vision of the night,** when deep sleep falls on men as they slumber in their beds, he may speak in their ears and terrify them with warnings, **to turn man from wrong doing** and keep him from pride, to preserve his <u>soul</u> from the pit, his **life from perishing by the sword.**

6. God <u>does very significant things</u> within dreams.
   (Genesis 15: 12, 13, 18)

For example, God established the Abrahamic Covenant in a dream and made Abraham **"<u>A PROMISE.</u>"**

7. God grants <u>supernatural gifts</u> through dreams. God promised he would give Solomon Wisdom to judge the Israelites. The living proof is the book of Proverbs. (I Kings 3: 5, 9, 12, 15)

8. What would you say the odds are of <u>you speaking with God</u> in a dream? Scriptures show we can converse with God in our dreams.

God spoke <u>with</u> Abemilich, <u>with</u> King Solomon and <u>with</u> Jacob in their dreams. There's a distinct difference in speaking <u>to</u> someone and speaking <u>with</u> them. Speaking with them is a dialog and not a monologue. Like them, God can and may want to speak with you in your dreams. God is no respecter of persons within the body of Christ! So, believe this principle and expect God to speak to you or with you in your dreams. This is scriptural! So, my friends, like the word of God says let it be done to you according to the measure of your faith!

Dreams are literal or symbolic pictures that surface in your being while you're sleeping. It didn't take me long after the beginning of my dream interpretation quest to find out that there are 2 categories of dreams. One being an "Ordinary dream," which is what I like to call a "Reflection dream" and the other being a "Prophetic dream"; below, I will share with you a biblical definition of the word dream, from the "Blue Letter Bible," which is an online resource site.

Dream has two definitions. (Blue letter bible online resource)
"Dream" in Hebrew is translated *chalowm*
     a) dream (ordinary)
     b) dream (with prophetic meaning)

As defined by the "Blue Letter Bible" there are two types of dreams; one type of dream is called an "Ordinary dream" and the other type of dream is identified as a "Prophetic dream." Here are some synonyms for the word "ordinary." Some synonyms are: average, common, everyday, normal, routine, run of the mill, standard, or unexceptional. A large percentage of the dreams we dream will be ordinary, but we can still learn very valuable lessons by learning to interpret and understand our so called "ORDINARY" dreams. Ordinary dreams will reflect the ordinary events of our daily life. So, as I mentioned earlier, ordinary dreams are what I like to call "Reflection dreams" and throughout this book I will use the term reflection, when speaking in reference to an ordinary dream. Each time we sleep we'll be dreaming one of the two types of dreams. We will dream a "Reflection dream" or a "Prophetic dream."

What is the difference, you ask? Well, a reflection dream is when a person is dreaming a story line with symbolic pictures reflecting the things that **have happened** in the ordinary events of your everyday life; or secondly, you can be receiving revelation from God in your dreams about something He wants' to reveal to you through a dream in the night and this type of dream is called a "**Prophetic dream.**" Please note that there are **4 types** of prophetic dreams, one being a "**Reflective & Prophetic Combination,**" secondly a "**Night Vision dream,**" which the bible refers to as a vision in the night, third is what I like to call a "**Wisdom or Knowing dream,**" and finally a "**General Prophetic dream**" in which, I will thoroughly explain all four throughout the following pages. So, whether it's a reflection dream, which is a dream that shows a series of mirroring pictures that reflect and emotional story about your ordinary daily life or a prophetic dream, which is a dream that comes from the depths of God's Spirit within your soul to give you a supernatural message from the Holy Spirit to minister to you, concerning your earthly purpose in God, or about your relationship with Him. It's important to note that both types of dreams are trying to send your "natural man" a message, so you can be enlightened and grow from what you observe about yourself or the message within the dream. So hang with me as I elaborate, further on reflection and prophetic dreams in chapter seven and eight. But, just incase you were wondering what I think about Lucid dreams and why I did not count it or teach on it as a dream type, here is my response to an e-mailer.

LUCID DREAMS

Hey Vonda, I love watching your Heart Hope shows on you tube. It's been such a blessing and you are a light. I've always been curious about my dreams because they have always been so vivid and at times lucid. "**Lucid dreaming**" (any dream in which one is aware that one is dreaming and then able to control it). I've always been so intrigued by them because since a kid, I have always had many lucid dreams, its like, I'm asleep and dreaming and I'm truly aware of the fact

I'm sleeping and in the dream state; I get to control the dream and be who I want and do what I want (my conscious is aware of my subconscious.) I can even tell myself in my dream to wake up, and I always wake up in reality. Would you tell me about it, give me some insight on these types of dreams? Thank you and **God bless, Shavon**

Hi, **Shavon**, thank you for your question! Now concerning "<u>Lucid dreams</u>." Lucid dreams do not need to be interpreted because you as the dreamer are controlling the dream, thus you are the motivating factor of the dream and its storyline, in the sense that you create the storyline while being conscious of your dream.

When you're conscious of what you're dreaming and consequently start to play a part in the dream making it a lucid dream, you take out the unknown factor and play the part of what is known in the dream. You're doing your own thing in the dream and you decide the storyline of your dream, not God. In doing this, you're creating your own story and what good is that?

But, when you are dreaming a regular dream from within the subconscious you are **not aware**. Your conscious thoughts are shut down while you are asleep. Hence, taking **NO PART** in determining how the dream starts, plays out or finishes. And since you don't have anyway of knowing what is going on in your dream concerning the reflective message it contains or the prophetic message that may be possible, then this is why you would need to interpret it. Why? Well, because you took no part in its development, so you don't know what it means!

<u>I would spend absolutely no time, whatsoever on lucid dreaming or considering their interpretations</u>. The only type of dream that contains any real worth are Reflection dreams that show you or mirror your faults in its content so you can learn, change and grow from them; or a Prophetic dream that is created and contains revelation from the Holy Spirit to bring you an unknown message for His great purposes in your life. I hope this helps you! **Blessings, Vonda**

Chapter 7
REFLECTION DREAMS

Genesis 50:6 says, "so Joseph died, being one hundred and ten years old and they embalmed him, and he was put in a coffin in Egypt"; the "*Quest Study Bible*" records, Daniels prophetic ministry began in 605 B.C. as a youth and it ended in 536 B.C., in which he spent approximately 69 years in Babylonian leadership. Biblical accounts reveal that both Joseph and Daniel lived long and prosperous lives and modern science has proven that every person dreams in their sleep, whether they remember their dream or not. So, as we take both of these facts into consideration, I think it's very important to point out that out of all the years Joseph lived, scripture only records two prophetic dreams concerning him and his personal life. And Daniel only recorded two personal prophetic dreams through-out his governmental leadership in Babylon, concerning Gods future will within the earth and its dominion thereof. Please note, I'm not referring to Daniels visions or angelic visitations. And if two prophetic dreams seem like a low number, to you, it's vital to remember that the other dreams that are mentioned in the book of Daniel were Nebuchadnezzar's dreams and Daniel only interpreted the dreams for him. And yes, it's possible that Joseph and Daniel may have dreamt many more dreams than biblically recorded; however, let's work with the biblical facts that scripture supports and let's explore the math ratio concerning "Reflection Dreams."

Mathematically speaking, since Joseph lived 365 days per year, multiplied by his 110 year lifespan, this equals 40,150 days and within all of those days Joseph only had two prophetic dreams concerning his God given calling. Then we have Daniel who lived 365 days per year until his 90's, who most likely spent approximately 69 years of his governmental nights dreaming, in which multiplied by 365 days equal 25,180. And yet, he too only recorded two prophetic dreams? So, if science is correct and they were dreaming every night, then I think it's fair to say that statistically speaking, the percentage of "Prophetic dreams" as opposed to "Reflection dreams" are extremely small and minuet, when we are considering the actual percentage bracket. Wouldn't you agree?

Between these two revered and great biblical Israelite dreamers and dream interpreters, they lived 65,330 days; if, our modern scientific facts are correct and they dreamt every time they went into a REM sleep state, then it's fair to say that 99% of their dreams were reflection dreams and their prophetic dreams were way below 1%. This percentage is so low it's really closer to zero then one percent. Thus, supporting my rough estimation concerning Christians, rarely dreaming prophetic dreams. Please note that I'm not saying this as an iron clad rule, because now as Spirit filled believers we are extremely blessed to have the Holy Spirit living within us and we are under a new and better covenant, which provides us with God's unlimited comfort and edification. And even though, I'm not currently having any prophetic end time dreams, I am happy to report that I've have had 40 or so prophetic dreams concerning my personal life and I have literally received thousands of visions, from God. So, be encouraged because it's God who decides, when and how much revelation He chooses to reveal to His children! God has much to say and He rewards those who diligently seek Him! But, overall the majority of my dreams have been reflection dreams and the majority of your dreams will be reflection dreams too, so let me share some insight with you concerning **"Reflection Dreams."**

I have learned, reflection dreams, reflect what is in your heart; Jesus says, "The good man brings good things out of the good stored up in his heart, and the evil man brings evil things out of the evil stored up in his heart." Luke 6:45a

Proverbs 27:19 says: As water **reflects** a face, so a man's **heart reflects** the man.

My personal interpretation or understanding of Proverbs 27:19 is that God is saying; just as water can show you a reflection of what your face really and truly looks like, **(pretty or ugly)** so does a man's heart **(because dream pictures, surface as symbolic pictures of one's heart)**, it really shows you what the man looks like on the inside and reflects the man.

Daniel shares another very important dream principle, with us; let's read the scripture. Daniel 2:28-30(NKJV) "But there is a God in heaven who reveals secrets and He has made known to Nebuchadnezzar what will be in the latter days. Your dream, and the visions of your head upon your bed, were these: As for you, O king, thoughts came to your mind, while on your bed, about what would come to pass after this; and He who reveals secrets has made known to you what will be. "But as for me, this secret has not been revealed to me because I have more wisdom than anyone living, but for our sakes who make known the interpretation to the king, **and that you may know the thoughts of your heart**."

Daniel said, God wanted Nebuchadnezzar to know the thoughts of his (kings) heart. So, even though the dream Daniel was referring to in this scripture was a prophetic dream. We can still use this principle as a "rule of thumb" within our outlook, concerning our Reflection Dreams and use his wisdom to see how it's very advantageous for us to monitor, watch over, and know the thoughts of our hearts!

King Solomon the wisest man on earth said, "Too much activity gives you restless dreams; too many words make you a fool (Ecclesiastes 5:3 NLT.) I don't know about you but, I want to understand my dreams, so I can monitor the pretty, ugly, or restless thoughts of my heart! Solomon the wisest man on earth said, "above all, watch over your heart with all diligence, for from it flows the springs of life" (Proverbs 4:23.) Okay, I hear ya and your interest is peaked. So, now you're asking me to tell you more about reflection dreams. Right? Right! Well, I'm glad you asked!

Dream Type: Reflection: Dreams

Reflection dreams are dreams that consist of or reveal and solely reflect or mirror, what a person is or has emotionally experienced; as well as the thoughts of a person's soul, "which are the thoughts of your heart or mind" (**heart in Daniel 2:30 NKJV**) or (**Mind in Daniel 2:30 NASB**). These thoughts can be known thoughts or unknown thoughts.

1. **Known thoughts** are conscious thoughts of your heart or mind.

2. **Unknown thoughts** are unconscious/sub conscious thoughts of your heart or mind.

Reflection dreams are literal or symbolic pictures that surface in your being, while you are sleeping and these pictures usually reflect or mirror, what is going on in the **negative** or **positive** emotional realms of our hearts. The pictures that make up our dreams are symbolic pictures representing things that have happened to us during the day, inside our spiritual, emotional or physical man. So, in our daily life, if our hearts are torn up, oppressed, hurt, hateful, frustrated, envious, lustful, angry, abused, depressed, traumatized or broken; then it is extremely likely that the symbolic pictures that surface in our dream, while asleep, are going to be an encoded dream with similar feelings and storyline that parallels the negative situation in your life, which would be a negative reflection dream. Essentially, understanding the dream and its interpretation can help us to face these resolved, unresolved or suppressed emotions within our lives. Moreover, helping us to deal with our issues and to grow within our soul realm by applying God's Word to these negative issues in our lives. On the other end of the spectrum, if our heart is excited, expectant, faith filled, peaceful, joyful, loving, caring, happy, hopeful, healed, and whole, then most likely on a regular basis your dreams will tend not be so negative in context. But, can reflect the happiness, hope and heart health, you feel and are truly experiencing in your life.

For example, instead of having a bad or troubling dream concerning a negative issue, you my dream that you are lying on a beach in Hawaii with a cold beverage in your hand as you joyfully relax and bath in the sun! It would not be uncommon for someone to have a reflection dream, like this as they are about to start packing to go on their long awaited vacation! So, as we can see reflection dreams can be positive or negative, based on the emotional feelings of the dreamer. But, as with most things, there is an "__exception__" to every rule, so hang with me and I will elaborate further through this example.

I have learned that all negative or positive reflection dreams can be identified and interpreted by the dominate "__FEELING__" or a specific "__THOUGHT__" within the dream; but the one exception to the rule is, there are times when you will have a very strong feeling and because of the intense feelings in the dream, you think it's a reflection dream. But, as you consider the dream you'll discover that it's not a reflection dream at all, but it is a prophetic dream with an induced feeling given to you by the Holy Spirit, which has absolutely nothing to do with the reflection of your hearts health!

For Example: My Friend Died: (Vonda's dream)

In the dream, I was extremely upset and devastated because my friend died. In the dream she left me her inheritance, but I did not care about the inheritance! I just wanted her to be back in my life.

When I woke up from this dream, I was crying and I felt devastated; it seemed so real. However, every which way I tried to apply the dreams feeling of devastation, into my life, it just did NOT fit! It reflected absolutely NOTHING I was going through at that time in my life. The feeling of the dream was that I was devastated and I knew that this could not have been anything I was reflecting, because as a newlywed, life was good. And I had never been happier!

101

So, I called my friend and told her about the dream and God ministered some prophetic words to us, about me inheriting her spiritual mantle, after she literally dies in real life. However, I truly did not know what to make of this dream. So, I just left it alone and continued to work on my other dreams.

Fulfillment: Sure enough 3 months later, my friend and I had a falling out and she decided to sever our friendship. She did not die literally, but because she did not want to continue the friendship any longer, she became like dead to me. Now, I see in hindsight that God was trying to give me a heads up and prepare me for the fall out, but I just didn't get it until after the event. Therefore, making this a prophetic dream, which predicted the devastating death of our severed friendship.

So, when it comes to reflection dreams this is "**the exception to the rule.**" Meaning, there may be times when the feelings of your dream, DO NOT reflect anything that is currently going on in your life. And no matter how many ways you try to relate the feeling to a real life occurrence, it just will NOT fit, thus making the dream a strong possibility of being a prophetic wisdom or foretelling type of dream. And if that is the case then most likely, you will not know 100% for sure, what it means until after the prediction comes to pass in your life. These types of prophetic dreams can happen to the best of us, even if you're sanctified, joyful and perfectly happy, because God is allowing you to dream of an up and coming negative issue that's on the horizon; also there will be times you can be struggling with a isolated issue in your life that makes you have a dream that reflects the one isolated, yet negative issue and since nobody's life is "PERFECT" all the time, this is going to be an ongoing **"exception to the rule,"** throughout your life. Why you ask? Well it's because we are always learning and growing, as people and things are going to come up. And throughout our lives some drama will occur periodically, even though it's not the norm! (Additional Example: "Left behind dream" pg. 126)

102

So, the bottom line is, no matter what type of dream it is, we should try with all diligence to understand what our soul is relaying to us or what God is trying to speak to us through the dream's message.

When you dream a reflective dream there will be many times when we will be aware of what the dream is reflecting and then there will be many times when we don't have a clue what the dream is reflecting in our lives. The times we don't understand the message the dream is trying to relay to us, may be because we have ignored, overlooked or suppressed our emotional feelings concerning the dramatic issues in our lives. Normally, we tend to think of things like divorce, death, sickness, abuse or poverty as the dramatic issues; however, to the soul realm, dramatic issues could be things like rejection, loneliness, depression, embarrassment, fear, insecurities, jealousy, covetousness, anger, anxiety, worry, envy, self esteem, or failure. As a person you may think, just because you are functioning in life, this means that you're ok! And that is true to some extent but, God is not just concerned about your ability to function daily. He is also intensely concerned about your ability to walk in godliness, righteousness, peace, and joy in the Holy Ghost.

Jesus died on the cross for our sins and our healing and it is through the Word of God and the blood of Jesus that was shed for us, that God wants to bring us healing and wholeness; not just to our physical body, but He wants to bring healing to every area of the heart and soul that has been traumatized. So, whether, it's because of the fall of man and the sin that once reigned in our lives, a onetime burst of anger, or the trauma that has come from the events and people in our lives, who have hurt us; God wants' our hearts pure, healthy, happy and whole, not hurt, murderous, sinful, and evil!

For Example: The Killing dream

Let's say you have a dream that you're at your job and for some reason things are really dark in the dream and you're fuming mad at one of your co-workers; then before you know it you're yelling at him or her and it leads into a fist fight with them. Then all the sudden you find a knife in your hand and you stab them and kill them. Then you wake up thinking? Oh man, what in the heck was that all about?

Well, if this dream is reflecting a real life hostile environment at your job then the interpretation of the dreams setting is a "no brainer," because in real life you already know that this is symbolic of you're ongoing hostile work environment. However, regardless if you know it or not, the dreams storyline is showing you that you killed the person! This negative reflection dream is most likely a true reflection of your feelings. This dream could be using the killing as a parallel that you killed them with the sharpness of your tongue or in other words it could be showing you that your feelings towards them are angry enough that you could kill them! You know how we playfully think or say to people, when they really mess up; oh man, "I could have just killed him for what he did"! (Exception: Sometimes dying can be good, see pg, 215)

Matt 5:21 (NASB) You have heard that the ancients were told, YOU SHALL NOT COMMIT MURDER' and 'Whoever commits murder shall be liable to the court.'

Matt 5:22 (NASB) "But I say to you that everyone who is **angry** with his brother shall be guilty before the court; and whoever says to his brother, 'You good-for-nothing,' shall be guilty before the supreme court and whoever says, 'You fool,' shall be **guilty enough to go** into the fiery hell.

Matt 5:27-28 (NASB) You have heard that it was said, 'YOU SHALL NOT COMMIT ADULTERY'; but I say to you that everyone who **looks at a woman with lust** for her has **already committed adultery** with her in his heart.

104

1 John 3:15 (NASB) says, everyone who hates his brother is a murderer; and you know that no murderer has eternal life abiding in him.

If you're a Christian, Jesus says that these feelings are sin and sinful feelings are a deep concern to God; and if you or I, as Christians ever have these feelings in our heart then they should be of a concern to us too and we should ask for forgiveness and repent! We should quickly deal with these ungodly feelings, according to the Word of God. The word of God says, sin and its desires are conceived in the heart and mind first, before it becomes and action, therefore giving birth to sin.

James 1:14-16 (NKJV) says....
But each one is tempted when he is drawn away by his own desires and enticed. Then, when desire has conceived, it gives birth to sin; and sin, when it is full-grown, brings forth death. Do not be deceived, my beloved brethren.

Let's look in the word and see what Daniel said to King Nebuchadnezzar, regarding the reason God gave him this dream. You know the story. The king is in his bed and thinking on the things that are to come and God gives him a dream about a large tree that has been chopped down by an angel. The King demands the dream to be told to him by supernatural means, as well as its interpretation made known to him or heads are going to roll! So, just as God wanted the King to know the thoughts of his heart and mind, concerning Nebuchadnezzar being a chopped down tree. God also wanted him to see his **prideful heart** and repent from his wicked ways. Just like Nebuchadnezzar the Lord Jesus wants' you and I to know the thoughts of our hearts and mind, concerning the issues or sin that may be birthing in our lives. Remember the earlier example I shared with you about that anger issue with the person at your job that you could "just kill"! Well, the word of God says that everyone who hates his brother is a murderer; and you know that no murderer has eternal life abiding in him. (1 John 3:15)

105

So, if we can understand the negative reflection messages that our dreams are trying to relay to us, then we can confess our sins unto the Lord and know that He is faithful and just to forgive us and to cleanse us of all unrighteousness and ungodliness. When we keep track of the thoughts of our hearts and minds, and seek forgiveness we can maintain a godly heart, through the crucifixion of our flesh and maintain right standing with God, through the blood of the lamb because God is able to cleanse our hearts and minds through our confessions to Christ. When we understand the messages our souls are trying to relay to us through the interpretation of our negative reflective dreams, we can examine our hearts, confess our sins and seek His forgiveness, long before it is ever birthed into an actual sin. For believers, understanding your dreams is a great tool for the Holy Spirit to work through, because by Him showing us our true selves He can bring correction to our mindset and attitude, when needed. Therefore, leading us to apply the Word of God in our lives and moreover we continue to please God, by walking in godliness. And in turn, we can maintain the enjoyment of all His wonderful benefits! Remember, the word of God says, if we judge ourselves then we will not have to be judged. So, let's heed Gods wisdom and let's regularly review or judge our own hearts!

Now, please let me share with you a personal example of a negative "**reflection dream**" and how the correct interpretation, with counseling could've been used to minister the **healing power** of Christ to my broken and traumatized heart.

Reflection Dream: The Car Accident (Vonda's Dream)

When I was 22 years old I dreamt that my boyfriend was driving in his red 300 ZX sports car and from out of nowhere he was tragically hit by another vehicle and killed instantly. Suddenly, my boyfriend was dead and I was traumatized by his sudden death in the dream. It was very tragic to me, so tragic that the next day I went looking for him to see if he really had died or if, it was just a dream.

Let me share a little background about me, before I share the interpretation of the dream. I was saved at a young age, but not living in the light of God's Word. During this time, I was seeing a man who sang in a band and he had become my "so called" boyfriend, but honestly between you and me, IF he was faithful to me, I'm persuaded that it was only for a very short time, like a week. Okay, moving along with the story, for the short time that he was supposedly my boyfriend, there was one day when I went over to his house to visit him and when his mom answered the door she told me he was outside, inside the back of the bands truck, building some type of stage lights for the band. So, I walked out to the truck and knocked on the door and as he rolled open the back door of the truck, to my surprise I saw another woman in the back of the truck with him and she was helping him make the band lights. This is when I found out that I had been replaced and that he was seeing someone else. When it finally dawned on me and I realized what was going on, I tried to hold my head up high as I walked away, but in my heart I was truly devastated! And to make matters worse, I became even more heart broken as the seconds, minutes, hours, and days passed as I realized that he was not coming after me, to even try to make up with me. So, hurt and wounded, it became extremely obvious to me that He did not care about me or my feelings and that He had decided to stay with her. He never even attempted to show me an ounce of respect by saying that he was sorry for, not being man enough to tell me he was interested in someone else. It was after this event that I had the dream that he had tragically died in a car accident.

My Interpretation: Car Accident- Reflection dream

I dreamt that my boyfriend was driving in his red 300 ZX sports car and his car was suddenly and tragically hit by another vehicle; he was killed instantly. In the dream my boyfriend was dead and I was traumatized by his death.

This dream was showing me pictures of my feelings. In real life he really did drive a red 300 ZX. The fact that he was driving his real car in the dream was putting the dream in the "present tense" realm. Eric dying, with no notice in a tragic accident was a symbolic parallel of the fact that he had suddenly, and tragically died in my life the day I caught him with the other woman. As my boyfriend and future mate he was like dead to me because he had removed me from his life and, like in the dream it all happened suddenly, with NO prior notice to me. Prior to the dream, in real life I had NO idea that he was not going to be active and ALIVE in my life anymore. So, in the dream the bottom line was that I was **tragically sad and devastated** at his death in my life. And in real life this left me sad, hurt, and very heartbroken that he was no longer in my life.

Can you see how this dream was a "reflection dream"? Meaning the dream was showing me internal imagery or pictures of my intense and wounded feelings within my soul realm of the traumatic heart break I had just suffered, through what recently happened in my life. In reflective dreams your soul puts your feelings into pictures as a type of processing one's emotions and these pictured feelings (dreams images) show up in our dreams. Countless, pictures and images we have seen throughout our lifetime are stored in our memory bank. When we sleep our soul pulls out specific pictures that we have downloaded in our memory bank over the years, to show us a little internal movie as a mirror or reflection of what we have been going through in our lives. This is what I call a **"REFLECTION"** (ordinary) dream. Understanding the meanings and parallels of your reflection dreams are important for many reasons, one being, that at times God can and will intertwine His revelation into a reflection dream at His discretion, placing it in the prophetic dream category; so, this dream type is called a **Reflection & Prophetic Combination** and I will share more insight later in the prophetic dream section. (see pg 138)

108

The dream I just shared with you was **NOT** a prophetic dream and it was NOT saying that my ex-boyfriend would REALLY die a literal death in real life. How do I know that you ask? Well it is because he is still alive and kicking, to this very day twenty years later. Nor, was this dream foretelling me that he would be, like dead in our relationship with me. Why you ask, because it happened **after the fact**, of me finding him with the other woman. So, it could not have been a dream, foretelling the future. But, this dream was merely a storyline of symbolic pictures or images, of the devastation that my soul had suffered after he had broken my heart. After his selfish departure I waited 10 years in bondage with a broken heart, meanwhile waiting for him to see "the light" and finally come back to me. And after 10 painful long years of waiting, it never happened!

Even now, as I share this dream and its interpretation with you, I firmly believe, if there would have been a Christian person around me that I respected who was able and equipped in dream interpretation, empowered by the Word and Spirit of God operating in their life. God could of used them greatly, to minister healing to my broken heart and possibly saved me a lot of wasted time. There are many people in our world, just like me in the past who have been abused, battered and broken, who desperately need the ministry of the Holy Spirit to heal, deliver and set their captive hearts free! Let's allow God to use us in dream interpretation or in any other unconventional way He chooses, without limitations to the traditional methods of man. So, as you can see, **when one is trying to interpret a reflection dream the feelings in the dream are of the utmost importance** (see chapter 11); here are several reflection dream examples and their interpretations, concerning how they reflect to positive or negative issues, within the dreamers' heart.

Teeth Falling Out: "Reflection Correction" Dream

Recently, I (Vonda) helped a lovely young Christian woman who had been having a reoccurring dream. In the dream, all of her teeth were rotten and they were falling out of her mouth and into her hands.

The Interpretation: Because of my experience, as well as the quickening of the Holy Spirit, I automatically asked her. <u>Do you have a ROTTEN mouth</u>? And with a very surprised look on her face, her eyes got real big as she had her "AHA" moment After the light bulb went off, she then humbly and truthfully admitted " <u>yes</u>," I do have a rotten mouth and she went on to share with me that she struggled with cursing.

So, I asked this person how long she had been saved and she said that she had been saved for a few years. So, I was quick to mention to her, that spiritually speaking, we all are at different places in our walk, at different times. And I reminded her of Ephesians 2:8-9 (NKJV) For by grace you have been saved through faith, and that not of yourselves; it is the gift of God, not of works, lest anyone should boast. But, I also told her, since one of the functions of the dream is to act like a mirror of the soul. It is extremely important to note that dreams do show the <u>truth</u> about who we are and the issues we are struggling with. And it's my opinion that at times, God isn't so much as concerned about our faults, but I believe He is even more concerned about our attitude and our obedience towards Him and His Word, when the Holy Spirit does <u>reveal</u> the <u>truth</u> concerning our sins. When we address these soulish and sinful issues with obedience and live by the LIGHT of HIS WORD, this is truly GROWTH. When it comes to dreams and visions, the Holy Spirit is NOT always tickling our ears by telling us were going to get married or come across a million dollars. For the word of God says "what does it profit a man if we gain the whole world but, loose our souls" So let's remember, God is concerned with our SANCTIFICATION as well as our EDIFICATION. Colossians 3:8-10

But now you **must rid yourselves** of all such things as these: anger, rage, malice, slander, and **filthy language** from your lips. Do not lie to each other, since you have taken off your old self with its practices and have put on the new self, which is being renewed in knowledge in the image of its Creator.

Her reflection dream was easy for me to read because of my ability to read symbolism, intertwined with the action, within the dream's storyline. This dream exposed the dreamer as having a seriously "rotten and foul mouth" and I encouraged her to repent and apply the earlier command of Colossians 3:8 to her sin. And I reminded her of Gods forgiveness in which "there is therefore now no condemnation to those who are in Christ Jesus, who do not walk according to the flesh, but according to the Spirit." I told her, It is Gods will for us to put away our sins and allow Him to transform us, into His image and to grow in our daily walk Him (Romans 8:1 NKJV.)

James 3: 10 (NKJV)
Out of the same mouth proceed blessing and cursing. My brethren, these things ought not to be so.

James 1:22 (NKJV)
But be doers of the word, and not hearers only, deceiving yourselves.

So, when we have dreams and visions, let's not put God in a box, but let's be willing to receive the correction of the Holy Spirit, with humility. For it was through Christ death, He was humiliated for our benefit.

Reflection: E-Mail Dream Interpretations

With the permission of the dreamers, I will now share some word for word e-mail correspondences, so you may observe specific examples of how dreams can reflect the strengths or weaknesses of the dreamer.

Serving People: Reflection Dream

Recently, Rosebenlie wrote to me about her dream; she says.........

I normally have dreams, where I'm always serving others and in the dream they **are never pleased** with my service; it **feels** like what I'm **doing is never good enough.**

My Interpretation: I shared with Rosey, in the dream she **feels** "that no matter how much she serves others, the dream shows, she cannot please people"! And the **action** of the dream shows that the people are discontent with her service concerning them; whether its family, friends, work, or school professors, people are expressing to her that she's not measuring up with their expectations.

I ministered the previous interpretation to her, via YouTube on "Heart Hope" and I really tried to encourage her that she needed to be the one to evaluate herself and if she needed to step it up, then by all means she should step it up! But, if she believes she is fine and this is just negative oppression, coming from negative people around her; then as long as she was working with a spirit of excellence unto the Lord, it really doesn't matter what other people think of her performance. But, she only needed to be concerned with pleasing the Lord. I also, encouraged her to warfare with the Word of God, against the enemy's oppressive voice in her life. Below was her response to her dream interpretation.

Hi Vonda, Thank you for the word of encouragement, it really means a lot to me; I'm going to press towards the high calling, until what's inside of me becomes a reality, and I can be rewarded in the Lord!! You helped me to see, not to give up hope, but to keep watering those flower seeds until they blossom and it doesn't matter what other people think! But, I have to be sure and know who I am in Christ Jesus!!! Thanks, **Rosebenlie**

SIDS: Reflection Fear Dream

Vonda, My son called me and he had a really bad dream about his son dying from S.I.D.S. I think it's just from my son, his brother, died @ 3 months old from S.I.D.S., but I thought I'd ask you your thoughts. **Thanks, Yvette**

Yvette, yeah, I'd say you're right on track girl! That sounds about right! It's most likely, **(not absolute)** his heart is giving him a picture of his worst fears! At times, these kinds of dreams are going to happen; but to balance the Word of God, concerning dreams and visions, **IF** your son is a prophet or has a prophetic gifting of the Holy Spirit, then there is a small chance that this could be a night vision showing him a prediction of what's to come :o(Hear me out now :o)

If it's a night vision revealing a truth, then he should consider it as a warning and pray, while taking authority over the spirit of premature death"; but, if he is submitted to God, he is to actively resist the devil, so he will flee from him and his family.

If it's a God thing, like His ways are higher than our ways His thoughts higher than our thoughts type of thing, then there's nothing he can do but, plead for God to have mercy on his child. However, I truly believe that the first explanation I mentioned is the true interpretation and that his fears are surfacing through reflective pictures in this dream.

As we know, **IF** he's not a Christian then he does not have the privilege of standing on the promises of God, since they are promises made to His Covenant people. And if this is the situation then you would need to intercede on behalf of him and your grandson through your relationship with Christ.

But, if your son is a Christian, please tell him to literally warfare, by proclaiming the word of God, over his child's life. Even though, his son's "really dying" is very unlikely; one can never be too sure. It's better to be safe than sorry, by wishing we would have prayed.

If it's just his heart showing him his fears through this dream and he is a Christian. Then the dream is clearly a reflection of his fear and his response to this dream should be, him speaking the Word of God too his fears. If this is the case then this dream shows, he still needs to have his mind and heart TRANSFORMED by the washing of the Word. God does not want him" fearing" this or anything else in his life. So, if I were you I would encourage your son to exercise and use his mouth, to confess Gods word on a regular basis, about God's goodness (divine protection) towards his son, and his whole family! Hope this helps, **Blessings 2 U, Vonda**

BOW AND ARROW

Hello, Vonda, I would be so very grateful for help under-standing the following dream I had this morning. I am at a type of cross-road, with a friend and was asking the Lord last night what I was to do, as I have no idea what direction I am to go. I looked up the meaning of bows/arrows, but there's no gossip or ANY type of harsh words between us or from us toward anyone else, but felt it has a different meaning than this anyway - I just am very unsure what this dream could possibly mean?

In the dream this morning a friend was standing behind and above me holding a string tight as if they were a bow. I was crouching in front of them firing arrows from the string at a target, except they weren't arrows – they were sticks made of some type of synthetic with no points, but there was a target they were to hit. The final one I fired dropped to the ground as the string became a little slack and I said "I lost my focus." With gratitude and Blessings, Robyn

Hi Robyn, I read your dream... Is the friend a man or boyfriend? The dream relays the message that "you lost your focus."

Your dream has him (if it's a he) as the bow (boyfriend) the dream shows that he's a little slack in the teamwork of your relationship and it shows that your tools (arrows/weapons) are not sharp enough. Meaning, you're not keen enough to hit the target with him. Because he's a little slack, (slacker) and not on top of it (relationship skills.)

The fact that he's above you in the dream could mean that in the spiritual realm he's above you or over the top spiritually (a leader) behind you could mean someone who is showing up not in the front (not a leader) and not ahead of you spiritually (not as mature.)

115

Even though the bow and arrow are a pair that goes together..... Regardless, It's (**your teamwork**) just not working.......:o(**Vonda**

Hello Vonda, I'm so very grateful for your email reply to my bow and arrow dream. So much has been happening over the last few days involving bow and arrows.

The man who was behind me (in the dream) is the leader of my prayer group - he invited me to join when it started back in May. There has been an attraction between us for a while, but we have kept our distance from each other, sort of step around each other (we are both single, over 36 and never been married). Confirmation for joining the prayer/ intercession group was 2 Kings 13:15-19 (Elisha instructing Joash to fire the arrow out of the window then into the ground to declare defeat over Israel's enemies).

I was telling The Lord the other night that I couldn't be further from any fulfillment of any of His promises than I am right now, and had a vision of an arrow being drawn right back in the bow - it's necessary to draw the arrow **AWAY** from the target to give it power when released. Then the next morning (yesterday) I saw the attached photo on the front cover of our local newspaper- four archers with their bows drawn back about to fire arrows! Last night I relinquished everything including nothing eventuating with this man.

I had a dream this morning that I was in a church about to give my marriage vows to a man I didn't know (a very nice man) but, as I was about to speak, I heard repeatedly the name of my prayer group leader and knew I was about to marry the wrong man. I heard God speak to my heart in the dream warning me that the man in front of me was the wrong man.

I had considered leaving the group but felt very strongly that was not the right thing to do. I am so very grateful for your insight! Refreshing and abundant Blessings, **Robyn**

116

Hi **Robyn,** Good morning to you! I'm glad my interpretation was a confirmation to what the Lord has been speaking to you :o) I agree with you, leaving the prayer group is not the thing to do; and yes you should stay. The reason why you're there is to pray and not worship any guy: o).... not that you are :o)

Anywhere God ordains for you to be spiritually (prayer group, church, ministry, and work) there will always be adverse situations that will come up; the enemy will try to use these circumstances to try and move us from where God has called us to be. So, **staying** planted in that group, as unto the Lord is the right thing to do, whether you ever get married or not.

And most likely, when you finally do get married, then the enemy will try to use some cute guy to like you in a similar attack, while in the group; and you'll be tempted to leave there too, because of the temptation. But, if you ask me that's when you need to stay, endure, and defeat the temptation through your faithfulness to God.

My point is simply this, that no matter, what our circumstances. Satan, our flesh or the world's perverse system will always make the environment that we breathe, live and work in, conducive to temptation. Hence, trying to come against us while fulfilling the plans and purposes of the Kingdom of God.

But, it brings God glory when we are able to live on this earth, rise above and maintain the course that He has set before us. No matter what the obstacles! **Thanks, Vonda**

Hi **Vonda,** My apologies for the delay in responding to your email; thanks for your wisdom - I really appreciate it! This week I have seen some attacks coming against the prayer group and particularly the leader. The upside is that we **(he and I)** have had to get over ourselves and work as a team :o)..... lol. With grateful Blessings and prayers, **Robyn**

117

Cast Out From Heaven?

Recently, I received an e-mail from a Christian woman, who, had fallen for two "worldly men, one right after another, within a three year period. During this time, God clearly told her to stop seeing these men and she did not listen to the Lord. Finally, the Lord broke up the first 1 ½ year relationship and she was convicted by the Holy Spirit and eventually removed herself from the second relationship. Meanwhile, in her struggle, she said that on three different occasions, she felt the Holy Spirit lift off of her; then she dreamt this dream.

Hello Vonda, I had a dream where I fell in outer space; there were no other planets in space. I was so scared because I just kept falling and falling and it seemed like I would never land anywhere, but then I smacked down on this small dirt planet and just lay there on this dirt planet with outer space blackness all around me, and I lay there face down with my wings on my back and then I woke up.

Vonda, my problem is on three different occasions, I felt the Spirit lift off of me and go up through the ceiling, as if back to Heaven. I am just scared that this dream means, God has kicked me out of Heaven for having "fallen" for these worldly men, for having failed the temptation, for having put idols in front of Him, for having loved someone or something more than Him, etc. Maybe, I am not worthy anymore to serve God? Maybe, my heart has fallen from grace or has fallen out of love with God? I'm scared of my dream.

I'm scared God has kicked me out of Heaven or that I am a fallen angel because I fell for these two men. God has kicked me out of heaven, hasn't He? And He has taken His Holy Spirit from me. I know I failed the test and the temptation. Have I lost the Lord also? Time is short and we are all about to go home soon. I can't lose God. Has my heart "fallen" from grace? God help me. Sarah

Hi Sarah,

Thank you for your transparency and for sharing your heart with me! Please hear me, this dream is **NOT** declaring or predicting, anything of the sorts. This dream is **NOT** a prophetic dream! This dream is a mirroring of your souls disobedience during that time of your life. This was a reflection dream, which gave you a symbolic picture, scene or imagery of your willful disobedience (like the angels) towards God, concerning your rebellion in these "unequally yoked" relationships with these two different unsaved men. This was a dream picture, which REFLECTED YOUR HEART in the past, at the time of the dream. Sarah, God has laid these scriptures on my heart, to share with you.

Genesis 4:7 KJV
"If you do well, will you not be accepted? And if you do not do well, sin lies at the door. And its desire is for you, but you should rule over it."

Sarah, God wants your very best "sacrificial life's offering"; if you have repented and asked God's forgiveness, then I have a Word from the Lord for you! 1John1: 9 NKJV says, "if we confess our sins, He is faithful and just to forgive us our sins and to cleanse us from all unrighteousness. So, forget the things which are behind and reach forward to those things which are ahead (Phil 3:13 NKJV). For, "the LORD'S loving-kindnesses indeed never cease, For His compassions never fail. They are new every morning; Great is Your faithfulness (Lam 3:22-23 NKJV.)

Sarah, please know that you are forgiven and deeply loved by God. I sense God is saying, if you keep God first in your life, your latter days will be better than your former days! This principle can be found in Haggai 2:9. Be encouraged, God loves you more then you will ever know! It's not His will for one person to perish. Your disheartening dream picture, or the overall "big picture" of your dream, does **not agree** with the Word of God. It is true, there is NO

119

grace for fallen angels and they cannot be redeemed, but humans can always be forgiven and redeemed as long as there is still breath in their bodies! You are still living; therefore you can be forgiven! I can assure you that this was only a reflection of how you felt and not a prediction of what is to come! Choose you this day, whom you will serve! Please press on and move forward in the things of God!

So, hopefully you can see, through the reflection dreams, I've shared with you that as these children of God experienced positive or negative events in their lives, it caused them to have good or bad dreams depending on the good or bad thoughts of their heart concerning their daily life. After understanding what part of their life, their dream was reflecting I was able to bring the light of God's Word into their present tense situation and bring them correction, comfort, or edification, through the all powerful Word of God!

And finally, on a lighter note, let me share with you one of my recent, and very encouraging personal reflection dreams.

Sunburned Nose: Reflection Dream (Vonda's Dream)

God gave me the cutest little dream this morning;
I dreamt that I had spent so much time in the <u>sun</u> (<u>sun is symbolic for Jesus the SON</u>) that my nose was sunburned!

The reason it was my nose that was sunburned (<u>and not another body part</u>), is because I've been being nosey or nosing around and spending <u>a lot</u> of time (<u>burnt nose</u>), in His presence; this is because I'm soaking in the Lord (<u>soaking in the sun/Son</u>) to hear from Him, to know what God is saying so I can help others understand their dreams.

What an encouraging dream!

Reflection Dream & Interpretations:
Literal or a Symbolic Spiritual Parallel ?

Now, I will I give you two dream interpretation examples of the same dream, but show you how they can have different meanings depending on whether or not the dream is reflecting literal people, places, and things; or if the dream is using literal people places and things to reflect a dream parallel, with a different symbolic, yet spiritual meaning all together.

For Example: This is only one example of other types of reflection dreams. Let's just say you are a woman and you dreamt, you're at your regular hair salon and your regular stylist, who we'll call Hannah, is cutting your hair. And in the dream, she cut all your hair off and you get very upset with her and walk out the door, sad and crying.

Possible Literal Interpretation: If in real life your hairdresser's name, really is Hannah and you really do go to the same salon as in the dream and she really did cut all your hair off or mess it up and you really are upset and crying. If, you are dreaming this after this really, truly, and literally happened in real life, then this is what I call a literal "__reflection dream,__" __with a literal (not symbolism) interpretation.__

This dream is a reflection dream, which is reflecting the truth of your tragic event, because Hannah, in real life really is your literal hairdresser, who has really done this horrible deed to you. Therefore, in this case she would be representing the actual true/literal role of herself as a hairstylist in your life. And because the hair salon in the dream really is the literal place you go to get your hair cut and it just so happens that you really did get a botch job the last time she cut your hair; literally, really upsetting you and making you sad enough to cry when you left the salon that day.

121

Since, in real life you really did experience this and are upset and sad about what happened to you; it's important to note that the dream surfaced in your heart by, cause and effect. One of the dreams functions are to process your feelings. This type of dream is giving the dreamer, literal pictures that are a simple reflection. These pictures are not symbolic, but they are exactly as they seem. They are functioning as literal pictures in your dream as to what literally happened to you. There is no symbolism involved here, therefore making this dream very simple to decipher. Now, let's take the same dream and use it as a symbolic yet, spiritual parallel to see how **other people and things can be symbolic, with a spiritual parallel** in the same dream (see pages 79-81.)

Spiritual Parallel
The example below is the same dream from above, but with a different meaning, which is a spiritual parallel.

Same Dream: "A Bad Haircut"
Let's just say you are a woman and you have a dream that you're at your regular hair salon and your regular stylist, who we'll call Hannah, is cutting your hair. And in the dream she cut your hair all off and you get upset with her and walk out the door sad and crying.

In this instance, it is true that in real life, Hannah is your hairdresser, but you also recognize her as a hairdresser who encourages you in the Word of God. Moreover, because she has the gift of prophesy, from time to time she has given you prophetic words from the Lord, while you're in her chair being beautified. So, not only is the salon, in the dream, the "real salon" you go to, but when you go there in real life, you notice that while you're at this salon, you're also being fed spiritually, and because of the environment, it makes you feel encouraged and built up; kind of like you're having church!

And in the past, in real life, you <u>know</u> that every time you've gone to the salon, you've received an EXCELLENT haircut; on the contrary, the truth is that you've never received a bad haircut from her, in all your time going to Hannah.

So, in real life, after you've experienced this type of "<u>bad haircut dream</u>," you might be thinking to yourself? Oh My Lord! I wonder, does this mean, I'm going to get a bad haircut next time? ha ha. And then, maybe you stop going to her for haircuts, because of the dream you had and you're afraid that this same thing is really going to happen to you. So, you start thinking, wow, this could be a "<u>Prophetic Dream</u>" and God could be warning me? When, really this is **not the case** at all and you have misinterpreted the dream. But, it just so happens to be a reflection dream of you and your devotional life with God. How you say? How could this dream represent my time alone with God? Well, I'll share it with you by, substituting literal meanings, with symbolic meanings.

<u>LITERAL</u>   +   Symbolic Meanings
Hair Salon   = feeling like you're at church
Hair   = Your beauty or Glory (1 Cr 11:15)
Hairdresser   = A prophet who encourages,
affirms, guides, teaches, comforts, warns or corrects you through spiritual words.

Symbolic yet Spiritual Interpretation (spiritual meaning)

You dreamt that you're at your regular hair salon (<u>enjoying your real church being built up in the word</u>) and your regular stylist, who we'll call Hannah (<u>the prophetic part of you hears from the Holy Spirit</u>), is cutting your hair (<u>maintain your glory of beauty and godliness in the Lord</u>). And within the storyline of the dream Hannah, cut your hair all off (<u>the corrective word that was delivered reduced /chopped down your glorious appearance of godliness</u>) And you get upset with her and walk out the door sad and crying (<u>upset and saddened because the Holy Spirit's had to bring correction, in your life</u>).

123

Can you see that your emotions in the dream are the same as your emotions you recently felt at church, last Sunday (in real life)? Can you see it? But, this time the hair salon is symbolic for your time with God at church. Hannah is symbolic for the prophetic voice of the Holy Spirit, in your walk that normally encourages, guides, teaches, comforts, and at times corrects us; he does this by showing us things we need to change or let go so we can be cleansed from ungodliness, by the renewing of our mind, through hearing of the word of God! And to many Christians a woman's long hair symbolically represents her glory in the Lord (1 Cr 11:15); therefore making the dream a spiritual parallel.

In the action of the dream, her hair being cut off short is the opposite of her hair being long. So, symbolically this short haircut would represent a reduction in her glory. Meaning, her glory is not looking too good (ugly) or she's not looking too good in her sight or to others, but mostly to the Lord.

Finally, through this emotional dream, the dream is using this symbolic dream picture as a spiritual parallel that's "reflecting" the true emotions and recent happenings in her "spiritual life." As you can see this dream is a symbolic reflection dream, which shows an **encoded message** of the dreamer being upset and saddened because of a direct result of her recent experience in church, when she realized she needed to deal with her flesh or the enemy in her life.

So, whether your dreams reflect your spiritual growth, or a person's negative heart issues like brokenness, not being good enough, fear of death, disobedience, hatefulness, selfishness, lust, greed, cursing, anger, killing or seemingly, God's un-forgiveness. Please keep in mind that God, is concerned with every area of the heart and therefore it would be wise for us to address these wrong or sinful feelings, while they are still in the heart and not wait until the thoughts of your heart manifest and then become an action. I have learned that it is advantageous to understand my dreams and to use dream interpretation as a tool that helps me to keep a watch over my heart. For this reason understanding your dreams, will be a huge blessing to you throughout your Christian walk to better maintain a heart of godliness.

Throughout this chapter I have shown you several dream examples of how reflection dreams can vary depending on the experiences of the dreamer at the time of the dream. Please let me reiterate that all Reflection dreams are about you, the dreamer and will revolve around your feelings concerning the people, places, things and events that have taken place in your life. It has been my experience that roughly **98%** of your dreams will indeed be purely reflection dreams with no revelation from the Holy Spirit; thus leaving an estimated **2%** margin for prophetic dreams for the average Christian dreamer. However, it is also my experience that as a Christian matures and grows, when they have been given the gift of prophecy from the Holy Spirit this percentage rate will change. Hence, your reflective dreams will decrease and can be roughly **90%** or less and your prophetic dreams will increase to around **10%** or more, depending on the amount of revelation the Holy Spirit desires to share with you. Moreover, if you're a Christian who operates within the prophetic gifting's or the "office of a prophet", there will be times when you may have a dream that is extremely tough to identify, whether it is a reflection dream or a prophetic dream. These types of dreams will happen because, there is a specific type of prophetic dream that can put out such an intense feeling, it initially appears to be a simple reflective dream. But, you will find as you evaluate the dream, in comparison with the facts and truths of the current events in your life, you will see that this dream is NOT reflecting any current feelings or factual circumstance in your life and in no way shape or form is the dream relaying anything to you that you may have experienced. And this is when you will discover that this type of non reflective dream and its intense feeling was induced by the Holy Spirit, to give you a heavenly message for Gods own purposes; therefore, making it a prophetic dream.

Reflection or Prophetic?

For example: Left Behind

My pastor's name is Dan and one Sunday he preached a message about how Jesus has called and commanded every believer to "go into all the world and preach the gospel to every creature." Saturday night, the night before he shared this evangelistic message with us, he had the following dream.

Dan dreamt that he was standing outside, in the dark of the night. His wife Rhonda was outside too, but she was over a ways to the right standing with a group and she wasn't standing with him. At this time Dan looks up and suddenly notices the sky is lighting up a little, as if a great light is breaching the darkness in the heavens and he begins to get really excited, because it's the Rapture and he can see that Christ is coming to meet His people in the air! Dan, then looks over to the right and sees his wife and the group, as they all begin to ascend into the sky. But, as he looks around he realizes that he is not going up with them and he's still on the earth being "left behind." At this point, he gets extremely upset as a dreadful fear and terrible anguish grips his heart, while he tries to relate to what has happened and why is he not going up? In the dream, he knows he's saved and right with Christ, but does not understand how he has been left behind.

When Dan shared his dream from the pulpit, he told us that this dream was extremely disturbing to him, because he knows exactly, what the word of God requires for a person to inherit salvation! He knows, without a shadow of a doubt that his heart was ready and prepared for the Lords return; hence the reason his dream bothered him so bad.

He said, the morning of the dream he continuously sought God for the interpretation, since he knew it was not the literal truth, reflecting his current relationship with Christ. He said that the Lord answered him that morning and gave him the interpretation to his dream.

> The Holy Spirit said to him, Dan, I allowed you to experience the dream and the dreadful feelings within the dream, because I wanted you to experience the same feelings unbelievers would feel, when the time comes for them to be left behind. (Paraphrased by Vonda)

Since, Pastor Dan had most likely spent 2-3 days preparing for that sermon, it became obvious to me that God was using the dream to reveal and cultivate a specific aspect of the evangelistic sermon Dan could not get just from reading, studying and speaking the Word. Meaning, God allowed him to dream this because He knew that this dream experience would create a greater stirring in his heart concerning, evangelizing the lost. Dan already had a heart for the lost. However, now he had a greater sense of urgency to passionately remind the children of God to like Christ seek and save the lost through the heart, calling, and ministry of evangelism. Experiencing this dream caused Dan to have a greater stirring for his personal evangelistic calling and it simultaneously expedited him, in how he implements "winning the lost," in his leadership role and pastoral sphere of influence. And this friends, is the heart of Christ. God is passionately trying to lead everyone into the Kingdom of God and it's not His will that one should perish! So, this dream was allowing Dan, to feel these feelings to better identify with God's love, dedication and urgency for unbelievers to come unto Christ, before it's too late!

Pastor Dan's dreadful dream did exactly what the Holy Spirit intended for it to do. Because that morning as Dan shared the message of salvation and reminded the church of their God given assignment, I'm happy to say that many people came into salvation, as Dan gave the alter call for unbelievers to come and give their hearts to Jesus Christ!

That morning in church, as I Vonda, intently listened to his dream story, I knew his interpretation was spot on! Like him, I myself have been exposed to feeling specific feelings, in my dreams that do not reflect or relate to any similar circumstance or truth of my real life. Just recently, the Lord gave me a very disturbing dream that allowed me to experience, how it felt for some people I knew, too die. It was an awful, tragic, heart wrenching feeling that He allowed me to experience. However, by the Lord allowing me to dream this, He was preparing my heart and showing me that my relationship, with these people would soon suffer a type of death, due to negative and fleshy feelings on their part. So, when you have a dream, with unrelated and unidentifiable feelings concerning your life, it's important to note and extremely likely that these dreams are prophetically inspired from the Holy Spirit. Why you ask? Well, it's so we can learn something or receive insight from Him and in cases like these the Holy Spirit is most likely trying to protect you or expound on a particular burden, within His heart. When He does this it will enable you to greater identify with the people He loves or He's revealing something to you, out of His love for you. Pastor Dan's dream was just one example of how a dream with intense feelings of devastation, fear, anxiety and dread, won't in anyway shape or form represent an inward reflective feeling in your life. But, is in fact a God given dream with feelings that have been induced by the Holy Spirit, in order to relay a current revelation or prophetic message and most definitely, these are harder to decipher, for their interpretation and application.

So, whether it's a **reflection dream**, which is a dream that shows a series of mirroring pictures that reflect an emotional story about your ordinary daily life or a **prophetic dream**, which is a dream that comes from the depths of Gods Spirit, within your soul to give you a supernatural message from the Holy Spirit to minister to you. It's important to note that both types of dreams are trying to send your "natural man" a message, so you can be enlightened, warned, encouraged, or grow from what you observe about yourself or the message in the dream.

Throughout scripture, God often uses the words dreams and visions, interchangeably; and as you will see in the scriptures below, it's important to note that God says the heart of a dreamer can reflect and cause the dreams people dream, so let's consider His advice and heed His warnings! It's important to note that the warnings God gave us, are to people that were NOT having prophetic dreams from the Lord; because if they were truly prophetic dreams from the Lord, then God would not be rebuking them! So, these false prophets and false dreamers must have been speaking out of the reflections of their own hearts; therefore, being their own "Reflection dreams."

Jeremiah 23:16 (NKJV) says, Thus says the LORD of hosts: "Do not listen to the words of the prophets who prophesy to you. They make you worthless; they speak a **vision of their own heart**, not from the mouth of the LORD."

Jude 1: 8 KJV Likewise also these [filthy] dreamers defile the flesh, despise dominion, and speak evil of dignities.

It's my opinion that the principle the Lord is trying to relay to us concerning this scripture is, depending on the heart of the man there are times that people can have dreams that are from the profane nature of their own heart and not from the heart or nature of God.

Jeremiah 23:25-26 (NKJV) says, "I have heard what the prophets have said who prophesy lies in My name, saying, 'I have dreamed, I have dreamed!" How long will this be in the heart of the prophets who prophesy lies? Indeed they are prophets of the deceit of their own heart."

So, please evaluate your dreams thoroughly; check yourself and make sure your heart is right, because when we share a dream and its interpretation we want to be sure that we are not misreading or misinterpreting the dream to say something that it does not mean. God has a problem when we say things are a "prophetic word" from Him, when in fact they are NOT, but are indeed the "reflections", desires or deceitfulness of our own heart.

So, with all this being said about reflection dreams, you may be asking yourself, why you should bother with trying to interpret them? Well, learning to interpret your reflection dreams will be advantageous for many reasons.

1. Great practice for when God gives you a prophetic dream.

2. Helps you to develop your own symbolic meanings.

3. Teaches you to discern feelings, thoughts, and helps you to read dream storylines and see the parallels.

4. Aids you in ministering dream Interpretation to unbelievers, with the hope of evangelizing them.

5. Helps you to know the difference "for sure" when God interjects his revelation, turning it into a "Reflective Prophetic" combination dream. (see pg. 133)

Chapter 8
Prophetic Dreams

He said, "Hear now My words: If there is a prophet among you, I, the LORD, shall make Myself known to him in a vision. I shall speak with him in a dream. Numbers 12:6 (NASB)

Prophetic dreams are often visions in a dream or picture glimpses, while one is sleeping, that give the dreamer divine revelation or an unknown message. So, when and if you have a prophetic dream, it's usually because the Holy Spirit wants to reveal some type of message, insight or revelation to you concerning your earthly calling, encouragement, correction, guidance, warning, or a foretelling about some particular promise that you can expect from Him, concerning your future or the future of others in your prophetic calling, as you serve the Lord. As His children, God has many things He longs to share with us, so we can continue to prosper in this life, but He especially wants us to prosper in our relationship with Him! And if you're called to represent the Lord as one of His prophets, then you will find yourself hearing from God concerning yourself, and at times hearing from God concerning others to deliver confirmations or revelatory messages to those He appoints for you to share His insights with. Until Jesus returns, there are always going to be the Ezekiel's and Jeremiah's within the body of Christ and it's my belief that God will usually, start you off in understanding dreams and visions concerning you, before He sends you off to minister as a prophet into "the world." Correctly, understanding what God is showing us for our personal lives, will in turn help us to be more seasoned and better equipped to be able to relay His revelation to others as our calling and influence expand throughout the Kingdom of God. Below are many reasons why God may choose to speak to you through a prophetic dream.

1. Restrain from evil   Gen. 20:3
2. Reveal God's will   Gen. 28:11–22
3. Reveal future   Gen. 37:5–10
4. Guidance   Gen 46:2-5

5. Encourage	Judg. 7:13–15; Acts 18:9-10
6. Judgment	I Sam 3:15-18; Daniel 4: 25-26
7. Warning	Isaiah- 21:2-6; Matt 2:12
8. Release a Gift	1 Kin. 3:5–10
9. Direction	Acts 16:9-10
10. Action to the Lord	Acts- 26:19-20
11. Instruct	Matt. 1:19-24; Matt 27:19

12. Insights or Confirmation of the thoughts of the heart or mind (Daniel 2:30)

It's rare, but it is possible a person can have a dream that is meant for another person or for others, like a group or nation; but, scripture reveals this type of dream was usually given to a King, concerning his nation and governments. A perfect example is the dream interpretation story concerning Daniel, when he ministered to Nebuchadnezzar of Babylon. Remember when Daniel dreamt of the gold, silver, iron, and clay statue? He did this, by the inspiration of the Holy Spirit. Daniel dreamed, Nebuchadnezzar's exact dream, so God could use Daniel to interpret and speak for God. Nebuchadnezzar, benefited by receiving revelation of the kingdoms that were to come and Israel benefited, in regard to receiving new scriptures and revelation concerning God's sovereign power of the up and coming earthly domains. Prophetic dreams will always consist of unknown knowledge, revelation or wisdom, which is relayed to the dreamer, through a dream, while sleeping. There are two reasons why a dreamer may have a prophetic dream. One, being that God is trying to relay a foretelling type of message to you about a current worry, concern, desire or situation that you've been struggling with in your life or you may have a prophetic dream because God wants to reveal, teach, warn or share with you something particular that's on His heart concerning **you or others**. It's been my experience that there are 4 styles or types of personal **prophetic dreams** ; one being called a **"Reflective & Prophetic Combination," "Wisdom or Knowing Dream," "Night Vision Dream,"** which the bible refers to as a vision in the night, and finally **"General Prophetic Dreams"**, in which I will thoroughly explain all four throughout the following paragraphs.

132

Reflection & Prophetic Combination Dreams

A "Reflection & Prophetic Combination" dream is a dream which entails literal or symbolic reflective symbols of your past, present or future concerns, intertwined with some type of prophetic revelation from the Holy Spirit that He has injected into your reflection dream; thus making it a prophetic dream because it contains revelation from His Spirit.

For Example : Nebuchadnezzars Dream

In Daniel 2:31-45, Daniel interprets the large statue dream for Nebuchadnezzar and obviously the interpretation goes straight to his head, because all of the sudden in Daniel 3:1-7 he has a similar statue built, for his people to worship him! So, some time goes by and God decides to deal with Nebuchadnezzar's **prideful** heart through another dream, but with the intent to usher his soul into repentance and walk in humility; however, the King did not heed the dreams (God's) warning, nor Daniels advice. Nebuchadnezzar's tree dream is a perfect scriptural example of a "**Reflection & Prophetic Combination**" dream.

Let's Read: Daniel 4:4- 37 (NKJV)
NOTE. The dream below Identifies the past, present and future.

⁴I, Nebuchadnezzar, was at rest in my house, and flourishing in my palace. ⁵I saw a **dream** which made me **afraid**, and the thoughts on my bed and the **visions of my head** troubled me. ⁶Therefore I issued a decree to bring in all the wise men of Babylon before me, that they might make known to me the interpretation of the dream. ⁷Then the magicians, the astrologers, the Chaldeans, and the sooth-sayers came in, and I told them the dream; but they did not make known to me its interpretation.

[8]But at last Daniel came before me (his name is Belteshazzar, according to the name of my god; in him is the Spirit of the Holy God), and I told the dream before him, saying: [9]"Belteshazzar, chief of the magicians, because I know that the Spirit of the Holy God is in you, and no secret troubles you, explain to me the **visions of my dream** that I have seen, and its interpretation. [10]"These **were the visions** of my head while on my bed: "I was looking, and behold, A **tree** in the midst of the earth, And its height was great.[11]**The tree grew and became strong**; Its height reached to the heavens, And it could be seen to the ends of all the earth.[2]Its leaves were lovely, Its fruit abundant, And in it was food for all. The beasts of the field found shade under it, the birds of the heavens dwelt in its branches, And all flesh was fed from it.[13]"I saw in the visions of my head while on my bed, and there was a watcher, a holy one, coming down from heaven. [14]He cried aloud and said thus: 'Chop down the tree and cut off its branches, Strip off its leaves and scatter its fruit. Let the beasts get out from under it, And the birds from its branches.[15]Nevertheless leave the stump and roots in the earth, Bound with a band of iron and bronze, In the tender grass of the field. Let **it** be wet with the dew of heaven, And let **him** graze with the beasts On the grass of the earth.[16]Let **his** heart be changed from that of a man, Let him be given the heart of a beast, And let **seven times pass** over him.

[17] 'This decision is by the decree of the watchers, And the sentence by the word of the holy ones, In order that the living may know that the Most High rules in the kingdom of men, Gives it to whomever He will, And sets over it the lowest of men.'

[18]"This dream I, King Nebuchadnezzar, have seen. Now you, Belteshazzar, declare its interpretation, since all the wise men of my kingdom are not able to make known to me the interpretation; but you are able, for the Spirit of the Holy God is in you." [19]Then Daniel, whose name was Belteshazzar, was astonished for a time, and his thoughts troubled him. So the king spoke, and said, "Belteshazzar, do not let the dream or

its interpretation trouble you." Belteshazzar answered and said, "My lord, may the dream concern those who hate you, and its interpretation concern your enemies! ²⁰The tree that you saw, which grew and became strong, whose height reached to the heavens and which could be seen by all the earth, ²¹whose leaves were lovely and its fruit abundant, in which *was* food for all, under which the beasts of the field dwelt, and in whose branches the birds of the heaven had their home ²²it is you, O king, who have grown and become strong; for your greatness has grown and reaches to the heavens, and your dominion to the end of the earth. ²³And inasmuch as the king saw a watcher, a holy one, coming down from heaven and saying, 'Chop down the tree and destroy it, but leave its stump and roots in the earth, bound with a band of iron and bronze in the tender grass of the field; let it be wet with the dew of heaven, and let him graze with the beasts of the field, till seven times pass over him'; ²⁴this is the interpretation, O king, and this is the decree of the Most High, which has come upon my lord the king: ⁵They shall drive you from men, your dwelling shall be with the beasts of the field, and they shall make you eat grass like oxen. They shall wet you with the dew of heaven, and seven times shall pass over you, till you know that the Most High rules in the kingdom of men, and gives it to whomever He chooses. ²⁶And inasmuch as they gave the command to leave the stump *and* roots of the tree, your kingdom shall be assured to you, after you come to know that Heaven rules. ²⁷Therefore, O king, let my advice be acceptable to you; break off your sins by *being* righteous, and your iniquities by showing mercy to *the* poor. Perhaps there may be a lengthening of your prosperity."

²⁸All this came upon King Nebuchadnezzar. ²⁹At the end of the twelve months he was walking about the royal palace of Babylon ³⁰The king spoke, saying, "Is not this great Babylon, that I have built for a royal dwelling by my mighty power and for the honor of my majesty?"³¹While the word was still in the king's mouth, a voice fell from heaven: "King Nebuchadnezzar, to you it is spoken: the kingdom has

departed from you! [32]And they shall drive you from men, and your dwelling shall *be* with the beasts of the field. They shall make you eat grass like oxen; and seven times shall pass over you, until you know that the Most High rules in the kingdom of men, and gives it to whomever He chooses."

[33]That very hour the word was fulfilled concerning Nebuchadnezzar; he was driven from men and ate grass like oxen; his body was wet with the dew of heaven till his hair had grown like eagles' feathers and his nails like birds' claws.[34]And at the end of the time I, Nebuchadnezzar, lifted my eyes to heaven, and my understanding returned to me; and I blessed the Most High and praised and honored Him who lives forever:

For His dominion is an everlasting dominion,
And His Kingdom is from generation to generation
[35]All the inhabitants of the earth are reputed as nothing;
He does according to His will in the army of heaven
And among the inhabitants of the earth. No one can
restrain His hand Or say to Him, "What have You
done?"

[36]At the same time my reason returned to me, and for the glory of my kingdom, my honor and splendor returned to me. My counselors and nobles resorted to me, I was restored to my kingdom, and excellent majesty was added to me. [37]Now I, Nebuchadnezzar, praise and extol and honor the King of heaven, all of whose works are truth, and His ways justice. And those who walk in pride He is able to put down.

It's important to note that the **tree** was **symbolic** for the **King**, concerning his **past, present, and future;** but the **angelic message,** of his impending **judgment was prophetic and literal,** concerning the **action** of the dream along with the **consequences**. Meaning, in this dream God showed him a "**reflection**" of who he was (**past**), and of what he had grown into (**present**), and what he would become (**future, which is not reflection, but it is predicting; thus making it prophetic revelation**), through the symbolism of the tree. Moreover, the angel in the dream declared a **prophetic message,** concerning the Kings gloomy destiny, if he did not change his wicked ways. Scripture reveals that he did not heed the warning and his judgment was executed and the dream's message was fulfilled and he lived, like an animal, in anguish for 7 years. Like Nebuchadnezzar, God who is rich in His mercy and grace desires to deal with us gently and warn us of our trespasses in Christianity; He often does this through His Word and the conviction of the Holy Spirit, but scriptures reveal that He has also been known to warn people through a dream or a vision. This dream is a scriptural example of what I call a "**Reflection & Prophetic Combination**" dream; which entails some literal or symbolic reflective symbols intertwined in prophetic revelation from the Holy Spirit. Like the pervious dream, in the following dream, I will share with you a current example of how God still uses this type of "**Reflection Prophetic Combination**" dream today; to relay a prophetic message, hidden in symbolic language that either reflects a current issue of your heart or a message from the heart of God into your spirit, concerning you or the calling on your life.

137

The Baby
Reflection & Prophetic Combination Dream

For a current example, please read along, within this e-mail conversation as I share and elaborate point by point, with Kristie concerning her "**Reflection & Prophetic, Com-bination Dream**." Just so you know, I have been working with Kristie for a little while now and she has really become pretty good in understanding many of her dreams. As you will read, she has already provided interpretations for most of the symbols in her dream and now we are just doing some fine tuning I thought would benefit her, as well as be advantageous for the readers. So, here we go!

The Baby: Reflection & Prophetic Combination Dream

Reflecting the **specific thought** "I can't talk to her" and the feeling "**I know something is wrong**".

Hi Vonda, Hey, hope you are doing well. I have to share something with you. We took my daughter Brittani to Vancouver to get on the plane to Germany. She went to be a part of YWAM (Youth with a Mission). It will be 7 months in total. The YWAM in Hernnhut Germany is a "Marriage of the ARTS." She will be in Germany for about 3 months studying ART and training and spiritual growth. Then the team head will head out somewhere in the world. It will be centered around social injustice. In the past they have worked to get women off the streets. I hear really good things though and they are non denominational, I think?

I have been worried about her as she didn't contact us at all and looking into it, I could see that her plane was delayed and wondered how she would make her connections in London. It's very hard to send your first born 17/18 year old off, like that all by herself. I was woken up at 2:00 am to pray for clarity for her and to be able to make the next plane. I knew she was in trouble somehow (a mom just knows).

I had a really weird dream last night and was weirded out and disturbed by it. When I woke up, I thought to myself and told God that, it MUST be that we just have weird dreams, that don't mean anything once in a while. I tried to ignore it and as I began to try, to find out where Brittani was and worry and wonder all of a sudden the dream was revealed to me. Here is the dream; I know you're going to laugh because I KNOW you will see it right away!

My Dream: In the dream I was watching a father throw his baby up in the air and letting the baby fall into the water. The baby didn't seem to mind, but I was uncomfortable with it. As the dad threw the baby up in the air the second time the baby fell deep down into the water and almost drowned. He scooped up the baby and catapulted the baby so hard and fast up into the air onto the sandy beach. The poor baby's face was smashed and I ran over to the baby and pried the eyes open. I KNEW something was wrong, the eyes were blue and wouldn't work. I couldn't talk to her. Someone said to me that "everything will be okay, and to just give it time until the baby can see you and talk again."

Kristie's, Interpretation: I felt like God said, "look at the big picture to detail, not detail to big picture." All of a sudden I SAW it, Brittani was the baby; the sandy beach was Germany and the dad, was God her father! On the way to Germany, she had 3 planes to catch and 2 lay over's. Both were delayed, which made her sink further behind (symbolic for baby sinking in the water). God made sure she made it there. The message was that she will be okay, just give her time to be able to talk. So I will rest in this and trust and wait that it was a message for us.

Wow, eh! I had to chuckle as I told God that he could have told me a little bit nicer! Looking at it from detail to big picture (if I had figured out what it was about); I would have her falling into the ocean and washed up on shore in a plane crash somewhere. I guess HE wants me to learn something through this, like just because it is disturbing doesn't mean it is. Any ways.......thought you might like to hear that.

HUGS...Kristie!

Hi Kristie, Well, well....:o) This would be a good dream/letter for me to put in my book, HINT HINT ? This is a good teaching dream and there's a tad bit more to it than you realize. **Thanks, Vonda**

Hi Vonda, You go for it GIRL. I would be honored and I can't wait to hear. I can't imagine what I have missed. I have to add also that, when I looked into the eyes I saw white spots covering the pupils and iris's and it was like electrical or something. It was at the 2:00 POSITION. Both eyes were the same.

By the way, we heard from Brittani. She got there safe. She could only let us know she got there okay and can't talk to us for 2 weeks (rules they have). Made me wonder if that was the 2 eyes??? 2:00 (2 weeks)? Or am I just reaching for things? **Thanks, Kristie**

Hi Kristie, I must be slipping, because as I'm re- reading this, I thought you wrote to me, that a **woman** said to you that, **"everything will be okay, and to just give it time until the baby can see you and talk again"**?

In the dream was it a woman's voice, man's voice, or did it appear to be neutral genderless voice, or more like just a knowing?

140

Also, concerning the eyes with the white spots at 2:00 p.m. Just forget about the dream for a minute and come into your real life and tell me what 2:00 p.m. means to you? For example, 2:00 for me is the time I like to make all my appointments. When I need to be at the dentist, oil changes, hair appointments or meetings, I prefer 2:00. So, 2:00 p.m. to me means appointment times because I hate early appointments. I'm an afternoon person.

So, what does 2:00 p.m. mean to you? Lunchtime, nap time, break time, quitting time, favorite TV show time, time of day you call and check in with hubby or time to take your medicine (if on any)? What does 2:00 p.m. mean to Kristie? :o) Thanks, Vonda

Hi Vonda,
No, it was NOT a woman's voice for sure. When I stop and really think about it, I would have to say it was a **male/genderless voice**. He was standing behind me so, I never saw him. Some times when someone says something in a dream, it is very much remembered WORD FOR WORD. This wasn't like that. So I would have to say that it was also more of a just knowing what he said (like trying to remember as best I can what he said.)

And concerning the white spots and time position on the eyes, I wouldn't say that it was PM or AM.....Wait a second here.....I would have to say, it was maybe trying to tell me if it was A.M or P.M because the eyes were not dark; but light blue like a blue sky with the white spot on the almost looking like a fluffy/electrical cloud. When I think of A.M. I think of DAY and P.M. NIGHT. But the fact is, at 2:00 A.M, it is always still dark out, like night.

141

Now, back to your question, about 2:00 P.M.? The only thing I can think of is NAP time. I have tried for years to lie down and REST for an hour or so, and nap before picking the kids up from school. I am MUCH calmer when I do that and enjoy them more. It's like pushing the RE-START button for me. God suggested this to me years ago and I have tried to stick with it. If, I was to think about 2:00 A.M, I would have to say, that's the time God usually wakes me up to pray for something.

Out of curiosity, what would it mean if it WAS a woman that spoke to me?

I also had more revelation on that dream. The child's face was smashed, and bruised???? could just tell that it had HIT THE SAND HARD). This represents, Germany **(the beach)** will have a GREAT IMPACT ON HER.....changing her. She will come back a different person; it's all GOOD.

P.S. The first part of the dream was only observing. The second part was my bending down and speaking and prying open the eyes. I was kneeling down when the person standing behind me spoke to me. I didn't know who the person was.

I JUST thought of something.........I bet because then I saw both eyes (I had said that both eyes looked the same?) Well the one I remember was the right one (her left) and I am guessing that the other one was the same. It was the same as far as the white spot on the 2:00 position, but not sure if the eye actual looked identical. I have a feeling that one was darker and smaller? And one was lighter. This could mean (I am trying to guess here)... for me to **REST and PRAY?**
Thanks, Kristie

Hey Kristie, Okay, this is what I wanted to share with you. I know you know the interpretation concerning the dreams real life context and that you understand the dreams setting and symbols concerning the first couple of paragraphs. But, I'm going to spell it out for the readers and my insight about the voices will come later and should be some good food for thought, when interpreting your dreams.

But, first things first! Believe me, when I say that every single dream means something and just because the dreamer cannot figure it out, or relate to the dream at the time of the dream does not mean it is meaningless. There's no such thing as a pizza dreams. Okay? Now, put that in your pipe and smoke it! He he ha ha lol... just playing around girlfriend :o)

Now, this dream you had was a **"Reflection & Prophetic Combination"** dream and your interpretation was good, now that I see I was mistaken about who said what! It is obvious that the symbols and storyline **reflect and parallel** your daughter's new journey to Germany; but your dream was **prophetic** because the end of the dream did not stop with you experiencing your present tense thought process, and end in just wondering, if she would be okay?

But the genderless voice of the Lord spoke into your dream concerning the circumstances of your real life situation and He made a declaration to you! As you already know, this is the prophetic twist to the dream.

The reason why I asked you if it was a woman, man or genderless voice is because it is very important not to say God said something, if He did not say it. Meaning, we always need to stay with the storyline and the action of the dream.If your answer to me would have been YES it was an unknown woman's voice, then I would have interpreted it to be one of the alternate voices of your own heart or thoughts that made this declaration. And if that is the case then it would not be considered prophetic because it most likely would have been the voice of reason and experience.

Let me explain further. Often, there are many inner "VOICES" in our heads and hearts; there can be voices of faith, doubt, insecurity, worry, fear, hope, reason and wisdom, just to name a few. However, I will give you some examples, to elaborate further on this principle.

You, as a mother, whose 18 year old daughter just independently ran off to Germany; you may experience these types of voices in your head, at the time of her departure.

A voice that says,

1. Oh NO, what if she gets kidnapped by some European sex traffickers and I never see her again!

2. Or, what if she gets killed in a plane wreck and she is lost in the ocean!

3. Or, what if she goes there gets married and I never see her again!

4. Or, what if she gets sick and I'm not there to help her and then, after you think all these terrible things, the voice of reason steps in and pulls you together and you think to yourself.....

5. Stop worrying everything will be okay! She will be fine! God's got it!

So, back to the dream, in the dream you heard a voice, if it was a woman's voice, then it would have been your inner voice of reason; the part of you that is correcting your negative thinking and knows the faithful God you serve. It's the inward voice of your heart that puts your trust in God and knows that everything will be fine, if you just give her time to come, too or get back to normal. (after the 2 weeks.)

So, when you as a woman dream, if the voice is female in gender, first consider if it could be the realistic thoughts you would or did have in the context of your waking life, at the time you dreamt it. The same principle would apply if it was a man dreaming, with a man's voice.

Because, if it was just another one of the voices of your thought process that was showing up in the dream, then it would have been an **INCORRECT** interpretation to say, that "God Said" she would be ok, when in retrospect it was really your own reflective thoughts and inner voice.

Because as you know there are many Christian people, my mother being one of them, that lose their children at an early age in some type of premature death. It's one of those "His ways are higher than our ways and His thoughts are higher than our thoughts" type of tragedies. So, consider this principle when it comes to unknown voices in your dreams.

However, for a balanced view, if it was a female voice that you recognized as a prophetic voice, like mine. Then the second interpretation for woman's voice declaring the phrase "**Everything will be okay, and to just give it time until the baby can see you and talk again,**" could make it a prophetic message.

If it was a woman's voice that you recognize to be a prophet then God is using that person's voice in the dream to represent Him, which would make this a prophetic declaration and not the voice of your inner man or conscience; but being a definite Word from the Lord! :o)

Another, possibility would be, if it would of been the father in the dream that said "**everything will be okay and just give it time until the baby can see you and talk again,**" then that too would be considered a definite word from the Lord, because the father in the dream was playing the role of the Heavenly Father.

145

And now to the good part, since your answer to me, was that it was a **genderless voice** then this is definitely the Holy Spirit speaking; I don't know exactly how He pulls it off, but there have been many occasions where I hear Him speak in a dream or vision and His voice is always GENDERLESS! It's neither male nor female, it's just neutral! So, I'm happy to say that I misread your first e-mail and that it was not a woman's voice. But, it indeed was the genderless voice of the Holy Spirit! It's equally important to note that the voice was coming from behind you, which can be symbolic of your God, who is your rear guard or support system! When someone is behind you it can mean "**Hey I've got your back**" or "**I'm backing you up,**" it can imply that they are standing behind in a supportive sense!

Finally, in the story line of the dream, her eyes were sky blue with some clouds; this showing that the time is 2:00 p.m. in the afternoon, because 2:00 a.m. it would be dark blue if not close to black. You said that, most likely 2:00 p.m. in the afternoon means nap time to you. So, when you were looking over the lifeless body of the baby, (**symbolic for Brittani**) you associated the white spot markings in her eyes, with 2:00 p.m. In the dream you were very concerned for the baby, so the interpretation is that God was telling you to rest (**nap time**) then the Holy Spirit said "**everything will be okay, just give it time until the baby can see you and talk again.**"

Also, based on the encouraging, prophetic and verbal message of the Holy Spirit, I don't think **REST AND PRAY** is the correct interpretation. However you can be the judge.

The reason being is because, in a worrisome situation like that, I believe prayer is hard work and it is the opposite of "**resting**" in the Lord. The Holy Spirit basically seems to be telling you to chill out and everything is going to be okay and that it's just going to take some time for her to be in a position so she can touch base with you.

146

So, you did a great job interpreting this and I do apologize for misreading or not remembering correctly. But, what you wrote gave me an opportunity to stress the important facts that every dream means something, while all symbols have meaning, and how extremely important it is to stick to the storyline or action of the dream, adding nothing and taking nothing away, in order to arrive at an accurate interpretation!

Does this make sense to you? I hope what I shared, with you about the different types of voices helps you with further dream interpretations! **Much Love to you! Vonda**

Hi Vonda, Oh, ya.....ya, now that you say that. Yes I agree. .... Although, I had the dream after PRAYING MY HEART OUT AT 2:00 a.m. right before going back to sleep and THEN having the dream. I woke at 2:00 am with a word in my spirit to PRAY, "BRITTANI NEEDS_PRAYER AND IS IN A BIT OF TROUBLE." I was shocked, because I went to sleep feeling really at peace. So I prayed my heart out and then left her in God's hands and then I went back to sleep and had that dream. I think the dream may have been showing that the prayers worked, and now I can REST? **Thanks, Kristie**

Hi Kristie, Yes, if that is the TRUTH of what happened, then it is reflecting the real happenings. Since you had the dream after God told you to pray then **one eye** was a **reflective symbol**, representing that you had prayed and the **other eye** was **prophetic encouragement** for you to rest in HIM.

Sounds about right, do you think?

147

See, you always have to continually check within your heart as you walk through the dream and you must compare the happenings in the dream with the current events of what you went through in your waking life. Walk through all the symbols and evaluate them with how they can relate to the events you have already experienced. <u>The ones that fit are reflections, the ones that have not happened yet are most likely predicting or showing you a new message</u>.

At the time of the dream if you would of been able to properly evaluate the eyes and what they were trying to show you, then you would of seen that since you already had prayed that the other message was to now rest (other eye) thus supporting the message of the voice saying "<u>everything will be okay, and to just give it time until the baby can see you and talk again</u>" Thanks, Vonda

Hey Vonda, OH yes! We nailed it! Yes, I totally hear ya, Good point! I thought of that too....It should "support the message". Because before I heard back from you on it I began to think...."hummm the cloud on the eye could also be "CLOUDED VISION." But, then I thought that, it wouldn't fit the message from behind me and could trail me off in a totally wrong direction, of the voice saying; "<u>everything will be okay, and to just give it time until the baby can see you and talk again.</u>"

I also forgot to tell you that the 2:00 thing <u>(along with the "voices" concept)</u> was a huge eye opener! 2 great things you caught that is going to really be helping me. Thanks, Kristie

Hi Kristie, Awe thanks I'm glad it helped, but one last thing about this dream, earlier when I was explaining the different voices to you I wanted to stress that the same would be true if it was a negative voice with a negative message that is contrary to the Word of God.

148

For example, maybe in the past on television you heard a demonic sounding voice that represented Satan and the evil side really well. Well, that voice is also stored in your internal memory bank and could be used in your dreams to represent the devil and his false evil messages. So, this is just one more example of how a voice could play a specific part in your dreams. Scripture also reveals that Satan can come across or appear to us as an "Angel of Light." So, always check the message and how it would apply to the current situation at hand for you, as a daughter and princess of the Most High God and the promises He made to you in and through His Word!

Okay, that's all folks! Lol..... **Bye Bye, Vonda :o)**

So, as we can see this dream's symbolism and storyline initially appeared to Kristie as a simple reflection dream that merely reflected a mothers concern for her daughter who had ventured out into "uncharted waters". But, upon further evaluation it was much more then that! We discovered that the Holy Spirit had interjected and intertwined a prophetic message to comfort and encourage her that "<u>everything will be okay, and to just give it time until the baby can see you and talk again.</u>" So, this prophetic message was the Holy Spirit declaring His comfort to a mother within the midst of a terrible reflection dream concerning the matter of her not hearing from her daughter. I'm so gad that we didn't miss what God was trying to say in this seemingly reflective dream that actually turned out to be a prophetic message dream. <u>Reflective Prophetic Combination</u> dreams can be very tricky to interpret and these we can't afford to misinterpret because they are so extremely valuable to us as believers who desperately need to be nurtured from the Spirit of God.

Night Vision Dreams

Then the secret was revealed to Daniel in a night vision. So Daniel blessed the God of heaven. Daniel 2:19 NKJV

Night visions are the same as day visions, except you are asleep and receive the vision in a dream, whereas one is awake during a day vision; both are revelatory. In Acts 10:1-4 Cornelius had a day vision. "At Caesarea there was a man named Cornelius, a centurion in what was known as the Italian Regiment. He and all his family were devout and God-fearing; he gave generously to those in need and prayed to God regularly. One day at about three in the afternoon he had a vision. He distinctly saw an angel of God, who came to him and said, "Cornelius!" Cornelius stared at him in fear. "What is it, Lord?" he asked. The angel answered, "Your prayers and gifts to the poor have come up as a memorial offering before God."

Like Saul, before he was Paul, and Cornelius a gentile (unsaved) who was seeking Gods will for his life, I have heard several stories of people who have received a type of "salvation revelation" message from God through a vision or a prophetic night vision dream. It's my opinion, it was because they were seeking God intensely and may not have had access to the gospel or a Christian messenger to present the good news of Jesus to them. So, I believe when there's a person who is not saved and they have little or no understanding of who Jesus is, it's my belief that God will do anything and everything He needs to do in order to reveal Himself to them, whether it's in a dream or a vision. But, I have usually found that the revelation that God gives to un-believers is in reference to their needing to become believers, is usually limited to just that; their salvation. I'm not saying that it's a lesser revelation, on the contrary it's the most important revelation they or we will ever know. However, after the person believes and receives Jesus this will now open the door for the believer to have more night visions or prophetic dreams. Let me share a prophetic night vision dream, with you from the bible.

150

<u>Paul and the Macedonian:</u> (Night Vision)
Direction Dream

Acts 16: 6-10, Paul and his companions traveled throughout the region of Phrygia and Galatia, having been kept by the Holy Spirit from preaching the word in the province of Asia. When they came to the border of Mysia, they tried to enter Bithynia, but the Spirit of Jesus would not allow them to. So they passed by Mysia and went down to Troas. **During the night** Paul had a **vision** of a man of Macedonia standing and begging him, "Come over to Macedonia and help us." After Paul had seen the vision, we got ready at once to leave for Macedonia, concluding that God had called us to preach the gospel to them.

Night vision dreams are usually very short action scene dreams that can contain, literal or symbolic images; these scenes are Gods revelation and response to a concern of your heart or may be His revelatory response to you concerning a prayerful issue about the lives of people, within your sphere of influence. Unlike reflection dreams, night vision dreams are always prophetic and share unknown information from the Holy Spirit, with the intent to make you aware of prevalent information the Holy Spirit feels inclined to make known to you. Below, I will share some modern day examples of how God still speaks prophetically, this way today!

<u>Wonder Bread:</u> Money Promise (Vonda)

In April of 2010, God made it very clear to me (Vonda) that it was time for me to transfer out of my hair stylist job, and into working for Him, full time in my ministry. In my heart, I really longed to get out of the hair business and I wanted so badly to be in full time ministry, but I was extremely concerned about not having enough money in my pocket!

This was when God showed me a loaf of Wonder Bread! As you know, bread is a synonym we often use to describe money and it in this case it was a very well known symbol, of Wonder Bread. So, the interpretation was, God was telling me that it would be a **wonder** and I would get some **money**! God was showing me ahead of time, I would have some money and this was a very comforting message to receive from the Lord at a time when I so desperately needed His encouragement. So, I trusted God and relieved myself from my duties and sure enough two months later, I did get some money and it truly was a wonder! Out of all the years I had owned my own business, I usually ended up being in the red when it was tax season. Before Clae and I were married my husband had paid out the ying yang most of the year, as a single man. But, because we married we fell into a much better tax bracket and ended up getting quite a bit of money back! And this was a wonderful financial surprise, just like God said! Knowing this revelation ahead of time, encouraged me to trust and see that God's sovereign provision was in store for me, because of the hand of God working for me, within the realm of Gods timing as well as Him blessing my husband's prosperity!

BRIDE IN A SHOPPING CART: Warning and Foretelling

Vonda, years ago I had a dream about being in a white wedding dress, standing in a shopping cart while it was rolling down train tracks....I think there may have been animals around me. Do you think this could have foretold my crazy (**bad**) marriage? Or does it mean something else? **Amanda**.

I ended up answering Amanda on video, but the answer is yes! Amanda shared with me that she got married on a whim and that didn't really know the man she was marrying! So, as you can see the Holy Spirit was trying to show her that as a bride her marriage would be on a fast track down hill. God put the animals in the dream because He was trying to show her that her marriage was **wild in its nature** and that she was marrying in the heat of the flesh!

God was trying to warn her **NOT** to marry this man! At the time of the dream she did not understand what God was trying to say to her and as a result she did marry him and to this day he has cheated on her several times. She continues to trust the Lord for guidance.

Dead Chick on the Ground: Foretelling or Prediction

I Vonda, saw a scene of a small yellow chick laying face down in the dirt and it was dead.

The dead chick is symbolic of me and its death is a parallel to how the dream teacher part of me would be killed; the revelation was obvious, I would never be allowed to fly from that nest! When I received this revelation from God it was at a time when God had positioned me and my husband at a new church. God sent us there for several reasons, but one reason being, so at the appointed time, I could teach on dreams and fully equip this church in the area of dream interpretation. God was showing me that even though I tried to fly, I wouldn't make it; but instead, I would suffer a premature death, concerning the church I was partnering with. It's not Gods will that a chick dies, without never being able to soar and it was not His will that my purpose as a teacher at this church died a tragic death. However, right or wrong, God did allow the pastors to reject my services. But, immediately after their rejection became obvious, God wasted no time in moving us to another church where teaching on dreams and dream interpretation were welcomed and highly appreciated.

Three planets lining up: Encouragement and Confirmation

In a glimpse of a scene I saw, the dark universe in the night and in it I saw three planets as they horizontally lined up and they were all coming inline as they sat side by side.

I'm not into astrology, but throughout my life time, I've been exposed to certain terminologies and sayings. And I knew what it meant when the Holy Spirit showed me a scene of 3 planets lining up in the universe. To me the night is symbolic of the unknown things or things that are in the dark. Simply meaning, things have not come to light in the realm of my knowledge or understanding and the universe is symbolic for the spirit realm. The action of the dream showed that the planets were almost aligned. "The planets are aligning". When I saw this I really got EXCITED! Because God is showing me that even though I don't have knowledge of it and I'm still in the dark as to when things are going to line up; but I can rest assured that things are lining up for me in the spirit realm! Meaning, God is setting things in line for me. He's setting it up and it is coming together.

During this time I had been waiting for God to open 3 very specific and very large doors for me. One door being an opportunity for me to teach on dream interpretation for an online bible college and secondly, a door to open up for me to go back onto the radio and last, an opportunity for me to start recording for Heart Hope, my prophetic television show. And even now as I'm typing this, I can assure you that things are lining up!

Night Visions: Literal Symbols
All of the Night Vision dreams I have shared with you, until this point have been night visions that have contained symbolism in them, to relay a message to the dreamer from the Spirit of God. However there will be times when God will show dreamers literal people, places and things that are **not** symbolic of anything, but really do mean the same literal meanings in the dream that they literally mean in real life.

For Example:
Debbie's Night Vision Dream: Literal Not Symbolic
The Blue Coffin – (Dream of Foretelling)
Debbie dreamt that her mom died and she saw the blue coffin being placed in the ground.

154

Debbie's Interpretation:

At the time of this dream Debbie's mom was not sick, but soon after the dream her mom was diagnosed with cancer and died quickly thereafter. When Debbie's father made the funeral arrangements, it just so happened that he purchased a blue coffin for his deceased wife. Debbie never told her father about the dream or the color of the coffin; so her father had no previous knowledge to make him pick out a blue coffin. So, it's important to note that in this dream, the Lord was not speaking in symbolism, but He was showing literal truths about a literal death that would be taking place and revealing the literal blue coffin. God was showing Debbie a picture that was literally foretelling this tragic event that was about to take place in her future.

So, you're asking yourself why God showed Debbie something terrible like this? Well, at the time even though she loved her mother very much, her relationship with her mom was a little stressful. So, this gave Debbie time to make sure everything got worked out between them. God revealed this to Debbie so she could prepare her heart so, it would not be as tragic to her, like it would have been if her mom died suddenly, without fine tuning their relationship. Debbie, knowing this and having a heads up about her up and coming death, helped her to prepare her heart for her mother's departure.

As you can see this Night Vision dream was a revelation from the Holy Spirit that was sending her head or mind a foretelling message that predicted her mom's death. And this night vision needed little or no interpretation skills. These types of dreams are very clear because they say what they mean and mean what they say!

Wisdom or Knowing Dream:
(Prophetic revelation)

On page fourteen of Kenneth E. Hagins book "Gifts of the Holy Spirit" he teaches us to; "Remember that the revelation the word of knowledge brings, is never about the future. The word of knowledge brings revelation concerning things past or present. The word of wisdom, on the other hand, brings revelation pointing to the future including the plan and purpose of God." So, Kenneth Hagin says, a word of knowledge is the Holy Spirit revealing supernatural knowledge concerning something that has previously happened or something that is presently happening; whereas a word of wisdom is Gods revelation about something that is currently happening or something that will come to pass in the future. And I believe, if you're sleeping, when the Spirit of the Lord decides to reveal it to you, since this is during your sleep/dream state, then it definitely makes it a dream! At times we will have short little prophetic "Wisdom or Knowing Dreams"; these are usually very simple dreams with little or no symbolism, but the emphasis is on knowing a "specific phrase, short scene, or thought" of revelation that you did not know, prior to the Holy Spirit sharing it with you. Below are some examples of prophetic "Wisdom or Knowing Dreams".

Wisdom or Knowing Dream: (prophetic revelation)

I Vonda, dreamt, it was dark and I was sleeping and in the dream, my husband Clae put his hand on my left shoulder to wake me and then he said "its 9:18". He was not trying to tell me I've slept too long but, it was as if he was gently trying to awaken me.

156

Background: For a couple of years there were a couple of things I had been asking God about and the timing of when they would happen? For one, I had been wondering about, when Clae and I would be moving to Texas and I had also been wondering about, when I would start working on the TV show, God promised me.

My Interpretation:

Clae is my husband and scripturally speaking, he is also the <u>priest of our home</u> and God has used him in the role of a <u>prophet to speak to me, as well as prophetically sharing with some men on his job</u>. In this "<u>Wisdom dream</u>", I believe God is using him to speak a prophetic revelation to me.

When Clae said, it's 9:18 it's because God was using my husband to speak a **prophetic** time into my life. The time 9:18 is symbolic for SEPTEMBER 18th or 9/18, which is a specific day. However I'm not sure of the year because God did not reveal the year in the dream. So, in this "<u>Wisdom dream</u>" God was revealing a time concerning something I had been praying for and He was doing it by giving me a specific date. The interpretation is a MONTH and DAY not a TIME of DAY.

In this dream, the reason I'm in the dark, is because In real life, I'm really in the dark about the exact time God will move us to Texas or the exact time He will let me be on my TV show. And the reason I'm asleep is because this represents an area in real life that I'm **not conscious** of knowing this information. Meaning, in real life when we are asleep we are not privy to the things that are happening around us. So, in this sense, like when one is sleeping, I'm not privy or conscious of the "exact time" I will get to walk into the promises God has made me. At the time of the dream, me sleeping was a correct symbolic representation of my current state. So, since I've been praying hard about when we would be moving to Texas. I believe God is telling me that we will be moving to Texas September 18th; now the exact year, I'm not sure! Hopefully, it will be this year 2010.

Well, 9/18 2011 has come and gone and we did not move to Texas and I have now discovered that I have misapplied the prophetic date, to the wrong subject matter. However, it did turn out that the interpretation was predicting the date and time I would start recording for my long awaited television show! Even though I applied 9/18 to the wrong prayer request, the date was the correct interpretation of the time in the dream. For more on misapplication, please read chapter 13.

WISDOM DREAM: A New Anointing (June 26, 2010 Sat. night)

While sleeping, I felt the hand of God touch me on my left leg. When He touched me, He said "**I give you a new anointing to go onward and upwards from this day forword**. I literally **felt** the impact of His **touch**; it went throughout my whole body and into the very core of my soul and being. I've never experienced this feeling before. It was very **intense** and I was in awe!

After this I was somewhat awakened, but still in an in between sleeping state and then the Lord brought a woman named Tamara to my remembrance. At this point the Holy Spirit spoke these words into my spirit; "**now is the time for Tamara to go abroad and teach.**" It was, as if the Holy Spirit was announcing a commissioning to me!

Several years ago, I had met a woman named Tamara and she shared with me that she really desired to go abroad and be a teacher in other countries. So, God was using Tamara, symbolic of the part of me that also desires to go abroad and teach on dream interpretation. So, through this wisdom dream, God is declaring that a door is going to open up for me and He is telling me that **now is the time to walk in the calling**, concerning teaching people of other places and nations

It's funny to me that after dreaming this a year ago, I'm currently waiting to receive an invitation from a man, who will offer me a spot to teach on dream interpretation in his online bible college! Since this is an online opportunity, I feel confident that some students will be Americans as well as students from other nations; hence, the declaration and commissioning to teach abroad! This was a wonderful wisdom dream to have and I'm extremely excited for the teaching opportunity that God is lining up for me, as well as for the equipping of the saints, within the area of dream interpretation for the Kingdom of God. God is good!

Scraping the bottom of a grape jelly jar: KNOWING DREAM

I woke up knowing that there was a knife scraping the bottom of a grape jelly jar. There was no jelly inside, just a little bit on the bottom edges and sides.

At the time of this knowing dream, I had been seeking God about a woman I was ministering to and God had given me several visions concerning her situation. And the day before I woke up to this knowing, I sensed that God had already shown me all the revelation that I needed to know concerning her and the insight for her situation. I'd planned on ministering to her the next day, but I just needed confirmation from God, that the Holy Spirit was completely finished with what He was showing me about her. When I went to bed that night I had gone to bed about 99% sure that He was done talking to me about her. But, I wanted to be a 100% sure, I had received everything from the Lord that I needed to know. That was the night I had the grape jelly jar night vision dream, concerning her and here is my interpretation.

My Interpretation: To me, grape jelly is a "bread" (Word of God) condiment. It's sweet fruit that makes the bread taste better. So, God is showing me that the bread is the (scriptural counseling word) I have for her and the grape jelly is the fruit (visions) that make the word sweeter to the taste. The bread is GOOD, but the bread (Word of God) with jelly, (visions) taste much better and sweeter when hearing from God. Having His logos word plus the rhema word is very tasty! So, by God showing me this, He is showing me that He's done speaking and that I've hit the bottom of the jelly barrel and there is nothing more to dip into (in the spirit.) So, I now know I can give her the word and that it's complete. This is awesome!

Clae not going to work today: Wisdom Dream

It was early one morning, while I was sleeping the Holy Spirit spoke into my spirit and said, "Clae's not going to work today"! When God said this, I was awakened and in my groggy state, I looked over at my husband and noticed that he was still asleep and I went back to sleep.

It was about an hour later and Clae, while still in bed next to me, says "I'm not going to work today." Then I told him that God had already told me that he was not going to work.

There were no symbols or scenes to this revelation it was a simple sentence of revelation from the Lord that He wanted to make known to me. So, this was a Wisdom dream from the Lord and until this day I don't have a clue why God felt the need to tell me that Clae wasn't going to work that day. But, God wanted to tell me and I'm thankful!

I love having these types of dreams because they are very easy to interpret and they are very encouraging to me as a child of God! I'm so excited when God talks to me like this because it really nurtures my soul.

General Prophetic Dreams:
Longer in symbolism and detail.

General prophetic dreams are dreams that usually have some type of symbolic story line (**non reflective**) that is intertwined with a prophetic **message** that gives the dreamer a specific revelation about a specific area of their life. At times God may choose to speak to you literally and not in symbolism; however, it's my experience that He usually speaks symbolic and not literal. Within general prophetic dreams, often the dreams symbolic storyline will give you enough symbols to represent information, so you can interpret the specific, subject area of your life that God is referring too; as well as an obvious or encoded message of revelation that supports the theme of the dream. In "**general, prophetic dreams**" their symbols won't differ from the dream's theme. Meaning, the symbols won't reflect a health issue, but then give you a prophetic message about financial prosperity. The dreams prophetic message will match and support the related symbols and storyline of the dreams theme.

For example, on the next page in my general prophetic dream, God used certain symbols and a particular storyline to represent me "**having it made**" and the dreams prophetic revelation of Psalms 128, speaks of a married couple who had been blessed and they too will have it made! So, in the dream below the celebration, while lounging on a yacht, all have to do with a life of luxury and having it made in the shade! Then, Psalms 128, which is the Holy Spirits revelation in my dream, makes it even more specific in how this will come to pass. And it's through the blessing of marriage! Let's walk through the dream point by point.

161

Psalms 128: Prophetic Dream (Message, Promise Dream)

Many years ago I had the following prophetic dream and this is a dream, I could not have been reflecting because in real life, I definitely was not in a place of luxury. Moreover, in my own thoughts and mind I had absolutely, **NO CLUE** what was written in Psalms 128. So, this dream was Gods revelation and encouragement to me, concerning my future and financial prosperity in marriage.

A long time ago, God told me in a dream that when I got married, I deserved all I had coming. The story goes like this, I dreamt that I was in a state room on a yacht and everyone else had left the yacht and gone home. It was as if, we had thrown some type of party or something. And in the dream I knew that my dad (**father**) had gone to check and make sure that everyone had gotten off of the boat. He was checking to make sure the boat was secure and that no one was still left on board. While he was securing the boat, I was in a stateroom or cabin room of some sort and I was lying on the bed and talking to my friend Pam on the telephone. Pam was talking to me and telling me about this awesome scripture, which was Psalms 128. And in the dream I said to her, oh I know! I know! I've got it written down in my journal and in the dream as I looked down I saw that I had written that scripture down in my personal journal. At this point, I saw my mom in the room with me and she was laying in a day bed over to the right side of the room. As she laid there trying to get some shut eye, she heard Pam and I getting really excited and in her groggy state she asked me what were we talking about and wanted to know what was going on? (**The End**)

When I woke up from the dream I had no clue what Psalms 128 said, but, since in real life Pam is a prophet, I knew God had given me a prophetic message in my dream, while I was sleeping!!! This is the exact scripture version I read that morning.

162

All you who fear God, how blessed you are! How happily you walk on his smooth straight road! You worked hard and deserve all you've got coming. Enjoy the blessing! Revel in the goodness! Your wife will bear children as a vine bears grapes, your household lush as a vineyard, The children around your table as fresh and promising as young olive shoots. Stand in awe of God's Yes. Oh, how he blesses the one who fears God! Enjoy the good life in Jerusalem everyday of your life. And enjoy your grandchildren. Peace to Israel!

Symbolic meanings

Psalms 128 = Declaration of Gods abundant blessings for His newlyweds.
Yacht = I've got it made, financially and I'm cruising in the things of life.
Dad = My Heavenly Father, checking to make sure there's no thief onboard in my life that can breach my financial security. God's locking things down!
Pam = A prophet who proclaimed or pointed out a prophetic marriage blessing in scripture.
Journal = Represents, where I had written down all my previous prophetic words from the Lord.
Mom = Someone who is nosy (she is playing the nosy part of me that wants to know what God is saying concerning my future marriage)

My Interpretation:

As soon as I woke up I looked up Psalms:128 and it was obvious to me, that in the dream, I had already received this word in my heart, but in real life I didn't have a clue what Psalms 128 meant before the Lord revealed it to me, in my dream. So, I read it, researched it and I learned that it was a wonderful declaration, of blessing and prosperity that was spoken over newlyweds among the Israelites. I also found

163

out that this particular Psalms is the only Psalms, in 150 chapters that is interpreted, as <u>literal material</u> prosperity. I knew Psalms 128 was for me, because in the dream I had already written it in my prophetic journal. In real life when I write things in my prophetic journal it means that it applied to me and that I had documented it for later review! The yacht is symbolic of me being in a place, where I've financially got it made, because in my mind if, I'm on a yacht then it means I'm like Donald Trump and I've financially got it made! In the dream the Holy Spirit was using my real life father to be symbolic of my Heavenly Father; even tough, I could not see my dad's face, I knew he was securing the boat. So, in real life God was saying that **He is** going to make sure that my financial security is on lockdown and that **He is** making sure that there is no breech in my security. This reminds me of Genesis 15:1, when God told Abraham "I'm your Shield and your reward will be great"! God is so awesome!!! Finally, God was using my friend Pam, a prophet who I know in real life to be in the dream, so I would know this is a "PROPHETIC WORD", concerning His promises for me and my husband. The unknown scripture of Psalms 128 was made known to me in this dream as a FABULOUS PROMISE that was declared to me from the depths of Gods Spirit; thus intertwined with **non reflective** symbolic dream pictures, to promise me a wonderful message for my married life! I praise God for this wonderful message and I look forword to the Lord performing His word in my life today.

Recently, the Lord called me out of my job and I have started working in my ministry full time and currently I do not get paid. So, my friends, I take great comfort in knowing that God has got my future on lockdown and that He has financially secured my boat! Hallelujah!!!! God is good!

164

Heidi Baker: Prophetic Correction Dream
(by Micheal King)

I dreamt that I am talking to Heidi Baker, and we are alone in a room in a house together. I'm not sure it is my house, but we are both staying there temporarily (for a day or two). I'm fairly certain that she is just passing through the area.

I am just putting around the room, cleaning or something, and nervous about talking to her. I want to ask her to prophecy over me, but I don't want to be rude and impose, especially since I would be putting her on the spot. After a while, I sheepishly ask her something I am wondering (in the dream). I ask her if she remembers me from when she prophesied over me at the Voice of the Apostles Conference in 2005. (Which actually happened, in real life?) I mentioned that it was about the immense favor she saw on my life, and asked if she could tell me if she still saw that favor, and that amount of favor, on my life. I was apprehensive about hearing her response, because I think I was expecting a "no."

This is what she replied, "At the time I spoke that over you, your heart was almost as open as it could be."

At some other point in the dream someone, whether me or her, mentioned something about revival. Heidi said in response to that, "God is more than one kind of tree." With her words came an impression that if I were to look up different trees in the bible (Cedars of Lebanon, Pine, Oak of righteousness, cassia, etc.) that I would discover something unique about the character of God and the different ways in which he works and manifests himself on the earth, or at least something profound like it. It was like her words were not just about trees in general, but specifically about something hidden in the Bible.

165

The interpretation for this dream is fairly simple.

Heidi Baker is a woman who has a massive ministry with miracles, signs, and wonders, including raising the dead, in Mozambique Africa. The ministry began as a ministry to the orphans and has expanded into over 10,000 churches since the 1990's. She represents the voice of the Father to me, but not just any voice. She represents His voice of love and compassion. If you've ever been in her presence, you can feel the love of God exuding from her being, and it's wonderful. In the dream, I'm wanting a prophetic word, more specifically about favor, and she gives me one, although not what I might have hoped for. The prophecy itself is basically the point of the dream. While there are other dream symbols this dream is actually a gentle correction from the Lord dealing with the condition of my heart.

As a side note, I have had numerous conversations with people in dreams, and even people that represented the voice of God, but rarely have I remembered what they said like in this dream. When I had this dream, it was about a year and a half after my wife and I had been wrongfully kicked out of a church, and it had been a very hurtful thing to us. Additionally, to include something about God's humor and timing, I had this dream on a Sunday. I truly HAD closed off my heart in a number of areas, and wasn't letting people get as close out of an underlying fear that if I let them get closer, then they would hurt me too.

The message in the dream was short, but you have to read its corollary to get the full picture. What the Lord was saying to me was that my heart was closed off and implied also that I was lacking in favor, but the flip side of that is that if I were to open my heart up again, the favor that I had previously experienced would come back. What struck me as so wonderful about this dream is that when I woke up, what she said really hit home. It is safe to say that it 'pierced my heart' to produce the necessary changes.

This is a dream where the Lord corrected me by pointing out a heart condition that didn't line up with His character. While it was a correction, it wasn't mean, hard or angrily delivered. I truly believe that it is God's desire to deal with us gently as a loving Father, instead of as a righteous Judge. He is both, and if we have a heart's desire to please Him and be obedient always, no matter what He says, then we can expect Him to be gentle with us because He won't need to do it any other way. But, if we choose to ignore His gentle course corrections and continue in our ways, then God has to get drastic, and then He's very difficult to ignore.

I hope that I always have a supple heart before the Lord and am both open and obedient when I hear his voice, both waking and in dreams, so that those times never come.

My Friend died: Prophetic Dream (foretelling a specific event)

In the dream, my (Vonda's) friend had died, I was extremely upset and devastated because of her death; even though she left me her inheritance, I did not care about the inheritance; I just wanted her to be back in my life.

When I woke up from this dream, I was crying because it seemed so real; however, every which way I tried to apply this dream to my life, it just did NOT fit! There was no possible way this could be reflecting any event that had recently corresponded in my waking life.

The feeling of the dream was that I was devastated, crying and very upset and I knew that this could not have been anything I was reflecting, because as a newlywed, life was good and I had never been happier! So, I called my friend and told her about my dream with her in it; and at this point the Holy Spirit then used her to prophesy to me and she ministered some things to me about how, after she dies in real life, I would receive her mantle as a spiritual inheritance. However, after all was said and done I knew that this dream meant something more but, I truly did not know exactly what to make of this dream; so, for the time being, I just left it alone and continued to work on my other dreams.

167

Fulfillment: Sure enough 3 months later, my friend and I had a falling out and she decided to sever our friendship. She did not die literally, but because she did not want to continue the friendship any longer, she became like dead to me, even though I made several attempts to reach out to her. So, in this dream, God was trying to give me a message about the future of my friendship with her; this dream was "foretelling" a specific event that was sure to happen. Now, in hindsight, I can see that God was trying to **prepare my heart**, so I wouldn't be so devastated when this event finally did transpire between us; but, I just didn't get it until after the event took place.

Burned to the ground: (Prophetic Promise of Harvest)

This is an e-mail, between me and a woman named Bev; I thought you would enjoy and learn from reading this dream interpretation.

Hi Vonda, I dreamt my home (we rent) burned to the ground and we were living in a motel sort of place, then my husband's father made a loan and gave him 9,000. I am confused about this dream, there is NO WAY my husband's father who is over 80yrs old, who does not work and has no money could do this for us ; just wondering what you may think? **Thanks, Bev**

Hi, Bev, I read your dream about your house burning down. I wanted to know how you felt in that dream. Were you angry, sad or devastated? What was the feeling while you were dreaming that? **Blessings, Vonda**

Hi Vonda, Sad, like what's going to happen to me? I felt abandoned, having nothing left, why? **Bev**

168

Hi Bev, What or where at in your life do you feel sad and abandoned? The dream shows that in the house you rent (**where you live daily in the present tense**) that it is burned down and ruined? Is there anywhere in your life that you feel "you've been burned" by someone or some issue? Like your finances, or bills?

Also, I noticed in your description of your father-in-law, in reference to your dream, you implied that he (in the natural) was incapable of helping you. When you think of him what comes to your mind? For example...Do you see him as helpless? poor? unproductive? What comes to your mind?

Also, does 9,000 have any significant meaning to you? Have you ever purchased anything for that amount? Do you want anything that cost that specific amount? Like a used car, education, any ideas? **Blessings, Vonda**

Hi Vonda, Yes, I feel sad and abandoned in my marriage and with my children; yes, I feel burned in many areas. I cannot think of anything concerning the 9,000.00 dollars. As for my in-laws, they have NOTHING; no home (they rent) they live on Social Security and have a **POVERTY MENTALITY** and I NEVER want to wind up like them. So, FOR HIM TO LOAN US MONEY WOULD BE IMPOSSIBLE! I THINK THE DREAM IS BASED ON FEARS THAT I TRY NOT TO THINK ABOUT or WALK IN. **THANKS A BUNCH, Bev**

Hi Bev, Thanks for your reply!

It appears that even though the dream seems negative at the beginning. I think the last part is a good part. Because your father in law is making a loan to your husband and that is the positive part of your dream. The dream shows that even though it's a loan for 9,000 there is provision for you!

169

In the bible 9,000 means that your fruit is ready for harvest (Ira Milligan's book "Understanding the dreams you dream".) The dream started off that way (negative) because God was trying to show you which part of your life He's talking to you about or referring too. If, the number 9,000 doesn't mean anything significant to you, then the Holy Spirit must be revealing it or using it to give you a clue (the 9,000.00 figure) through your spirit man, in your dreams.

So far we have?

I dreamed my home that we rent, which represents (your present life because you live there now) burned (your life or soul is burned or your feeling ruined and devastated in your marriage and children) to the ground and we were living in a motel sort of place (a motel is temporary place, unless it has another meaning to you so, the dreams shows that you're in a temporary place) then my husband's father made a loan and gave him 9,000 (fruit ready for harvest).

In the dream you're father-in-law appears to be helping the situation by loaning your husband money? This would put a positive character trait on your father-in law, because all of us have good and bad things about us, which can show up as negative or positive symbols. For example, Moses was the meekest man on earth, but he also had an anger issue. So meek would be a positive trait, while his anger issue would be more on the negative side. So, what do you think of, when you think of your father-in-law in a good sense? Like, was he funny, a hard worker, dependable, good husband, good father or was he faithful? These are just meant to be ideas but, whatever he means to you in a good way would be advantageous for you to figure out so you can understand your dream.

Also, I see in the dream that your husband receives a loan for 9,000 from your father-in-law. If, the 9,000.00 doesn't specifically, mean anything to you I would say that the dream is showing "that your fruit is ready for harvest." In the bible 9,000 means that your fruit is ready for harvest!!!!! (Ira Milligan's book, "Understanding the dreams you dream.") It appears that the fruit of your labor is coming into your life by whatever it is that your father in-law represents to you (the good part of him.)

And since in real life, you know that your father-in-law making your husband a loan is **the impossible**; then it would appear in the dream that what is impossible is being presented as possible! Meaning that maybe God is getting ready to do the impossible. Maybe, not through your real father-in-law, but through the part of you or someone else your father- in-law represents within the dream.

For example, if your father-in-law represents some-one that has worked hard all of his life yet, has nothing to show for his self, then maybe God is getting ready to do the impossible through the hard working part of you that seems to have nothing! It could be a blessing through your job situation or something like that.

Whenever a dream is interpreted it's very important to get as much feedback from the dreamer as possible. So it can be very challenging over the internet. However, I just wanted to explore your dream with you and hopefully you'll get some ideas and hopefully our interaction has sparked something in your spirit that makes you say aha! I know what the dream is saying. :o) I hope this helped! **Blessings, Vonda**

Hi Dev, I'm sorry, but I meant to ask you if, after all, of our e-mailing, if you feel that your spirit enlightened you on the dreams interpretation? Do you feel like you know what it (the dream) means? **Blessings, Vonda**

Hi Vonda, YES... See the enemy was tormenting me with that dream. Telling me, that I would never get my own home and that I would always have NOTHING. My husband's family is CAJUN FRENCH and I AM NOT. They are ALMOST like the MAFAIA, IT'S ALL ABOUT DAFAMILY.

I am NOT IN THEIR CIRCLE, so I was thinking that his father giving him the money was just another pat on the back for my husband, and another rejection for me. NOW I SEE IT MEANS SOMETHING TOTALLY DIFFERENT. YOU MADE SUCH A DIFFERENCE IN MY LIFE!!! What state did you say you live in?? Let me know about those dream workshops. GOD BLESS You. PS: Keep in touch. **Love, Bev**

Hello Bev,
Dreams can be very tricky to work with because if a motel means temporary home (<u>vacation or moving transition</u>) to most people, it could mean something totally different to someone, who may have had to live in a motel for a year. Or maybe a person worked at the motel for a year and got free room and board.

Do you see what I'm saying about symbols being personal to the dreamer? :o) So, sometimes things I assume, while helping others with their dreams are overlooked as common, when in fact each person has personal symbols. I'm sure you have gathered by now; there is quite a bit of information that needs to be learned first, in order to have a foundation at interpreting dreams. Well thanks for the encouragement! I enjoyed lending a helping ear.

Hey, Vonda   3-01-07 (PRAISE REPORT) From Bev,

GUESS WHAT!!! THE DREAM CAME TRUE!!! AGAINST ALL ODDS OF MAN, I HAVE A NEW HOME!! BRAND NEW, got out of the RENTAL HOME, it was a MIRACLE!!! **Blessings, Bev**

The Anointing: Encouragement in the Gifts

The Lord gave me a dream about His healing anointing and Benny Hinn. In my dream I was walking on a sidewalk, past a house that I had rented for Benny Hinn while he was in town. As I walked by I decided not to stop in, because I didn't want to bother him. As I continued to pass by the house a guy named Ray (that I had met in real life who used to tour with Benny) saw that I was not going to stop; so he came over to me and put his arm around me in a brotherly way and said come on in we've been expecting you. And I said, no that's alright I don't want to bother him. But, Ray persuaded me and I went into the house with him and after I went in the room, we all sat down at a rectangular table. Across the table from me and my girlfriend Pamela, Ray sat to the left, Benny was in the middle and another guy was on Benny's right side. And one by one, they all three reached across the table and shook my hand as if to honor me. But, after Benny shook my hand I took my hand and reached over and rubbed the top of his hand; I rubbed it like a genies lamp. And as I did that Mr. Hinn looked at me and he asked me "what are you doing"? And I giggled, as I replied that I was trying to get some of that anointing. And then he looked me in the eye, winked at me and said; "**You are anointed**".

My Interpretation:

In this dream, Benny Hinn was not symbolic but he was representing himself in a literal form. In the dream I was rubbing his hand like a genies lamp and it was as if, I was trying to get some of his healing power. My friend Pam was with me because in real life she is a prophet. Thus, symbolic for the part of me that wanted a special gifting or word from the Lord to receive the gift of healing in a greater measure.

The message of the dream shows, Benny was reminding me that I am anointed! This dream is a dream picture that supports the word of God, because all believers are called to heal the sick and not just special Christians that walk in the healing gift.

So, when I woke up, I realized that God was reminding me that He has anointed me and it's not by any man's power or touch from them that I am able to heal others, but that I have indeed received the anointing through my covenant with Christ and His Holy Spirit. God was using Benny Hinn, in this dream to give me a message and remind me that the anointing of the Holy Spirit was already present in my life to heal the sick. This message was a message of affirmation, encouraging me of Gods promise that just like Benny Hinn, <u>I too, am anointed</u>!!!

And these signs will accompany those who believe: In my name they will drive out demons; they will speak in new tongues; they will pick up snakes with their hands; and when they drink deadly poison, it will not hurt them at all; they will place their hands on sick people, and they will get well."
Mark 16:17-18

Prophetic Dreams For Others

As you can see the messages God speaks to us through dreams will vary and the majority of our prophetic dreams will be **personal prophetic messages** that are meant for the dreamer; however there will be rare times when God may give us a dream that contains a message for others and not for the person who dreamt it. However, always try to apply the dream and its message to you, first and then if it does not fit you or your life you may consider the **very slim possibility** that it may apply to another person. Let me share you some biblical statistics proving how rare the occasions were that a person dreamed a dream for another person or for others, like a nation.

From their Book "Hearing God in your dreams" Mark and Patti Virkler, give these scripture references that support the principle that dreaming dreams to give messages to other people are extremely low in their overall percentages.

174

Gen.15:1-21 Abraham in interaction with God & sleeps = dream about himself.

Gen. 20:1-18 Abimelech and God in interaction = dream about himself.

Gen. 28:10-22 Jacob being spoken to by God= dream about himself.

Gen. 31:10-29 Jacob and God in interaction = dream about himself.

Gen. 37:1-11 Joseph and brothers in interaction= (2) dreams about himself.

Gen. 40:1-23 Cupbearer and Baker = (2) dreams about themselves.

Gen. 41:1-49 Pharaohs (2) dreams about 7 cows and corn = dreams for others.

Gen.46:1-7 Israel in dialogue with God= dream about himself

Judges 7:9-18 Loaf of bread hitting the camp = dream about himself.

1 Kings 3:5-28 God and Solomon trust and interact= dream about himself.

Daniel 2:1-49 Statue hit by stone = dream about others.

Daniel 7:1-28 Four Beast = dream about others.

Daniel 8:1-27 Ram and Goat = dream about others.

Daniel 10:1-12:13 Terrifying vision = dream about others.

Matt. 1:20-25 God spoke to Joseph= dream about himself.

Matt. 2:3-15 God spoke to Joseph = dream about himself.

Matt. 2:19-23 God spoke to Joseph- dream about himself.

Summary: Fourteen (14) dreams about the dreamer; five (5) dreams about others and usually applied to a nation or people. To learn more, purchase "Hearing God through your dreams" www.cwgministries.org

175

So, a person may have a dream for themselves or they may have a dream that concerns others. It's obvious to me that as these faithful men applied their dream messages to their individual life, they were blessed and, or became a great blessing to others in whom they led! But, unlike others who heeded Gods warnings, Nebuchadnezzar suffered greatly for **not** applying Daniels wisdom, concerning the dreams message. So remember, like Joseph listened to God and the message of his dream, when God speaks to you about your calling, many others will be blessed through your walk of intimacy, revelation and obedience to the God you serve! And concerning dreams for others, I do have to say that in my 8 years of serving in my appointed area of dream interpretation, I have only had one prophetic dream that was given to me that contained a message for someone else.

Two years ago, God appointed me to operate within the "Office of a Prophet" and it's my belief that the reason God gave me a dream for this person is because I was seeking God about his dream and its interpretation before I dosed off to sleep. This young man wanted my help in understanding his dream. Normally, God speaks to me through visions, to give me revelation for other people. But, this time God chose to speak to me about the young man's dream I was interpreting for him, through a dream. So, while I was sleeping God gave me a prophetic dream of encouragement for this guy. When I woke up I interpreted my dream and I shared Gods revelatory dream message with him, which God had given me for him. The message of the dream was a message of encouragement. In the dream, God let me know that this young man was an AMAZING man of God and that he was stewarding over the areas of his responsibility, extremely well in his life. He was an amazing steward. What a great compliment to receive from the God of all creation!

The Faceless Prophet: (Prophetic, Fame and Time promise)

I Vonda, had this dream from the Lord. In the dream I was at a church service and the prophet in the pulpit spoke to me. I could not see his face, but, I trusted his leadership. In the dream, I trusted his leadership because my pastor in real life was at the back of the room and he had obviously turned his pulpit over to him. In The dream the unknown prophet said that he was going to open up the floor for prophecy. The prophet in the pulpit was faceless, and he prophesied to 3 people; he spoke quickly to the first person and then I was second and then he spoke to a third person. I don't remember what the Lord said to the others, I only remember what he said to me and when it was my turn I was surprised that I was receiving a prophetic word. When the prophet looked at me he said, "you will be famous" And I looked at him with a look, like what did you say? Are you talking to me? I was surprised that he was saying this to me! And then He pointed at me and spoke "You will be famous within a couple of years." And then we all broke up and started to fellowship with one another. Then my pastor in real life, was in the back and he called the prophet over to him because he wanted the prophet to tell him what he said to the first person and the third person; because it all happened so quickly my pastor wasn't able to catch it all. So the prophet said to my current pastor "hold on a moment, first I need to talk to Vonda because I'm being drawn to her like a magnet" In the dream while all this was going on I was standing with and speaking to a girlfriend of mine whose name is Pam and in real life she is a prophet. Dream Interp. (#1. on pg 193)

This dream is a very personal and exciting dream that the Holy Spirit gave me concerning a very deep, private, and hidden desire of my heart. The paragraphs below will show more of my promise to fame, but please know that my desire to be famous was not something, I had asked God for nor, would I ever think of asking Him for. But, leave it to God to grant us the desires of our heart without us even having to

177

ask! After the dream I started to wake up and as I was half in and half out of my sleep, I said to the Lord "o.k. that's nice Lord but how are you going to do that? And He answered me; "**He said I'm going to give you a television show where you'll minister to people on the air.**" For some reason when God put this in my heart, I thought of Larry King; so I assumed that God was saying that people would call in on the phone like the TV show "Larry King Live". I don't know if that was the Lord impressing that on me or if it was me thinking it, because I would love to be on T.V.; but unless they were in the audience they would have to call up. Also, Larry King started in radio and then went to television. And now in the present 2008-2011, I have a prophetic dream interpretation radio show with callers and I'm sure this will lead to T.V. However, regardless of the specifics, it will be something of that nature. When the Lord said that it would be a TV show I thought to myself, wow Lord wouldn't it be great if I had a prophet there, like they do on the 1-800-hsyic line. But, unlike them, instead of using a fake prophet we can use a real prophet of God to speak to the people and give God's encouragement and direction. Then I woke up totally and looked at the clock and it was 6:22 am.

After I was fully awake, I thought wow Lord that's great, so I turned on the television looking for Joyce Meyers or someone to confirm the Word that God had just given me. And as soon as I turned on the TV, the commercial for Voice of Revival (my churches weekly show) was on and I saw my pastor inviting people out to church. Next, I flipped some more and stopped to watch this elderly black couple with salt and pepper hair and they said on their commercial; "Please join us here Sunday at 6:00 am as **we answer the questions you mailed to us and we minister the answers to you directly from God's Word**. And at that moment it was like God was saying, see I'm already putting this type of ministry into motion, it's already begun; I was in awe. Then I decided to read my bible and have my devotions. I was hoping for more confirmation, but not really. After all didn't I think I had already had enough? Ha ha.... I mean a dream and a confirmation all in one morning it would have been greedy for me to expect another? Yes I was greedy. At that time, I had just so happened to be reading the bible all the way through from the beginning to the end and I was in the book of Job. And as I read the second paragraph, Job's friend Elihu said, "don't you know that God comes to us late at night when were deep in sleep and shows us things to keep us from making some reckless choice or gives us a warning." At that moment, right then I knew for sure 100% that God had given me that dream. Before I was only 99% sure, but now I was fully persuaded. After I had the rest of my devotions I called my mom and told her everything and I said, wow I wonder if I should run and tell pastor what God has showed me. She suggested "I wait and think it over before I run to him." So, I decided not to tell him even though I was so excited.

Please note, if and when God chooses to reveal His great promises or times to you in a dream, you should always ask the Lord to confirm it to you and <u>you should NEVER chase after the promise or change your life based on just a dream</u>. Please know that as you continue to walk and grow in Him and the calling, where He presently has you placed, whether it's a job or ministry; <u>He can and will bring the blessing of promotion to you, in His divine timing</u>. Be sure to seek ye first the Kingdom of God and His righteousness and all these things shall be added unto you; faithfully walk in obedience, unto Him and let the Lord do the work in bringing the dreams promise to pass in your life. Also, on the flip side you can rest assured that when God has a great blessing in store for you the enemy will also bring you a counter offer, hoping that you will take the bait; but be wise and know that he is just offering you an Ishmael when the Isaac is on its way! Be forewarned that the other "counterfeit blessing" is just a distraction! How do I know you ask? Well, I should know because shortly after God made His promise to me, I was offered an acting position; but I knew the acting route was not the way, God laid out for me, so I declined! Please know, as in my acting alternative, satan's offer to you will be

179

tempting and look good, but he's only trying to divert you from waiting for the true promise. After the dream and as time passed by, I started to think. Maybe, it was just the devil giving me that dream trying to impart false hope into me. I thought to myself that maybe, the devil just wants me to be tricked, so I'll get mad at God when it doesn't happen by causing me to think that God let me down, while making me so angry that I would become disappointed with God; therefore making me turn away from the Lord. But, God knew what I was thinking in my mind and how I thought there could be a slim possibility that the devil could be toying with me. So, like God did with Abraham the Lord spent the next years validating His "Fame" promise to me. Here are 10 confirmations, I experienced after the Lord spoke to me through "The Faceless Prophet" dream.

TEN CONFIRMATIONS

Confirmation# 1- Answering Mail
I saw an older couple on TV first thing that morning, while watching them minister to viewers who had sent in questions about Gods Word. In my spirit I knew that God would use me in that same way, which is answering other peoples questions on TV, about the things of God.

Confirmation# 2- Dreams from God
Reading the passage of Job and seeing, how he often received dreams from God. This was in essence, confirming to me that God had just spoken to me in a dream.

Confirmation# 3- Fame and Wealth
On the way home from church Sunday a car was in front of me and the license plates noted **Deuteronomy 8:18**. The scripture spoke on how God gives the power for one to get wealth; and as we know, usually where there is fame there is wealth. But, God wants us to use our wealth and influence to do what He's called us to do!

Confirmation # 4 -Gods Girl and Healing

Later in about 1 1/2 weeks, while we were in consecration I felt like the Lord wanted me to pull away from the TV and spend more time reading. My mom had given me a book for my 37th birthday and the book was called "Daughter of Destiny"; it was the story of Kathryn Kulman. In the past, I'd started the book but I could not get past the first chapter. So, I knew that I was going to have to buckle down and make myself read it. A couple of weeks later, I picked up the book again. And this time, I literally spoke to the Lord and I said, Ok Lord I'm going to read this book since my mom was nice enough to give it to me. So, I got on my exercise bike and I was peddling away and I came to a part in the book, where the writer was saying that there came a time when Kathryn broke away from her sister and brother-in-laws ministry, because Kathryn and Helen the piano player had different visions for serving God. The book stated that when Kathryn and Helen started their own ministry they started billing themselves as "<u>God's</u> <u>Girls</u>". At that point, I literally had to stop peddling because, not long ago before reading this book, I had started a Christian Disc Jockey business and I called it God's Girl. I was awe struck because God had healed me and it's also my desire to see other hurting people healed. So, when I read that they called themselves God's Girls, like me. I felt like God was saying to me, "see you didn't think of that name all by yourself, I gave it to you." (Later my radio call name, was God's Girl: o)

Confirmation # 5- God letting me know that there would come a day, when I would be known everywhere I go.

Later that day I had to go to Tidewater C. College and that day I felt extra sensitive to the Spirit of God and I felt like He was showing me all of the sick people. I felt like God was saying to me that life will no longer be as I know it and that my life would no longer be my own. I would not be able to go places in solitude, but people would always be around me and I could not always be in a hurry. And that I should be prepared when in public to greet/minister to others when they approached me.

Confirmation # 6- "I would shake the Gates of Hell"

In this dream, I was in a grocery store. And I was standing in the isle and there was a man and he was of ethnic origin. Mexican, Hispanic, I'm not sure, but he had olive toned skin and his hair was very dark. And in the dream I noticed that he had pushed his wife aside in frustration or anger. And as I looked over I spoke to him and I said something like, you should love your wife she's a blessing. I'm not exactly sure what I said but, I was trying to minister to the situation, not trying to tell him what to do. And while I was speaking to the man he interrupted me and said, what's your name? And as I was about to tell him he interrupted me and said these words, as well as told me my name.

"He said No don't tell me He said I know your name. He said your name is Vonda, and everybody knows your name. And your name sounds kind of Hebrew, and that my name would be great for the Kingdom of God. He said, because you're going to sweep through Hollywood and shake the gates of hell and that I would do damage to the devils kingdom. He said, I would be unstoppable and that no one would be able to pull me down because my testimony would be above reproach!

After he spoke this, I looked at him strangely because he was saying so much so fast about me and I was wondering who he was and how did he know? And as I wondered I pulled out a piece of paper and asked him if he could write all of that down so as that I would not forget any of it. In my dream he did not write it down I woke up after that and that was that.

The reason the dream had me in the grocery store was, because I associate the grocery store with a place of ministry. When I'm at the grocery stores, I would always try to look for an opportunity to minister to people. So the store in the dream was symbolic for a place where I would minister a Holy Spirit type of message.

182

Confirmation # 7- "Voice (radio) and Visibility"(TV)

The Lord showed a prophet and friend of mine a vision and in the vision **my face was on the television screen**. It was a close up shot and my face was large taking up most of the screen. And then she saw that my hand was lifted up and I was proclaiming that someone was being healed of something in the television audience. Something like what Pat Robertson does. She said it wasn't churchie or church-a-fied. But that I was ministering to the people and the secular people were going to receive me better then the church people; and I would be very famous in the secular world. To the point that I would eventually evaluate and kind of question my calling, because I was so accepted in the secular world. But, she said I would still stand firm and continue to realize that this was of God and that this was God's call and doing in my life. And she said that in the church realm people like Jerry Falwell and those types of fundamental Christians would wonder and question whether or not I was of God. She said there would be opposition within the body of Christ about the way God used me.

The Lord showed her another vision immediately after that. She said "**Vonda I see bars!!!!**"; and I thought of a jail cell.

She said no bars, as in nightclubs. She said, Vonda, you're just going to pop up everywhere and out of no where. And people in the bars will say "who is she and where did she come from"? Kind of like why is she on? And others would say oh she's ok she's God's Girl. She said their going to watch you in bars from the roughest to the more easygoing places, like Apple Bees. She said, I don't know if the night club will come first or the TV show, but you're going to have influence in the secular world because they can identify with you because of your Christian bar and they'll receive you. She said, that I will have favor within the night club industry because of my club.

183

She said, God said that at this moment, God was anointing my hands for power and authority. And there would be power in my hands (releasing his power through the TV). And whenever, I lift my hand to tell the devil no you can't have this person or no devil you can't do that; there would be a source of power in the motioning of my hands.

Then she said "voice and visibility"! She said, God was going to give me voice and visibility and that I was going to the market place (a place where the fish are). She said that I would go to from nation to nation and to the utter ends of the earth!

At that time the Lord showed her a vision of a Muslim woman with her veil covering and she could only see out of her little peep holes and she said she didn't know exactly what that meant. But, I would have a voice in the Muslim world, but she didn't know if I would have visibility with Muslims. It could be both (voice and visibility) but, she didn't know for sure. So at that time she prayed for both. Then she said that God was going to use me to touch women of all generations and I would even cross over, and men would accept me too.

Then she prophesied and said, that I wouldn't be all by myself, but that the Lord was going to raise up a ministry team. People who would work with me by taking care of all the technical issues to support me. So, I could be free to just drop things and go at a moment's notice so that I wouldn't be hindered in serving Him.

Confirmation # 8- "Famous TV Evangelist"

One day I was crying at work because of all of my debts and I was wondering if things would ever change financially? Just then this salesman came into my salon and he was trying to sell me some magazines. So, I bought the magazines to be a blessing to him. He shared that He was a Christian and that he was trying to win a contest; he also mentioned to me that his brother was very sick. So, I took a towel, I anointed it with oil and prayed over it! I told him to take it and put it under his brothers' pillow and to trust God for his brothers healing. We talked a bit more and it was now time for me to sign my name on the dotted line for the magazine subscription I had just purchased. And when I signed my name on the dotted line he said to me. "Thank you very much for the signature, because I just know you're going to be a famous television evangelist one day and I'm going to be able to say that, I knew you when"!

Confirmation # 9- "May I have your autograph, please?"

One day I went to downtown Norfolk, to buy a city parking pass. I was taking a college class so I needed a pass to park in the garage. And when I paid the $10.00 on my debit card the lady, whom I didn't even know proceeded to hand me my debit card receipt, and then she said to me. "May I have your autograph, because I just know you're going to be famous one day"! My jaw dropped in awe of God's supernatural ability to confirm a matter again and again. I had several additional confirmations but, I don't want to bore you. The fact of the matter is that if and when God makes you a promise in a dream, if it's truly a God dream and not just a reflection dream, He will have NO problem confirming it to you! Don't chase the dream, but chase after God.

But seek ye first the kingdom of God, and his righteousness; and all these things shall be added unto you. Matthew 6:33 NKJV

185

Confirmation #10 "Superstar"

Not long after this dream, my friend's husband called me **Superstar!** After he said that, I asked him why he called me that and he said, it was because I look like a Hollywood superstar. But, little did he know that God was using him to confirm God's promise to me. Moreover, not long after he said that to me, a kid about 7 years old looked up at me and said these words to his mother. "She looks like a TV model." And even now my husband jokes with me and calls me "Hollywood" because he knows I love to get dolled up and make videos for Jesus! But, all in all it's really just another confirmation from the heart of God!

So, as you can see in my "Faceless Prophet Dream," the Lord did promise me fame, within a certain time frame as well as 10 confirmations, concerning this promise for my life. Even though this was so awesome, it's my opinion that all dreams are to be valued and esteemed for the Christian or the non Christian. Understanding and interpreting your "reflection" dreams correctly are a vital means of communication from your soul, to your natural man and for the Christian your "prophetic" dreams are a vital means of communication, from the heart of God, with the intent to bring revelation and understanding from the Spirit of God into the mind of your natural man. And for the non-believer, biblical history does show that at critical times throughout history, God spoke to the unrighteous through prophetic dreams as well as believers, regardless of their sinful state, in order to accomplish His will on earth. Now that we have thoroughly covered **Reflection dreams, Reflection & Prophetic Combination dreams, Wisdom & Knowing dreams, Night Vision dreams,** and longer and more detailed **General Prophetic dreams;** it is now time for me expound on time frames within a dream.

Chapter 9
Time Frames

In Daniel 2:31-45, Daniel interprets the large statue dream for Nebuchadnezzar and obviously the interpretation goes to straight to his head, because all of the sudden in Daniel 3:1-7 he has a similar statue built of him for his people to worship him! Go figure? So, some time goes by and God decides to deal with Nebuchadnezzar's **prideful** heart through another dream, with the intent to usher his prideful soul into repentance, and for him to walk in humility; however, the King did not heed the dreams (God's) warning, nor Daniels advice. After reading the scripture below, I will reference some important insights on time frames, within this dream.

Nebuchadnezzars Dream, let's read: Daniel 4:4-37 (NKJV)

[4]I, Nebuchadnezzar, was at rest in my house, and flourishing in my palace. [5]I saw a dream which made me **afraid**, and the thoughts on my bed and the **visions of my head** troubled me. [6]Therefore I issued a decree to bring in all the wise men of Babylon before me, that they might make known to me the interpretation of the dream. [7]Then the magicians, the astrologers, the Chaldeans, and the sooth-sayers came in, and I told them the dream; but they did not make known to me its interpretation. [8]But at last Daniel came before me (his name is Belteshazzar, according to the name of my god; in him is the Spirit of the Holy God), and I told the dream before him, saying: [9]"Belteshazzar, chief of the magicians, because I know that the Spirit of the Holy God is in you, and no secret troubles you, explain to me the **visions of my dream** that I have seen, and its interpretation. [10]"These **were the visions** of my head while on my bed: "I was looking, and behold, A **tree** in the midst of the earth, and its height was great. [11]The tree grew and became strong; Its height reached to the heavens, And it could be seen to the ends of all the earth. [12]Its leaves were lovely, its fruit abundant, And in it was food for all. The beasts of the field found shade under it, the birds of the heavens dwelt in its branches, and

all flesh was fed from it.[13]"I saw in the visions of my head while on my bed, and there was a watcher, a holy one, coming down from heaven. [14]He cried aloud and said thus: 'Chop down the tree and cut off its branches, Strip off its leaves and scatter its fruit. Let the beasts get out from under it, And the birds from its branches.[15]Nevertheless leave the stump and roots in the earth, Bound with a band of iron and bronze, In the tender grass of the field. Let **it** be wet with the dew of heaven, And let **him** graze with the beasts On the grass of the earth.[16]Let **his** heart be changed from that of a man, Let him be given the heart of a beast, And let **seven times pass** over him. [17] 'This decision is by the decree of the watchers, And the sentence by the word of the holy ones, In order that the living may know that the Most High rules in the kingdom of men, Gives it to whomever He will, And sets over it the lowest of men.'

[18]"This dream I, King Nebuchadnezzar, have seen. Now you, Belteshazzar, declare its interpretation, since all the wise men of my kingdom are not able to make known to me the interpretation; but you are able, for the Spirit of the Holy God is in you." [19]Then Daniel, whose name was Belteshazzar, was astonished for a time, and his thoughts troubled him. So the king spoke, and said, "Belteshazzar, do not let the dream or its interpretation trouble you." Belteshazzar answered and said, "My lord, may the dream concern those who hate you, and its interpretation concern your enemies! [20]The tree that you saw, which grew and became strong, whose height reached to the heavens and which could be seen by all the earth, [21]whose leaves were lovely and its fruit abundant, in which *was* food for all, under which the beasts of the field dwelt, and in whose branches the birds of the heaven had their home [22]it is you, O king, who have grown and become strong; for your greatness has grown and reaches to the heavens, and your dominion to the end of the earth. [23]And inasmuch as the king saw a watcher, a holy one, coming down from heaven and saying, 'Chop down the tree and destroy it, but leave its stump and roots in the earth, bound with a band of iron and bronze in the tender grass of the

field; let it be wet with the dew of heaven, and let him graze with the beasts of the field, till seven times pass over him'; ²⁴this is the interpretation, O king, and this is the decree of the Most High, which has come upon my lord the king: ²⁵They shall drive you from men, your dwelling shall be with the beasts of the field, and they shall make you eat grass like oxen. They shall wet you with the dew of heaven, and seven times shall pass over you, till you know that the Most High rules in the kingdom of men, and gives it to whomever He chooses. ²⁶And inasmuch as they gave the command to leave the stump *and* roots of the tree, your kingdom shall be assured to you, after you come to know that Heaven rules. ²⁷Therefore, O king, let my advice be acceptable to you; break off your sins by being righteous, and your iniquities by showing mercy to the poor. Perhaps there may be a lengthening of your prosperity."

²⁸All this came upon King Nebuchadnezzar. ²⁹At the end of the twelve months he was walking about the royal palace of Babylon. ³⁰The king spoke, saying, "Is not this great Babylon, that I have built for a royal dwelling by my mighty power and for the honor of my majesty? "³¹While the word was still in the king's mouth, a voice fell from heaven: "King Nebuchadnezzar, to you it is spoken: the kingdom has departed from you! ³²And they shall drive you from men, and your dwelling shall *be* with the beasts of the field. They shall make you eat grass like oxen; and seven times shall pass over you, until you know that the Most High rules in the kingdom of men, and gives it to whomever He chooses." ³³That very hour the word was fulfilled concerning Nebuchadnezzar; he was driven from men and ate grass like oxen; his body was wet with the dew of heaven till his hair had grown like eagles' feathers and his nails like birds' claws.

³⁴And at the end of the time I, Nebuchadnezzar, lifted my eyes to heaven, and my understanding returned to me; and I blessed the Most High and praised and honored Him who lives forever: For His dominion *is* an everlasting dominion, And His kingdom *is* from generation to generation.

189

[35]All the inhabitants of the earth [are] reputed as nothing; He does according to His will in the army of heaven And [among] the inhabitants of the earth. No one can restrain His hand Or say to Him, "What have You done?"

[36]At the same time my reason returned to me, and for the glory of my kingdom, my honor and splendor returned to me. My counselors and nobles resorted to me, I was restored to my kingdom, and excellent majesty was added to me. [37]Now I, Nebuchadnezzar, praise and extol and honor the King of heaven, all of whose works are truth, and His ways justice. And those who walk in pride He is able to put down.

TIME FRAME: Past, Present, and Future

Pease note: Nebuchadnezzar dreamt, "I was looking, and behold, A **tree** in the midst of the earth, And its height was great. "The tree grew and became strong".

I'd like to point out that God's word says, the King was looking at a tree and then it grew and became strong; thus making this a smaller tree and then getting bigger, within the dream. Therefore, making the time frame from smaller (**past**) into growing and becoming a stronger tree (**present**); and finally the tree was going to be chopped down (**future**) if the King did not change his wicked ways. It's important to note that the **tree** was **symbolic** for the **King**, concerning his **past, present and future;** but the **angelic message** of his impending **judgment was futuristic, prophetic and literal,** concerning the **action** of the dream, along **with exactly 7 years consequence**.

In this dream, God showed him a **reflection** of who he **was** and of what he **had grown into**; moreover, a **prophetic** prediction of who he **would become**, through the symbolism of the tree. And the fact that this dream reveals the future makes it prophetic in nature; in addition to the heavenly angel, who declared the **revelatory message**, concerning his dreadful seven year punishment, if the King did not change his wicked ways. Daniel knew the Kings character and offered godly wisdom, but scripture reveals that he did not heed the

190

warning and his judgment was executed. Therefore, the dream's predictive message was fulfilled and he lived, like an animal, in anguish for **7 years (literal exact time)**. Like, King Nebuchadnezzar, God in His mercy and grace desires to deal with us gently and warn us of our trespasses, in Christianity. God often does this through the conviction of the Holy Spirit. But, scriptures reveal that He has also been known to warn or reveal His timing concerning the life of an individual through a dream. Nebuchadnezzar's dream is a great example of a **"Reflection & Prophetic Combination"** dream, with emphasis on an exact time frame, which was revealed through a dream.

Below are some personal, yet current examples of how God still uses a prophetic message dream to reveal His divine timing, meanwhile all wrapped up in some very detailed symbolism; remember my marriage dream, let's review.

Marriage Dream:
"For the Lord would say to you, "it will not be 10 years and it will not be five but, I was in the final stretch of the race and that I should hold on because I was almost there. And then God wanted me to look around because I was not running this race by myself but, there were others running the race with me."

In my walk with the Lord I have found that it is very rare that God actually gives time frames to His people. Since my **"marriage dream"** was my first prophetic dream ever, when I had this dream I really weighed it against the word of God because I didn't want to mislead myself in any way. We must remember that we are humans and at times we can mis-understand and make mistakes in our interpretations concerning the things God shows us; it's all part of the learning process. Since, I didn't want to accidentally mislead myself, I would ask myself what the word of God says about time promises and I tried to look at the dream from several other perspectives, because I would rather know the truth then believe a falsehood.

191

So, as I pondered the dream and the fabulous time frame God had revealed to me; I asked myself, could this be true? Has God in His Word, ever given anyone an exact time frame? So, as I thought over scripture I remembered that God told Abraham that "by this time next year you will have a son". So, I said to myself, yes, even though it's rare; God has been known to give time frames in His word. In our dreams and visions there are many ways God will show us time frames, if it's His desire to enlighten us!

A. He may choose to relay the first one or two scenes as reflection scenes and then make the third scene a prophetic or foretelling type of scene, where He chooses to reveal an unknown revelation to you within the meaning of the dream; making this a "**Reflection & Prophetic Combination Dream**."

B. Or, God may choose to give you a dream, where all the scenes are future. Meaning none of the dream will reflect any past information but, the dream will start with a future scene, with unknown information and revelation that He is trying to reveal too you by making it known to you, through the dream. Meanwhile, the dream progressively unfolds further into the future as the additional dream scenes progress into completion of the dream; making this a "**General Prophetic Dream**."

For Example: let's say for a long time you've wanted a new car. In the night vision dream, the first scene shows your personal car being sold or traded in. And the second has you driving off a car lot in a new Cadillac. These are two progressive future scenes unfolding in a prophetic dream. Neither dream scenes are you present tense truth, but God is showing you what is to come, if you have interpreted your dream correctly.

C. And there will be times He shares literal images or symbolic imagery with us to let us know the times and seasons, He has certain things in store for us. Besides the dream, that I would marry in 5 years, here are a few examples of things God has shown me, in order to relay a particular "**time frame**" message to me.

1) Remember my "Faceless Prophet dream"? In the dream, the faceless prophet said "**you will be famous within a couple of years**"? In that dream, my old pastor was in the background and now he really is in the back ground. Meaning, he is not my pastor anymore. This dream had placed me in a **future setting**, which I now know as my new church with my new pastor. God was showing me then, that I would be commissioned at my current church (not the old one) and that from the point of my prophetic commissioning, I would be famous within 2 years. This dream and it's time frame did not start the day and the time I had the dream; but, the 2 year promise will start from the time of my prophetic commissioning at my current church.(Dream on page 177)

2) Once in a dream, the time **9:18** was spoken to me in a dream and this was a time code, symbolically re-presenting the 9th month and 18th day. So, when the time **9:18** was spoken to me, God was telling me that the thing I was praying about would take place on **9/18**, which was September 18th. This was the exact day I started recording videos for Heart Hope, which is my prophetic TV show and even though I didn't plan it. It happened just when God said it would!

3) One time I was praying, about when something would happen and the Holy Spirit suddenly reminded me of the freshly made, hot rotisserie chickens, which are sold at Food Lion grocery store and are only available from **3:30 p.m.** and are usually gone or sold by **8:00 p.m.** So, God was using my knowledge of this rotisserie chicken,

193

window of time to tell me that what I was praying about would happen between the dates of 3:30 or March 30th to August, which is the 8th month. Thus, 3/30 to 8/00. So, how about them apples? Ha ha

4) Once, I was praying about when I would go somewhere and God said **JFK president's day**, which was on the 21st of February 2011. At the time, I thought God was talking about when my husband and I would pack up to move. But, I soon found out that God was referring to when I would pack my things for a trip I was scheduled to take.

5) August 15^{th,} 2011, upon awakening the Holy Spirit said to me "**you will go up on 12:05.**" Since, in the past God has used a time to represent a date, I believe God could be saying that the Heart Hope shows are going up on the air December 5th. However, even more recently, in visions God's been showing me that **I'm going up to the front of my church,** and it's as if, I've won some type of a prize. In real life going up front is symbolic to me, of me receiving recognition. A while back God showed me that a couple at my church would sponsor Heart Hope and put it on TV. So, I believe God is saying that in church I will be going up front to be recognized for my Heart Hope TV show. When and if this happens it would be after worship, offering, announcements and before the pastor preaches. This would be right around the time of 12:05! So, I will continue to seek God, on the specific area I'm to apply the date too. But, whatever He's referring too, I believe it's this year. But, even though I'm believing for this year, I must remember that God **did not** give me a specific year to go with **12:05.** So, unless God reveals more, only time will tell!

6) Once God showed me an older clock where the time flaps would normally flip, but instead of a time I saw the date **Dec 13**[th], which represented a literal date something I had been praying about, would take place.

7) Once in a dream I watched my old roommate pack up her house. In the dream she told me that she had until **May 7**[th] to move out. My old roommate in the dream was a domesticated homebody in real life and lately I've been a homebody too. So, God was using her to represent the domesticated homebody part of me, while giving me the very important message in the dream that I would be moving out on **May 7**[th]. I believe that the college I will teach at will have a place for me to stay, while I'm there, and after the class is over I believe God is saying I will have until **May 7**[th] to move out.

8) Let me share another way God reveals times too me, this is a vision story. Because, I'm very familiar with birthstones and the months they represent, often God will show me **birthstones**, within the story of my dream to represent a month or a window of months, concerning the time I've been seeking Him about.

Birthstones: January is a Garnet, February - Amethyst, March - Aquamarine, April - Diamond, May - Emerald, June - Pearl, July - Ruby, August - Peridot, September - Sapphire, October - Opal, November a Citrine and December is a Blue Topaz.

Now, in my life as I continue to hear from the Lord through **dreams** and **visions**, He will often show me a birthstone, to represent a particular month of the year. He shows me these birthstones because they are symbolic of a particular month and they represent a time that God is declaring that the thing I've been praying about, will come to pass in my life! The following "**birthstone type of vision**" is another example of God's divine time frame, concerning my life.

195

<u>Silver Emerald Goblets</u>: For example, this year, I had many visions from the Lord showing me that it was time for me to quit my job as a hairdresser and begin to work in my dream interpretation ministry full time. I had been waiting for many years for God to give me the go ahead and now He had finally given me a yes! The time frame message God gave me to quit my job was in a vision. In the vision God showed me a royal couple sitting on the ground on a beautiful rug. The man looked like a nomadic prince and the woman looked like a princess as they sat on the ground drinking from a pair of exquisite silver champagne goblets, these drinking goblets were made of very thick silver and were old world style. They looked like the type of goblets that kings in the bible would drink from and imbedded on the outer part of the silver goblets were some very large and beautiful emerald stones.

My interpretation of this vision was that the Word says, as Christians, me and my husband are of a royal priesthood; therefore the "royal couple" is symbolic for me and my husband. And to me silver is symbolic for refinement, while the champagne and the goblets themselves represented, a time of celebration or a type of celebratory action. As far as the emeralds are concerned, in my real life I like jewelry and I'm pretty familiar with birthstones, so in the vision God used the emerald stones that were imbedded in the silver to specifically communicate to me a representation for the month of May. So, can you see it? God gave me this vision while I had been seeking him on the timing of me quitting my job. God had showed these champagne goblets to let me know that I had been refined and that the month of May would be the time of celebration, concerning me taking much joy in ending an old phase of my life as a hairdresser and coming into full time ministry!

And it turned out that I quit my job May 30, 2010, which was the exact birthstone month God showed me in the vision. I had not planned it. It just worked out that way because of certain circumstances in my life. The salon owner that I rented a booth from told me that she was selling the salon and it would be under new ownership and in her notice to me she shared that her lease ended May 31, 2010. So, just like God divinely showed me, my time was over as a hairdresser on May 30th and it really was a time of **great** celebration, because I had been waiting on the Lord to transition me for a long, long time.

But, concerning my marriage promise, for those 5 long years, I had to consistently believe, hope, rest, wait, and declare that it would come to pass. So, we must understand that there is a part that we play in bringing the promises of God to pass, in our lives. In my marriage promise, I stood and I shared my promise with so many of my friends that when my husband finally did come he was famous among all my friends. Some of my friends told me after my husband showed up, that they were getting a little concerned for me because the promise had not yet manifested until the very last minute. But, I do have to say that while I was waiting for him to come into my life, I **NEVER** doubted God. Not for **one single moment**! After we married my husband said to me, your friends act like they know me. And I said, they do know you and they've all been waiting with me and are happy because like me, they have been expecting you too and they are joyful to see that you finally came!

Like me, has God made you a promise in a dream, concerning something fabulous for your life? If so, please remember, with any promise of the Lord there is a factor of testing and timing. Innocent Joseph, while in jail waited from about age 17 to 30 for his promise to come to pass in his life. And like Him, we will have to go through a time of endurance and testing, as we stand in faith on the Word of God for His promises to come to pass in our lives.

"He sent a man before them—Joseph—who was sold as a slave. They hurt his feet with fetters. He was laid in irons. Until the time that his word came to pass. The word of the LORD tested him."
Psalms 105: 17-19 (NKJV)

197

Like Joseph, I have learned to wait on the promises of God. It was 18 years ago that I first desired to go into full time ministry, and that has just recently come to pass in May of 2010. I waited 15 years for my husband to come into my life and have waited 8 years, for the promise of my television show to manifest. The past 2 years my husband and I have been waiting for God to move us to another state. So, I said all of that to say. I have learned that the promises of God take time, patience, and obedience in order for them to come to pass in my life. In my walk with God I am and have become a professional waiter and up until this point in my life, God has never done a suddenly for me, but I happily anticipate and wait with expectation for a **suddenly in my life**!

One final thought concerning Gods timing, unlike many others in the body of Christ that I've met, I don't know exactly why God chooses to share some of His time frames with me. However, I do sense that He may share timings with me because of the type of end time prophetic calling I will walk in, as a prophet of the Lord. I believe part of His plan for my life is to use me to declare end time prophecies about what will happen in the earth. So, if God shares timings with you as well, please bear in mind, my friends that we cannot put God in a box. We cannot tell the Almighty God what information and revelations to entrust to us. God gets to decide what we get to know and when we get to know it! So, let's believe that He will share with us exactly what we need and love Him for who He is in our lives! And remember, if God makes you a promise it's our duty to activate the Word by declaring His word with our mouths and believing it in our hearts. It is imperative that we co-labor with the Holy Spirit by faith in bringing to pass the promises He gives us for ourselves, to release into the earth for His will. God's promises are conditional upon our belief, faith, endurance and obedience! So, if God makes us a promise, let's choose to respond like Mary did, when the angel of the Lord told her that she would conceive the Son of God. Like her, let's say "Let it be done unto me according to thy word"!

Chapter 10
Evangelism through Dream Interpretation

THOSE WHO HAVE INSIGHT WILL SHINE BRIGHTLY LIKE THE BRIGHTNESS
OF THE EXPANSE OF HEAVEN, AND THOSE WHO LEAD THE MANY TO
RIGHTEOUSNESS, LIKE THE STARS FOREVER AND EVER.
(DANIEL 12:3 NASB)

Up until the time of currently writing this book, through the leading of the Holy Spirit I have personally lead 153 souls to the Lord and I have always had an extreme love and passion to win the lost to Christ. Like me, you too can use dream interpretation to bring others to Jesus. Once a person shares a dream with you, it gives you an open door into their heart that they might not have normally opened up to you. Dreams are a secret way to find out what's going on in a believer or unbelievers life and after they share their dream with you, there's now an open invitation to usher Christ into the specific area their heart needs help with! Like Daniel and Joseph, you can help them with their dream; meanwhile, ready to share with them about how rich your God is in wisdom, to solve their personal dilemma or to save them from the soul's hurts and wounds. Please walk with me, as I share a personal story of how I led a young woman to Jesus, through dream interpretation and finally I will share a "**general prophetic message dream**" the Holy Spirit gave me declaring, "**I would shake the gates of hell and do damage to the devils kingdom**" for Jesus Christ, through ministry.

One For Christ:

July 2006, in my earlier years of my "Dream Quest," I remember very clearly as if it was just yesterday. I drove from Virginia to a dream interpretation seminar in Mount Pilot North Carolina, with my parents and a friend of mine. And it was at this conference, I found out by experience that good dream interpretation skills could bring the opportunity of salvation to the lost. How exciting it was when this precious young soul was harvested in, for the glory of Christ Jesus.

The story goes like this. The hotel I was staying at had a pool, PRAISE GOD; because I'm a beach girl. So, one day I went out by the pool to get some sun and as I laid there basking in the sun reading one of my dream books, I was laying out by another young lady who was in the chair beside me. We were the only two out by the pool that day. Anyway, that hot July afternoon we made some small talk about why each of us was in town. And as she inquired about more information on the subject of dream inter-pretation, it just so happened that I found myself sharing one of my dreams and low and behold, before I knew it, I was sharing the interpretation of my dream as well. Then suddenly she decided to share one of her dreams with me and I then found myself helping her and interpreting her dream too. And believe me she was wowed that her dream actually meant something! It was amazing to say the least, that interpreting her dream for her, gave me an open door into her heart. Simply because the dream and its interpretation revealed a private issue that she had been struggling with in her life. Ministering to her in this way gave me an open door into her heart and allowed or enabled me to counsel her in the light of God's Word that may not have been possible, otherwise. One thing led to another, so I went out on a limb and presented the gospel of Jesus Christ to her, right then and there. It was in the pool that afternoon that she believed and received the gospel of Jesus Christ and was saved for all of eternity, through the skill, or realm of dream interpretation. This was priceless! So, this, my friends, is an example of how the Lord can and will use us to rescue the lost and usher them into a thriving relationship with Him; hence, "<u>shaking the gates of hell</u>" and doing great damage to the devils kingdom through the realm, or skill of Christian dream interpretation.

"Shaking the Gates of Hell": A Prophetic Message Dream

I Vonda dreamt, I was in a grocery store and I was standing in the isle and there was this man, who was of ethnic origin; Mexican or Hispanic, I'm not exactly sure, but he had olive toned skin and his hair was very dark. And in the dream I noticed that he had pushed his wife aside in frustration because she had not picked the correct item off of the shelf. And as I looked over I spoke to him and I said something like, you should love or be kind to your wife because she's a blessing from the Lord. When I spoke this to him I spoke this with the intent to minister to the situation, not trying to tell him what to do. And while I was speaking to the man he interrupted me and said, what's your name? And as I was about to tell him my name was Vonda, he interrupted me at the Von part and then he proceeded to tell me my name.

"He said no don't tell me. He said I know your name. He said your name is Vonda, and everybody knows your name. And your name sounds kind of Hebrew, and that would be great for the kingdom of God." He then said, "because, you're going to sweep through Hollywood and shake the gates of hell; and that I would do damage to the devils kingdom and be unstoppable and that no one would be able to pull me down because my testimony would be above reproach"!

And I looked at him strangely, because he was saying so much so fast about me and I was wondering who he was and how did he know these things? And as I wondered, I pulled out a piece of paper and asked him if he could write all of that down so as that I would not forget any of it! I woke up after that, and that was that.

My Interpretation: "Shaking the Gates of Hell"

I dreamt, I was in a grocery store (<u>a place, where in real life, I would be on the lookout so I could be used to minister to people</u>) and I was standing in the isle and there was this man, who was of ethnic origin. Mexican or Hispanic (<u>symbolic of my love to minister, in an international type of ministry</u>), I'm not exactly sure but, he had olive toned skin and his hair was very dark. In the dream I noticed that he had pushed his wife aside in frustration (<u>a person needing to hear about Gods ways</u>) because she had not picked the correct item off of the shelf. And as I looked over, I spoke to him and I said something like, you should love or be kind to your wife, because she's a blessing from the Lord. When I spoke this to him I spoke this with the intent to minister to the situation, not trying to tell him what to do. And while I was speaking to the man he interrupted me and said, what's your name? And as I was about to tell him my name was Vonda, he interrupted me in mid-word, at the "Von" part and then he proceeded to tell me my name.

"He then said No don't tell me. He said I know your name. He said your name is Vonda, and everybody knows your name. And your name sounds kind of Hebrew, and that, would be great for the kingdom of God." He then said, "because you're going to sweep through Hollywood and shake the gates of hell; and that I would do damage to the devils kingdom and be unstoppable and that no one would be able to pull me down because my testimony would be above reproach! (This was a clear cut Prophetic Message, being spoken)

Through this message, God is using this man to give me the message that I will be well known in Hollywood and in the world. And that in my/God's ministry, which I know as dream interpretation and me being in the prophetic, God will use me, through Christ to shake the gates of hell and do much damage to the devils kingdom. And in a sense, no one will be able to pull me down or point fingers at me because my testimony and the way I lived my life will be above reproach!

202

And then, I looked at him strangely because he was saying so much so fast about me and I was wondering who he was and how did he know? And as I wondered I pulled out a piece of paper and asked him, if he would write all of that down, so I would not forget any of it! (Since it was rare that I actually got prophetic words or messages at the time of this dream. It was very much like me in my real life to want to make sure any and all prophetic words were written down. So, in addition to the actual message of the dream, this last part of the dream is just another clue, confirming to me that was a prophetic dream.)

At the time of this dream, I received the "dreams message" by faith, even though I didn't understand how God would bring something this big to pass in my life. But, now that much time has passed and many things have unfolded in my life, I can now see, exactly how God will bring His declaration of promise to pass in my life. It will be through radio and television.

Since, I discovered that God speaks to us through dream's the call of God on my heart and life has been to use the skills, I've learned to help others to understand their dreams and visions; and to offer the plan of salvation to unbelievers in the process. After tons of practice on myself and others in July of 2006, God opened the door for me to have a Christian dream interpretation radio show, called "In Your Dreams." And as of Sept 2011, I began recording a prophetic, dream interpretation television show called "Heart Hope," which will soon air in God's timing. The mission of these media voices are to help the believer in receiving the interpretation to their dream or vision and to minister any type of deliverance ministry they may need; but, moreover to bring salvation and deliverance to the lost through the gospel of Jesus Christ. For example, I would now like to share a "Night Vision Dream" by Tammi Vaughan. It's entitled "The Narrow Path" and this is just one example of how the Holy Spirit can use a dream and its interpretation to evangelize the lost for the glory of the Lord!

The Narrow Path: Prophetic Night Vision

Hello Vonda, (e-mail dream request)

I am so glad to have found you! A friend of mine, Glynda told me about you and I certainly need your help. I don't know where to start. I began having dreams as far back as 10 years old. Finally, during my adult years I started having the dreams again. Although I knew they meant something, I did not understand at the time exactly what. I have researched the meaning of the symbolism and interpreted them according to what I feel the Holy Spirit has guided me to know. From what I have discovered thus far, all of them (except maybe one or two) are references to the "End Times."

I am a Fine Art Oil Painter, so I have been able to reproduce a very close likeness to the dreams. I began painting the dreams in 2004 due to the Holy Spirits persistence. I recently completed a painting of a dream I had when I was twelve years old. I had decided to paint this dream because I thought it would be a beautiful painting and I have clearly remembered it throughout the years, I had no idea that this dream meant anything related to God until I began painting it. Then very strange events happened that my immediate family witnessed and so together we quickly decided to look into the meaning of the symbolism.

I dreamt, Saturn was setting upon the earth in a field and there were some huge purple grapes that were growing along a fence and upon the ground right up to the planet. There was a path in the dream which I added to the painting. Then again, a strange event happened with this painting. Upon completion, my son asked me why I put the #4 in the clouds! I replied that the #4 was not in the clouds and I persisted with this until he explained that it was the Roman numeral IV (4).

I am hoping you can take the time to view my (Christian art and the stories of dreams and miracles that accompany them at your leisure). www.tammivaughan.com

I would definitely appreciate your opinion as to my interpretations and if I have overlooked or interpreted in error. **Thank you, Tammi**

Originally, when Tammi wrote me about this dream, I did not know that she had entitled it "The Narrow Path." I had merely read her dream. Because of the numerous dream interpretation e-mails I receive, I had not seen the painting or gone on her web site until after God had given me the interpretation. Afterwards, Tammi so graciously allowed me to share the dreams interpretation with her on "Heart Hope," my prophetic television show. The video dream interpretation is entitled, **"End Time Harvest."** If you would like to watch the live video interpretation you may view it online at, www.youtube.com/user/godsgirltv

Now, I Vonda will share with you the symbols, their meanings and the interpretation.

Symbols:

Sky = Spirit Realm
Roman numeral IV (4) = Dominion, Rule or Reign
 (Ira Milligan Understanding the Dreams you Dream)
Green Field = The World
Narrow Path = Christianity
Saturn's symbol is a = Sickle and a **sickle** represents **harvest.**
Saturn = is also where we named **Saturday** the **Seventh** day
of the week, which is the **Sabbath**, with the end result
meaning the **LORD'S DAY!**
Fence = A dividing boundary line
Plump Grapes = "Grapes of Wrath" are ready for Harvest.
Rev 14:14

My Interpretation: The "Action" or "Storyline" of the dream clearly shows that Saturn has already come out of the universe and landed in the world or on the earth! This is a symbolic, yet prophetic "Night Vision" dream in which the Holy Spirit is using today, to remind us of His Word concerning the "Final End Time Harvest" in Revelation 14:14.

The Lords Day (**Saturn**) has come down from out of the universe (**spirit realm and heavens**) and has come into the world (**green field**) to harvest (**sickle**) the Christians (**narrow path side**) and the unbelievers (**grapes of wrath side**) on the earth. The dividing boundary line (**fence**) has been drawn between the believers and the unbelievers. The Lord's Day has come and Christ will take dominion, rule and reign (**IV or 4**) after this final and "End Time Harvest."

206

At the age of twelve, when God gave Tammi this prophetic dream, He knew that she and I would meet, share and interpret this "Night Vision" dream for His Glory. So, please my friends, if you have not made Jesus Christ the Lord of your life, we pray that you will heed this warning today and accept Christ into your life Time is short. These are the End Times and even now through this dream, God is reminding us of Revelation 14:14 that the "End Time Harvest" is sure to come upon us and it is not His will that one should perish. (Matt 18:14)

I'm delighted to share with you, that the Holy Spirit has assured me that many will see this dream and its interpretation on "Heart Hope" and will heed the warning and accept Christ Jesus as their Lord and Savior! Friends, this is just another example of how Christian dream interpretation can be used as an evangelistic tool to win the lost for Christ! Even now, I am happy to report that many people are being enlightened, set free and delivered through this vein of ministry and my prayer is that each Christian would be effective within the realm of dream interpretation. Whether, it's understanding a promise for them or for assisting others the word of God says, in Philippians 2:13, "for it is God who works in you to will and to act according to His good purpose." All praise, glory, and honor, be unto the King of Kings and Lord of Lords!

Chapter 11
"Action" and "Feeling"

Below, in Nebuchadnezzar's dream it is important to note that the **tree** was **symbolic** for the **King**, concerning his **past, present and future**; but the **angelic message** of his impending **judgment was prophetic, literal and specific**, concerning the **action** of the dream along with his **consequences**. Please look at the words I have underlined below in the scriptures and let the record show that contrary to some misconceptions and beliefs, Daniel did not just "make up" Nebuchadnezzar's consequences nor did he get a divine revelation from the Holy Spirit, concerning the King's judgment. But, on the contrary Daniel simply read, relayed and reiterated the angelic message, within the dreams revelation. Notice, when Daniel interpreted Nebuchadnezzar's gloomy judgment sentence, Daniel did not add or take away from the dreams message; but, he interpreted it as the angel spoke it, and exactly as the dreams storyline revealed. Before I noticed this, I had often wondered how Daniel knew, the King would turn into the beast of the field, but like me, if you look closely you can see that the angel of the Lord revealed this miraculous event when he spoke the message within the dream. Let's read!

Daniel 4: 10-17
"These **were the visions** of my head while on my bed: "I was looking, and behold, A **tree** in the midst of the earth, And its height was great.[11]**The tree grew and became strong**; Its height reached to the heavens, And it could be seen to the ends of all the earth.[2]Its leaves were lovely, Its fruit abundant, And in it was food for all. The beasts of the field found shade under it, the birds of the heavens dwelt in its branches, and all flesh was fed from it.[13]"I saw in the visions of my head while on my bed, and there was a watcher, a holy one, coming down from heaven. [14]He **cried aloud and said** thus: 'Chop down the tree and cut off its branches, Strip off its leaves and scatter its fruit. Let the beasts get out from under

it, And the birds from its branches.[15]Nevertheless leave the stump and roots in the earth, Bound with a band of iron and bronze, in the tender grass of the field. Let it be wet with the dew of heaven, And let **him** graze with the beasts On the grass of the earth.[16]Let **his** heart be changed from that of a man, Let him be given the heart of a beast, And let **seven times pass** over him.[17] 'This decision is by the decree of the watchers, And the sentence by the word of the holy ones, In order that the living may know that the Most High rules in the kingdom of men, Gives it to whomever He will, And sets over it the lowest of men.'

Daniels Interpretation: Daniel 4: 19-26

[19]Then Daniel, whose name was Belteshazzar, was astonished for a time, and his thoughts troubled him. So the king spoke, and said, "Belteshazzar, do not let the dream or its interpretation trouble you." Belteshazzar answered and said, "My lord, may the dream concern those who hate you, and its interpretation concern your enemies! [20]The **tree** that you saw, which grew and became strong, whose height reached to the heavens and which could be seen by all the earth, [21]whose leaves were lovely and its fruit abundant, in which was food for all, under which the beasts of the field dwelt, and in whose branches the birds of the heaven had their home [22]**it is you**, O king, who have grown and become strong; for your greatness has grown and reaches to the heavens, and your dominion to the end of the earth. [23]And inasmuch as the king saw a watcher, a holy one, coming down from heaven and saying, '**Chop down the tree** and destroy **it**, but leave **its stump and roots** in the earth, **bound with a band of iron and bronze** in the tender grass of the field; let **it** be wet with the dew of heaven, and **let him graze with the beasts** of the field, till **seven times pass over him**'; [24]this is the interpretation, O king, and this is the decree of the Most High, which has come upon my lord the king: [25]They shall drive **you** from men, **your dwelling** shall be with the beasts of the field, and they shall make you eat grass like oxen. They shall wet you with the dew of heaven, and **seven**

<u>times shall pass over you</u>, till you know that the Most High rules in the kingdom of men, and gives it to whomever He chooses. [26]And in as much as they gave the command to <u>leave the stump and roots of the tree, your kingdom</u> shall be assured to you, after you come to know that Heaven rules.

<u>WARNING</u>: In dream interpretation, one cannot change the action or storyline of the dream. You <u>**MUST**</u> keep the storyline and action as it is, in order to arrive at an accurate interpretation. <u>In Nebuchadnezzar's dream the angel declares that the tree (king) became and "it" and the "it" became bound and the (bound tree/man) was given the heart of a beast for 7 years.</u> The Scriptures do not reveal Daniel hearing the Lords voice supernaturally in order to relay the interpretation to the King. But, on the contrary Daniel read the dream and repeated what the angel of the Lord revealed to Nebuchadnezzar within the reflection, prophetic message combination dream. Here are some more examples, stressing the importance of the action and storyline of the dream.

Joseph and the sheaves of grain: Genesis 37:5
Joseph had a dream, and when he told it to his brothers, they hated him all the more. He said to them, "Listen to this dream I had, We were binding sheaves of grain out in the field when suddenly my sheaf rose and stood upright, while your sheaves gathered around mine and bowed down to it."

The Action of the dream: The sheaves were <u>bowing down</u> to Joseph's sheave of grain that was <u>raised upright</u>!

The interpretation: Genesis 37:8
His brothers said to him, "Do you intend to reign over us? Will you actually rule us"? And they hated him all the more because of his dream and what he had said.

Can you see it? The brothers could interpret his dream and knew that Josephs dream revealed that he would be raised up and they would be bowing down; this implies that he would be some type of royalty and lord over them.

Josephs: sun, moon and stars dream in Genesis 37:9
Then he had another dream, and he told it to his brothers. "Listen," he said, "I had another dream, and this time the sun and moon and eleven stars were bowing down to me."

The Action of the dream: The sun moon and stars all <u>bowing down</u> to Joseph.

Josephs: sun, moon and stars interpretation: Genesis 37:10-11
When he told his father as well as his brothers, his father rebuked him and said, "What is this dream you had? Will your mother and I and your brothers actually come and <u>bow down to the ground before you</u>?" His brothers were jealous of him, but his father kept the matter in mind.

Later, when Joseph was in prison the chief cupbearer told Joseph his dream. He said to him, "In my dream I saw a vine in front of me, and on the vine were three branches. As soon as it budded, it blossomed, and its clusters ripened into grapes. Pharaoh's cup was in my hand, and I took the grapes, squeezed them into Pharaoh's cup and put the cup in his hand."

Chief Cupbearers Dream Interpretation: Gen 40:9 -11
"This is what it means," Joseph said to him. "The three branches are three days. Within three days Pharaoh will lift up your head and restore you to your position and you will put Pharaoh's cup in his hand, just as you used to do when you were his cupbearer."

The Action: The cupbearer was <u>working by serving</u> the Pharaoh, just like in the past. Genesis 40:16

Chief Bakers Dream: Gen 40:16-17
When the chief baker saw that Joseph had given a favorable interpretation, he said to Joseph, "I too had a dream: On my head were three baskets of bread. In the top basket were all kinds of baked goods for Pharaoh, but the birds were eating them out of the basket on my head."

Chief Bakers Interpretation: Genesis 40:18

"This is what it means," Joseph said. "The three baskets are three days. Within three days Pharaoh will lift off your head and hang you on a tree. And the birds will eat away your flesh."

The Action: In the chief baker's dream the **birds were eating from his head area**. I believe, Joseph and everyone knew, when the birds of the air are eating from a human head that "**surely someone is dead!**"

Fulfillment and End of the Story: Genesis 40:20-22

Now the third day was Pharaoh's birthday, and he gave a feast for all his officials. He lifted up the heads of the chief cupbearer and the chief baker in the presence of his officials. He restored the chief cupbearer to his position, so that once again he would put the cup into Pharaoh's hand; but, Pharaoh hung the chief baker, just as Joseph had predicted to them in his interpretation.

As you can clearly see, Joseph did not veer from the action or storyline of the dream. The dream's story line showed the chief baker with birds eating around the sphere of his head and the cup bearer putting the cup into the hand of the Pharaoh, which speaks of being back on the job! So, like Joseph, when interpreting a dream we **must** stick to the action or storyline of the dream by adding nothing and taking nothing away; which is imperative to arriving at an accurate interpretation!

Please note that all of the prior dream examples, were prophetic **night vision dreams** that were given by the Holy Spirit in order to predict, promise, enlighten, or warn them of an up and coming event in their life; thus making these prophetic dreams, containing **no inward feelings** to consider, like with reflection dreams. However, the same "**action**" principle still applies, when it comes to reflection or prophetic dreams. Please remember, prophetic dreams can predict, but reflection dreams are not a prediction. But, are the dreamers heart reflecting an ongoing situation that they've already experienced. Moreover in all dreams it's extremely important to stick to the storyline at all times.

The Waterfall dream: Reflection Dream

As a more current example, let's say you have a dream that you're drifting uncontrollably in a small boat that you know is headed for a dangerous cliff type of waterfall. And the dream ends with you fearing you will go over the edge and being killed; but in the dream you did not actually go over the edge but, you just feared it.

The dream is what it is, and in order to arrive at an accurate interpretation, you cannot add to the storyline or take away from it. You can't say I'm dead; I'm going to get killed! This would NOT be true!!!! The dream just gave you a symbolic picture of you about to go over the edge. So most likely this is a reflective dream that is showing you a picture, which is paralleling a specific personal struggle.

So, if it were my dream I would ask myself where at in my life, am I in an uncontrollable situation and about to go over the edge? It may be symbolic of some type of addiction or a situation at work, church or within a personal relationship, where you are about to go over the edge or you are about to go over the deep end, which is a metaphor!

So, please take note that you cannot say that the dream showed you going over the waterfall and dying, if the dream never showed that. You have to stay within the story line of the dream. The dream shows what the dream shows and you are in **error** if, you add or take away from the storyline of the dream.

Let me share some insights with you from Mark and Paul Virklers book, "Hear God through your dreams." Mark says,

214

"ask the Holy Spirit to show you the symbolism of the **action** in the dream. For example, if the symbol in your dream is that your car is going backward, ask, in what way do I feel I'm going backward, that I'm not moving forword in this area of my life? If someone else is driving your car in the dream, ask, In what way is this person driving or controlling my life (e.g., my reactions attitudes, behaviors) at this time? Or, how is the characteristic that this person symbolizes controlling me? If you are falling, ask yourself "In what way do I feel like I am falling, losing ground, or out of control in my life at this time? If you are soaring, ask In what way or what area of my life do I feel like I'm flying, that I am rising above my problems or my abilities? If you are being chased, as how and why do I feel like I'm being perused or hunted? If you are naked, ask" In what way do I feel like I am exposed and vulnerable? If you dream of dying, ask, what is dying within me? (This may be a good thing, for perhaps you are dying to pride, or to self, or to workaholism.)"

The Feeling in the Dream

I have learned that the dreamer only needs to identify the specific thought or feeling in the dream, when interpreting a Reflection Dream, Reflection Prophetic Combination Dream and Prophetic Dream mysteries. But, it is my experience that Night Vision Dreams and Wisdom or Knowing dreams **do not** relay a specific feeling to the dreamer, while dreaming the dream; therefore, the "feeling" is not a factor in the interpretation of the latter two prophetic dreams. When, Joseph and Daniel interpreted their prophetic night vision dreams, the feeling in the dream was not an issue, but they were dependant on the symbols, action or angelic message of the dream, as well as the revelation of the Holy Spirit for their dream interpretations

After you wakeup and you are remembering your dream, it's extremely important to ask yourself "How did I feel **in the dream**, while asleep or what was the feeling in the dream?

215

Here is a list of human emotions or feelings, my friend Kristie prepared for your review. These are just some of the emotions that a person may experience in the dreams they dream!

Amused	Doubtful	Hateful
Alienated	Depressed	Horrified
Adoration	Disjointed	Humiliated
Anger	Discouraged	Hysterical
Anticipation	Desire	Home sick
Aggressive	Disappointed	Humble
Awe	Excited	Honored
Annoyed	Embarrassed	Interested
Apprehensive	Ecstasy	Infatuated
Accepted	Emotional	Insulted
Aroused	Empathetic	Irritated
Anxious	Empty	Irritable
Artistic	Enthusiastic	Isolated
Angst	Entangled	Intolerable
Ambivalence	Encouraged	Joy
Approval	Energetic	Joking
Alone	Envious	Jovial
Bitter	Friendly	Jarred
Boredom	Fearful	Jealous
Brave	Fake	Kind
Betrayed	Fat	Lonely
Comforted	Fictitious	Love
Confused	Fabulous	Lustful
Conscientious	Fantasy	Longing
Content	Frustrated	Mad
Calm	Gratitude	Melancholy
Compassion	Greif	Modest
Compared	Grateful	Nonchalant
Contempt	Gratified	Nostalgic
Courageous	Guilty	Nosey
Curious	Glee	Non sarcastic
Clumsy	Gladness	Nervous
Defeated	Honoring	Negative
Defiant	Hopeless	Optimistic
Disgusted	Hopeful	Out of control
Disapproving	Helpless	Obsessed
Disengaged	Hurt	Overwhelmed
Distracted	Happy	Pain

216

Panic	Respectful	Shame
Peaceful	Regretful	Sentimental
Proud	Rage	Self Pity
Paranoid	Rejected	Self Love
Patient	Sorry	Silly
Passionate	Suspended	Trust
Pity	Shy	Terror
Pleasurable	Sad	Terrified
Pleased	Surprised	Tired
Remorseful	Satisfied	Tortured
Rested	Shocked	Unhappy
Repentant	Sympathetic	Vulnerable
Revengeful	Suspenseful	Wonderment
Righteous	Suffering	Worthless
Indignation	Social	Worry

Whatever the feeling, after you have successfully identified how you felt in your dream, now is the time to ask yourself, where or in what part of my life, do I feel the same exact thought or feeling as is felt in my dream? When you arrive at your answer, now you know the subject matter of your whole dream and all of the dream will be a reflection of that exact issue. (There's an exception to this rule, see page 101-102)

For example, maybe your answer was that you felt anger and in real life you've been angry at your husband or wife for something they did or did not do. So, the anger you are feeling in the dream is a direct result of the anger you feel towards your mate, because of a recent argument the two of you had. Well, **if** the dream is just a **reflection dream** and it's **not a prophetic dream**, then I can guarantee you that the whole dream will be about that argument you just had. The symbols, action, storyline and feeling will literally or symbolically all reflect that exact emotional struggle. However, if it was a "reflection & prophetic combination" dream, you will need to consider your **"feeling answer,"** in addition to the proper insight of your symbols, action, storyline and the dreams revelation from the Holy Spirit, in order to arrive at an accurate interpretation, concerning any prophetic message from the Lord about the dreams subject matter. (see Reflection & Prophetic combination dreams page 137-149)

217

Examples:

1. Where or in what part of my life, am I fearful?
2. Where or in what part of my life, am I worried?
3. Where or in what part of my life, am I unhappy?
4. Where or in what part of my life, am I bitter?
5. Where or in what part of my life, am I hurt?
6. Where or in what part of my life, am I sad?
7. Where or in what part of my life, am I surprised?
8. Where or in what part of my life, am I shocked?
9. Where or in what part of my life, am I annoyed?
10. Where or in what part of my life, am I hopeful?

If, your answer is that you're fearful about losing your job, then the whole dream will be about that issue. If, your answer is that you're sad about your pet dying, then the whole dream will be a reflection of the specific sadness of having lost your pet. ect ect ect.

Now that we have thoroughly covered the importance of understanding your personal symbols, time frames, feelings, and action of the dream, as well as identified how Reflection and Prophetic dreams can differ from one another. It's now time to learn and embrace my eight systematic steps of dream interpretation! Are you ready? If so, then let's go!

"WISDOM SAYS AFTER YOU DREAM A DREAM, PRECEIVE YOUR DREAM" Vonda Brewer

Job 33:14-15 NLT

For God speaks again and again, though people do not recognize it. He speaks in dreams, in visions of the night, when deep sleep falls on people as they lie in their beds.

Chapter 12
DREAM INTERPRETATION: 8 EASY STEPS

It is the glory of God to conceal a matter,
But the glory of kings *is* to search out a matter.
(Proverbs 25:2 NKJV)

After waking and remembering your dream, please follow these **8 steps.**

Step 1: Ask yourself: Was I active in the dream (reflection dream) or was I watching myself or seeing a scene's imagery, in a glimpse (night vision) or bird's eye view (night vision)?
If, determining the dream is a "**prophetic message dream**" (enlightening revelation or message being spoken) or "**night vision dream**," then <u>STOP</u> at this step because different and shorter steps will apply. But, after determining it's a "**Reflection Dream**" then you may continue with <u>steps 2-8.</u>

Step 2: Ask yourself: How did I **feel** in and during the dream? Not, after the dream, but **during the dream**; then write down your answer.

Step 3: Ask yourself: What was I **thinking** about in the dream or what was the <u>**EXACT**</u> phrase, impression or dominate line of thinking in the dream? Then write down your answer.

Step 4: Where do I feel or think this same things in my life?
Ok, for right now forget about the dream in itself and take your answers from steps **2 and/or 3** and ask yourself, this question; where do I feel this same feeling, thought or line of thinking in my daily life? What could it pertain to? Write down your answer!

219

When and after you answer this question in step 2-3, the whole dream will be about this "<u>specific subject</u>" in your life.

<u>For example</u>: If you said, I feel and think the same way in the dream, as I do about what is going on at my job, friendships, church, emotions, husband, money, children, ministry, health, college, or in-laws, ect, ect, ect. Then, whatever your answer was to step 2-3 and if you have pegged it correctly as a "Reflective Dream." Then I can promise you that the whole dream will be about that exact subject, and your symbols in the dream will make more sense to you, while supporting that specific subject. No doubt about it!

Step 5: Evaluate the Symbols (review chapter 5)

<u>Ask, yourself, if this whole dream is about my previous answer</u> (**step 4,** my God, job, teacher, class, homework, friendships, church, emotions, boss, husband, wife, money, children, ministry, health, vacation, house, car, friend, college, or in-laws, sickness ect, ect, ect,.) <u>then how would each symbol fit into the subject matter the dream is paralleling in my real life</u> ?

Now that you know the "<u>real life subject</u>" your dream is reflecting, you can begin to identify the symbols much easier and start to see the parts they're playing in your dream. Also, be sure to relate your symbols together in conjunction with the storyline of your dream! Now, any possible metaphors, similes, metonymies or idioms, in the dream will make more sense to you. And the symbols, whether people, animals, numbers, colors, places and things will fit in, with the feeling of the dream. Like pieces to a puzzle, your symbolism will SUPPORT your real life issue or struggle and give you more clarity pertaining to the subject matter of the dream, you're interpreting.

<u>For Example</u>: Let's say for some reason Donald Trump was in your dream and your thinking, "What in the world was Donald Trump doing in my dream? And how in the heck could he be symbolizing some part of me or someone else in my life"?

220

Well, let's pretend when you answered step 4 the answer was all about your job and in real life it just so happens that you work in or sell real-estate. Well, then Donald Trump could be symbolically, playing the part of you that is very successful in real-estate or if you're the big boss in real-estate, then he could be playing the part of you that will have to say "Your Fired", because in real life at the time of the dream you may have been pondering the fact that you may need to fire someone under you in your field of work. Or, he could not be playing a part of you, but instead be playing the part of your "real life boss" in real- estate, if you consider your boss to be a successful real-estate tycoon! And finally he could just simply, be symbolic for the part of you who so, very desperately needs to get a new hair style! Sorry Donald, ha ha! So, first apply the symbols to you, if they fit and if they do not fit you specifically, then see if it can apply to some other person related to the **subject matter** of what the dream is paralleling /representing in your real life.

Step 6: Identify the action and storyline.

Be sure to carefully observe the action and storyline of your dream and do not add or take away anything from the dream and the storyline the dream is showing you, mean-while looking at the overall "**Big Picture.**" (See key principle # 8 on page 47-50) Let me share another example in the dream below and what not to do, concerning adding or removing information from the storyline of the dream.

Adultery Dream:
Maybe in real life your feeling frumpy, overweight, unattractive and insecure with your spouse; and even though you know, your spouse has been completely faithful to you, somehow in your heart you have been concerned that your spouse may find someone else. So, let's pretend that one night you dreamt, your spouse had an affair with another person and in the dream you feel so insecure and upset.

Well, if it is the truth and in real life you're dreaming this because you really did feel this way about yourself and you really did **know for sure** that your spouse had an affair. Then this is a literal or **true reflection** of the thoughts and emotions of the terrible event that your heart had to process, as a result of the adultery in your marriage. However, you cannot add to the action or storyline of the dream and say that in real life your spouse is going to leave or divorce you for the other person, because the dream does **NOT** show this, in the **ACTION** or **STORYLINE** of the dream. Now, I'm not saying that the spouse will or will not leave. The spouse may or may not leave you because they do have a choice to exercise their free will in any circumstance. However, I'm just pointing out that you cannot add or take away from the dreams action or storyline. The dream showed that the spouse was unfaithful and it's what the dream showed, no more and no less.

Also, while considering the action or storyline of your dream, please note this **warning**. Most of the time, reflective dreams simply reflect the factual truth of events in your life or your feelings thoughts and emotions of the events in your daily life. But, everything we feel is not always the absolute truth and often it is or can be our "**perception of truth**." Reflection dreams, **never** predict, foretell, or validate any event in your day to day life, but they simply reflect the positive or negative issues of your heart.

For Example: Truth or Perception?

Maybe in real life you're overweight and you're feeling frumpy, unattractive and insecure with your spouse. And even though you know your spouse been completely faithful to you, in your heart you have been extremely concerned your spouse may find someone else. So, one night you dream your spouse had an affair with another person and in the dream you're upset.

222

Fact or Perception?

When you wake up and think about the dream, you can't claim it to be **a fact**, just because you dreamt it. You can't say the dream is showing you the truth and then go and falsely accuse your spouse with no real iron clad proof. Because, it's a 99.9% chance that this dream is solely a reflection of your inner thoughts and of the emotional insecurity you're experiencing in your heart and life concerning him. The dream you had, is your perception and thoughts of the way you've been feeling lately and it's not the factual truth of the matter. Later, I will use this same example again, in the "**Night Vision Dream**" interpretation section, so you may know how to recognize it, if it's a foretelling, prophetic message or some type of revelation that God is trying to relay to you; instead of an internal reflection dream.

Step 7: Write down your dream, meanwhile trying to identify any possible metaphors, similes, metonymies or idioms, in the dream. Some people say you should write the dream down as a first step. But, I always write mine down after I have understood it. It's really up to you when you choose to right out the whole dream.

❖ Then you have your interpretation! It's that simple; like anything the more you practice the better you will become!

Step 8: Counsel yourself in the Light of God's Word.
In every area of your life, allow the Word of God to be your guide and apply its truth to the positive or negative messages of your dreams.

After decoding the symbolic interpretation of a reflection dream, I always ask myself, is this the truth? Is this truly what happened <u>or</u> is it just <u>"my perception or feelings"</u> of what happened in my real life. Then, I always <u>COMPARE THE FACTS</u> of what happened in real life to the **Truths** based on the <u>God's Word</u>. Let me elaborate on this and demonstrate my thought process with you.

For example: In Christianity, un-forgiveness is not an option. So, if your dream really did reflect the unfaithfulness (<u>fact</u>) of your spouse and he/she really did cheat on you. Then the fact of the matter is, that at some point you must find it in your heart to forgive your spouse for the adultery and in turn this will aid you in the healing your heart so desperately needs! If, the spouse who cheated is truly repentant and sorry, it is God's desire to heal your heart and restore the spouse back to a heart of godliness and finally, restore the marriage, if both parties are willing to do God's will and not their own will. However, if the adultery dream is just based on your **perception,** and insecurities in your marriage, because of your outward appearance concerning your bodily image. Then you would need to use the word of God to combat and speak against those insecure areas of your heart and ask God to heal you from the way you **perceive** yourself; in addition to trying to eat right and go to the gym, while taking care of the one and only body God gave you! This is just an example of how a Christian should respond no matter what subject the dream is reflecting in their life. God's word should always be applied to dreams that are reflections of the thoughts, emotions, and events within your daily life.

Here are some detailed examples of these **8 Easy Steps** and how they are applied to "Reflection Dreams" only. The steps for Night Vision Dreams are similar, but much shorter and will be shared in the prophetic interpretation section.

Reflection Dream: Interpretation Examples

Reflection Example: Can't get up the mountain

I (Vonda) dreamt, that I was trying to walk up a mountain and about half way up some men stopped me and they would not let me pass. Then I went to another area of that same mountain and tried to get up that way and again, some men stopped me at the half way mark. In the dream, I tried four or five different routes and no matter which way I went or how hard I tried to get to the top of the mountain, these men would always stop me at the half way mark and they would not let me get to the top! I was upset and frustrated.

My Interpretation Answers:

Step 1: Ask yourself: Was I active in the dream (reflection dream) or was I watching myself or seeing a scene's imagery, in a glimpse (vision) or bird's eye view (vision.)

My answer: I'm **actively participating** in this dream and because I'm walking up the mountain, this makes this a <u>reflective dream</u>" NOT a "<u>night vision</u>" dream.

Step 2: Ask yourself: How did I **feel** in and during the dream?

My Answer - Frustrated and **upset!**

Step 3: Ask yourself: What was I <u>thinking</u> about in the dream, or what was the **EXACT** phrase, impression or dominate line of thinking in the dream?

My answer: My thinking was, "I really want to get to the top"!

Step 4: Asking myself, In what part of my daily life was I frustrated and wanted to get to the top?

My Answer: Serving at my church.

225

Background information:

At the time of the dream, I wanted to be a big leader in my church, like my pastor and it seemed no matter how many areas of ministry I served in at the church, I could never get to the top and really be somebody important and someone significant, with in my church family. It seemed that no matter how hard I served, everyone else was being spiritually promoted, but me! This was very frustrating and upsetting to me. So, as you can see this dream is a symbolic picture and "parallel" reflecting the exact emotional feelings that were going on in my soul realm.

Step 5: Evaluate the symbols: Ask yourself, how can each symbol (men, journey, mountain, and mountain top) relate to the subject matter at hand, which is the answer to step 4 (serving in church) and then write the meaning of your symbols down.

Now that you know the "real life subject" that your dream is reflecting you can begin to better identify the symbols and start to see the parts they are playing in your dream. Be sure to relate your symbols together in conjunction with the storyline of your dream! Now, any possible metaphors, similes, metonymies or idioms in the dream will make sense. And the symbols, whether people, animals, numbers, colors, places and things will fit in, with the feeling of the dream. And like pieces to a puzzle your symbolism will SUPPORT your real life issue or struggle and give clarity pertaining to the subject matter of the dream you're interpreting.

My symbolic meaning answers:

A. Walking up a mountain: symbolic of hard work

B. Men who stopped me: symbolic of only men that were in charge and that were being promoted at that church and not women. It's a man's world and they were in control!

226

C. The journey: Is symbolic of my spiritual journey with God, specifically ministry and my church.

D. Top of the mountain: Is symbolic of a great victory or success and achievement!

Step 6: Action or Story line: Ask yourself what was the action or storyline of the dream?

My answer: I can't get to the top of the mountain. The action and storyline of this dream, is an exact parallel to my real life experience and inner emotional struggle of what was going on in my church at the time of the dream.

In real life, when I had the dream, it was my opinion and experience, that I was being stopped from getting to the important, successful, visible or **top** areas of leadership at my church.

When you bring all this information together in the light of your real life struggles, then it is obvious that you have your interpretation of your dream. My dream was showing me an exact symbolic picture of how I felt. YES, I did feel, it was true that it was a man's world at my church. And it was true that there was no way, no matter how many areas I served in or how hard I tried to get to the top in leadership, I could not obtain my goal. As you can see this dream was reflecting the true feelings of frustration within my heart!

So, now you have your interpretation! It's that simple; like anything the more you practice the better you will become!

Step 7: Write down the dream and its interpretation.

Step 8: Counsel yourself. In every area of your life you need to allow the Word of God to be your guide and apply its truth to the positive or negative messages of your dreams.

227

After decoding the symbolic interpretation of a reflection dream, I always ask myself; Vonda is this the truth? Is this truly what happened OR is it just "my perception or feelings" of what happened in my real life. Then, I always COMPARE THE FACTS of what happened in real life to the Truth's based on God's Word. Let me elaborate on this and demonstrate my thought process with you.

Yes, it is true that I really did feel that it was a man's world at my church and that there was no way, no matter how hard I tried to get to the top, I was not able to get too or advance to the top. Also, the factual truth of the matter in real life was, within the 11-12 years I was at that church, I never saw one woman put into pastoral leadership, except for the pastors wife. I used to think to myself, you mean to tell me out of all these sold out strong Christian women, who are crazy in love with God and support this church, that there is NOT ONE woman that is qualified to operate in pastoral leadership except for the pastors wife? I found it very hard to believe, accept and swallow that this church was anything but, a man's world! So, in the private frustration of my heart concerning this very personal inner struggle, I needed to apply Gods Word to my situation. Romans 13:1 says; "everyone must submit himself to the governing authorities, for there is no authority except that which God has established. The authorities that exist have been established by God." So, the truth of the matter is that no one, not me, my pastor or anyone appoints natural or spiritual leaders. The real truth is that they're appointed by God almighty Himself! And during that time, I really needed to encourage myself with the Word of God. And allow the truth of the Word to correct my feelings, by actively believing and confessing that when the time is right, God will make absolutely sure that I'm where I need to be, when I need to be there and that no one can thwart what God has planned for me!

"For the LORD Almighty has purposed, and who can thwart him? His hand is stretched out, and who can turn it back?" Isaiah 14:27

228

Reflection Example: The Crocodile dream (Vonda Brewer)

I dreamt I was sitting and gently wading in very shallow water about waste high, when a crocodile slowly swam in front of me. I knew I didn't want to move an inch or I would get bit! As the crocodile trolled very slowly near my out-stretched leg, suddenly it quickly **snapped** its deadly jaws right down on my foot. However, I was not hurt because it just so happened that its teeth missed my skin and went perfectly right between the inner separation of each of my 5 toes and I did not feel a thing. Not even a scratch!

My Interpretation Answers:

Step 1: Ask yourself: Was I active in the dream (reflection dream) or was I watching myself or seeing a scene's imagery, in a glimpse (vision) or bird's eye view (vision)?

My Answer: I'm **actively** wading in the dream, therefore this is most likely a "reflection dream" and NOT a "night vision" dream.

Step 2: Ask yourself: How did I **feel** in and during the dream?

My answer: I feel like, "I'm treading in dangerous waters."
▪ Please note this phrase is a metaphor.

Step 3: Ask yourself: What was I **thinking** about in the dream, or what the EXACT phrase, impression was or dominate line of thinking in the dream?

My answer: My thinking was, "I knew I did not want to move an inch."

Step 4: In what part of my life did I know, "I shouldn't move an inch"?

My Answer: With my mentor, concerning a vision inter-pretation and discussion I recently had with her the day before.

Background: The day before I was at my mentors house and we were talking about a vision she had and her interpretation of that vision. I then gave my opinion to her about another possible interpretation. She firmly corrected me, but did not hurt my feelings. So, this whole wading in the water getting snapped at by a crocodile dream was about that specific talk with her.

Step 5: Evaluate the symbols - Ask yourself, how can each symbol (croc, shallow waters, my feet) relate to the subject matter at hand, which is the answer to step 4 (talking with my mentor) and then write the meaning of your symbols down.

My symbolic meaning Answers:

A. Crocodile: Like a crocodile my mentor, is very thick skinned; meaning she is tough and doesn't let much bother her. Crocs are known to be ancient mammals and like the crock she is aged in her years; she rules with much authority in the waters of the spirit realm, just like a croc rules in waters in the natural.

B. Water: To me the water represents the things of the SPIRIT

C. Wading in Shallow Waters: Is symbolic of me being in shallow waters, meaning I'm "NEW", I've only gotten my feet wet in the spiritual things of the prophetic. She, like the croc rules the in the spiritual waters and me being in the water with her is symbolic of me learning from her about the prophetic. At that time I was not real "DEEP" in the things of the Spirit, unlike her I was more shallow in my prophetic knowledge because her knowledge and experience is deeper and extremely vast.

D.   My feet: Are symbolic of my natural or spiritual walk.

230

Step 6: Story line or Action: Ask yourself, what is the **action** or **story line** of the dream?

My Answer: I'm wading in shallow, but dangerous waters with a crocodile and I should not move because I don't want to get bit (snapped at.)

Background information: The day before, in our conversation she snapped at me with her firm correction. But she did it very respectful and without hurting me.

Step 7: I wrote the dream and its interpretation down on paper.

So, now we have our interpretation! It's that simple. Like anything the more we practice the better we will become!

Step 8: Counsel yourself: In every area of your life, allow the Word of God to be your guide and apply its truth to the positive or negative messages of your dreams.

After decoding the symbolic interpretation to a reflection dream, I always ask myself, is this the truth? Is this truly what happened OR is it JUST "my perception of the truth or feelings" of what happened in my real life? I always COMPARE THE FACTS of what happened in real life to the Truths based on God's Word. Let me elaborate on this and demonstrate my thought process with you.

FACTS:

1. The **fact** is: This is an exact reflection of my feelings in picture form, concerning my previous interaction with her. The dream revealed no message or foretelling scene of revelation, but the content was all known or conscious information that surfaced through symbolic pictures and a similar story line reflecting my previous discussion with her, thus creating this cute reflection dream.

231

Gods Counsel: A Divine Appointment

I believe God has appointed her to me and she's a wonderful person and mentor. And I willingly choose to submit myself to her spiritual authority. So, regardless of whether my interpretation of her vision was correct or hers was correct, I still chose to willingly submit to her until God shows me it's time for us to depart into a new season.

2. Who's right?

Is she right in her interpretation or am I correct? Does it really matter, since symbolism is personal to the dreamer or receiver of the vision?

God's Counsel: Jeremiah vs. Hannaniah (Their prophecies differed)

After time Jeremiah was proven to be the true prophet!
So, **no** it was her vision from the Lord and God has entrusted her with the privilege of relaying the interpretation. Hindsight and only time will prove which interpretation was correct!

3. How should I respond to the dreams message or picture movie of what happened?

Should I remove myself from her authority or not be her friend just because she firmly corrected me?

Gods counsel:

No! This may sound like the A B C 's of Christianity, but sometimes I think we could all use some reminding at times because as you know we don't cut believers off, just because of a difference in opinion, mistake or conflict. If, she was wrong the bible says to forebear one another and be gracious with each other! If, she was right then she handled it appropriately. The truth of the matter is that **people** are Gods most precious treasures and they are extremely valuable in His eyes and should be regarded valuable in our eyes too. If, she really did hurt me in real life even though she did not, then we are to always forgive. There's no limit to our forgiveness. We do not have that option if, we want to have peace in our hearts and not to mention eternal life with Jesus!

232

4. No harm no foul! The dream shows, I did get corrected, but without getting hurt! It does show that. Doesn't it?

The Truth? YES,......I did not get my feelings hurt.
Even if, she's wrong she corrected me firmly and with full respect to me as person and respect for our relationship.

Lesson Learned: There was no particular lesson to be learned concerning the refection dream, but many times there are things we can discover about who we truly are through an accurate interpretation of our refection dreams. Some reflection dreams will enlighten us of our faults, shortcomings, sins or happiness and some will not mean anything. But, the more we can understand our dreams and know how to categorize them the more we can be certain of the interpretations concerning our prophetic dreams and with confidence, undoubtedly stand on the revelatory dreams, God gives us.

In other words, when you are able to correctly identify your dream as a reflection dream only, then you're less likely to assume it is a "prophetic dream." In the past, I've come across several Christians, who were disgruntled with God, because they think He gave them a promise in a dream and in "**fact**," He never promised them anything of the sorts. Because their dream was a reflection dream and they were dreaming of the desires of their own heart, yet took it as a prophetic word from the Lord, because of their dream interpretation ignorance and as a result they're left waiting and wondering why the "so called promise" has never come to pass in their life.

Hopefully, by sharing these examples, I have helped you to clearly see that when you have a reflection dream, your heart puts your feelings into a picture, which is called a dream and the dream is the hearts way of talking or expressing its feelings to your head and mind. When you are asleep the heart speaks with pictures, instead of words and like the old saying goes, "a picture is worth a thousand words"!

233

So, now that you've read the book and you've walked through the 8 easy steps, you should be able to successfully categorize and identify the subject matter of your dream in likeness to a past event in your life; as well as now, being able to clearly see or see in part how the dream is symbolically reflecting a specific event that recently took place in your life. If, now you have a general idea of what the dream is reflecting, but still do not have a complete understanding then continue to pray and meditate on the dream and its symbolism, and over time you will get more and more insight and all the pieces should come together. If, and only if, at this point you still have NO idea what specific issue in your life the dream is mirroring or reflecting. Then you should now consider the possibility that the dream could be reflecting a suppressed or underlying emotion that you are not currently conscious to.

For example, maybe you have a dream and in it you feel rejected, but in real life the reality is that you are very popular and you have many friends and loved ones. So, now you're thinking to yourself, hum? Nothing has happened recently to make me feel rejected or no one that I know is rejecting me! If, this is the case, then fine. It's okay! But, now we need to move on and try another way to understand the dream. This is where reflection dreams with suppressed emotions can come into the picture! Okay, so your answer was no, there is nowhere in your life that you are currently feeling rejected. Then secondly, you would need to ask yourself, if there was somewhere in my past I felt rejected or was rejected? And if the answer is yes, then identify who and when, it was? After you have the answers to these questions, you now have your dreams subject matter. Now follow the prior 2-8 dream interpretation steps because a dream that reflects suppressed emotions is still a reflection dream.

234

For example, let's say that after you asked yourself these questions that you get an aha moment because you realize or remember in the past an old boyfriend rejected you, and even though your seemingly fine now you really never got over it, entirely. Well, this type of hurtful event is something that has become a suppressed emotion.

Why you ask? Well, it's because you have learned to suppress it; and because you don't walk around and think about it every day you have learned to try and not think about it, while trying your very best to get over it and move on with your life. The reason you had the dream years later, is because the hurtful feelings from your past rejection are still in your soul realm. Even though you're not conscious of it or it's not on the forefront of your mind and in your everyday thoughts. This is just an example, of how you can have a reflection dream that does not reflect current conscious matters of the heart, but on the contrary the dream reflects an old suppressed or unconscious truth in your life. If, this is the case and you come to understand that your current dream is reflecting a suppressed issue, then you should interpret the dream, speak God's Word and ask Jesus to heal you from the brokenness, hurt or wound that is still lying dormant and deeply suppressed within your soul realm; therefore, causing you to currently have disturbing dreams.

Now, if your dream in any way, shape or form does not fit into the reflection category, it is now time to consider the possibility that your dream and its feeling could be a direct result of the Holy Spirit. He may have induced or caused the feeling, therefore making it a prophetic dream to give you a revelatory message concerning something He's trying to teach you or He wants to make something known to you through the dream that has not yet happened, but will happen in the future. (Review dream example on pages 101-102)

235

"Night Vision Dreams": Interpretation Examples

Please believe me when I say, interpreting "Night Vision Dreams" are much easier to interpret than "Reflection Dreams." With night visions you usually just identify the symbols and put them together with the action of the vision's scene and then for the most part you're done and you have your revelation from God! I have found that 99% of the time, the only thoughts you need to consider when interpreting a night vision dream are the thoughts or events that you're thinking about in your **waking** life. The thoughts you had before the vision or night vision dream in your waking life are needed, because you want to make sure you apply the dreams revelation to the correct area of your life. Where as in your reflection dreams, you need to consider the exact feelings, thoughts and emotions **in and during the dream**, as well as your exact thoughts, emotions and events in your day to day waking life.

Prophetic Examples: Night Vision Dream: Losing the weight

I Loretta dreamt, I saw my brother and in the dream he looked a little sickly and he had dropped weight.

Step 1: Ask yourself: Was I active in the dream (reflection dream) or was I watching myself or seeing a scene's imagery, in a glimpse (vision) or bird's eye view (vision)?

Loretta's Answer: this was a "Night Vision Dream", because I was not active and I only saw a scene in a glimpse.

Step 2: SKIP! Please note, since your feelings, while sleeping are only a factor in reflection or refection prophetic combination dreams we will skip this step and move on to the next question.

Step 3: Ask yourself, were there any knowing thoughts, wisdom information, words, sentences, phrases, scriptures or revelatory messages in the dream?

My Answer: (write down your answer, when God reveals it)

Step 4: Ask yourself, if the dream revealed any revelation then what part of my waking life could the thoughts, images, or message of revelation be addressing?

My Answer: (write it down)

Step 5: Evaluate the Symbols -The brother (review chapter 5)
Ask yourself, how each symbol (sickly brother) can relate to the subject matter at hand, which <u>is the answer to step 4</u> (whatever God reveals to you) and then write the meaning of your symbols down.

Loretta's Symbolic meaning answers:
1. **Loretta's brother:** Her brother is a very compassionate person, who loves and desires to help others and in this way she is very much like her brother, when it comes to being compassionate and desiring to minister and help others. Therefore, He is symbolic of a specific part of Loretta, which is the compassionate part of her that longs to serve God in full time ministry.
2. **Sickly:** The compassionate part of me (Loretta) is a little sickly because her strength is depleted because of her weekly job. She works so hard she doesn't have the energy to minister to others like she really desires too full time.

Step 6: **Storyline or Action-** Ask yourself what was the **action** or **storyline** that took place within the Night Vision Dream?

Loretta's Answer: Her brother dropped the weight (past action.)

Please Note: Since Loretta's brother is playing a part of her, Loretta is receiving revelation through the action within her vision; meaning the action did not literally apply to her brother because he is symbolic of her. But the Holy Spirit is showing her what she should do by having her brother who is symbolic of her, doing it. He (symbolic of her) has dropped the weight; so, God is giving her direction and showing her what she needs to do.

Step 7: Ask yourself; Since, Loretta's brother is symbolic of the compassionate part her that loves' to help others then <u>where at in her life does she need to drop the weight?</u>

Please Note: At this point it is important to take into account what is going on in your life, what are your emotions, thoughts, desires, and struggles about? Because when you receive a Night Vision dream, or as the bible calls it a "Vision in the Night;" it is God trying to give you some type of prophetic message concerning the things on your heart.

Loretta's Answer: For about a month and a half she had wanted to start an online radio show and was waiting because of personal reasons. But, shortly before the vision God had laid on her heart that she needed to make it a priority and get with it! So God was using this vision to confirm to her that the "compassionate part of her that loves to help/minister to others needs to drop the weight," which is symbolic of dropping the WAIT! Usually and **OFTEN**, God will use little symbolic word parallels, like this to get His message to us. This was a word of direction for her to drop the wait and get with it!

So, can you see it? The night vision showed her that she had dropped the weight (**wait**). When she asked herself, where does the compassionate, loving, and ministering part of me (**her brother**) need to drop the weight (**wait**)? Her answer was, in ministering on the radio show because in real life she knew that she had put the radio show on hold until a more convenient time! But, through this vision God was telling her she needed to drop the wait (**weight**). Meaning, stop waiting or GET GOING GIRL because the time is now!

Warning: If, you don't know, consider and are conscious of the things you desire, feel, and have been hoping, wishing, and praying for, when you try to interpret your "Night Vision dreams." I can guarantee you, it will be **EXTREEMLY HARD**, if not impossible to comprehend what God is trying to say to you. It's extremely important to put the revelation into the

238

correct subject matter you've been praying for or wondering about. So, please keep this in mind when you're meditating on the dream and its interpretation!

Step 8: Write down the night vision; they are usually short.

<u>Simple Night Vision Example</u>: <u>Loving and Fighting</u>
As a young Christian, I (Vonda) dreamt, I was passionately hugging and loving, someone on my left side and then I turned to my right side and karate kicked someone.

My Interpretation Answers: (simpler visions can require fewer steps)
Step 1: Ask yourself: Was I active in the dream (reflection dream) or was I watching myself or seeing a scene's imagery, in a glimpse (vision) or bird's eye view (vision)?

My Answer I'm watching myself in this dream and because it is a glimpse of me doing something and there is no feeling or thoughts in the dream. This was a "<u>night vision</u>" dream and NOT a "<u>reflective dream.</u>"

Step 2: Ask yourself what was the **action or storyline** that took place in the Night Vision Dream?
My Answer: On one side, I was loving very deeply and on the other side fighting hard or chopping down!

Step 3: Evaluate the Symbols: (review chapter 5)
My Answer: There was no symbolism because the people were blurry; it was just me, Vonda.

Step 4 Ask yourself, in real life, like in the night vision; am I a lover and a fighter? Or where at in my life am I, on one hand loving deeply; but, on the other hand, fighting hard?

My Answer. In my spiritual walk I love others hard; but I am quick to chop them down too, if they hurt me.

Step 5: Write it down.
Step 6: Counsel yourself (because it's a correction.)

239

At the time of this dream, I was very young in my walk with the Lord and I needed to ask God to help me to grow in the fruits of the Spirit; so, I could walk in His love towards others and not be quick to chop them down to size! As we know some things only change with maturity and by supernatural means! Today, I'm happy to say that even though I'm not perfect. I do believe, I've come a very long way through the power of Christ Jesus! God is good!!!

Night Vision: Literal in Meaning (full term pregnancy)

For example, three years ago I got married at the age of 42, and within the first month of our marriage I became pregnant. Shortly after, I told one of my clients that I was pregnant and at this point she told me that recently God had given her a night vision dream and in the dream she saw me as big as a house. She said, I looked full term and I looked as if I was about to give birth. So, the same day she told me her dream she encouraged me to take heart because she saw me full term. Since, I was in my latter child bearing years I thanked her for the encouragement!

Her interpretation: In the dream, I (Vonda) was really representing myself, and in the dream I really was pregnant and in real life I was really pregnant. So, God was not speaking in riddles here; it appeared that it was a straight foreword dream with a straight foreword interpretation for an identical real life situation. At the time, we interpreted it to be that God was trying to tell or encourage me that I would go full term in my pregnancy. So, as you can see this night vision dream was not symbolic, but was indeed literal in its meaning.

I Vonda, was and still am very happy that she spoke up and shared this night vision dream with me even though it turned out that I miscarried that baby and then miscarried again a year later. I'm still appreciative of the dream because in hindsight we now realize that God gave her that dream and its encouragement, NOT only for then, but for later too! God knew that I would miscarry twice. Moreover, the Lord

240

prepared my heart for the second miscarriage too, because He gave me visions about the second miscarriage before it happened. So, because of her revelation and encouragement from the Spirit of the Lord, I now know and have peace that it does not matter how many miscarriages I may or may not have, but in the proper time, I will eventually go full term and I will have a child. When the Holy Spirit showed my client that revelation in her Night Vision dream, God was DECLARING that I would go full term as **truth** in the Spirit realm and since, I believe it by faith it will happen because nothing is impossible for those who believe! God is good and He will withhold **no** good thing from those who love Him!

So, as you can see this Night Vision dream was a revelation from the Holy Spirit that was sending her head a foretelling message that predicted my full term pregnancy. And as you can see this night vision dream needed little or no interpretation skills for the dreamer to interpret. Even though, the interpretation was a misapplication of the "specific time" in my life that I would go full term within my pregnancy. Please remember that these literal types of dreams clearly say what they mean and mean what they say!

Interpreting
"Reflection & Prophetic Combination" & "General Prophetic"

Please note that you will need to combine your 8 "**Reflection Dream**" steps and your "**Night Vision**" dream steps together, when you are interpreting your "**Reflection & Prophetic Combinations**" and your "**General Prophetic**" dreams. Remember, symbols can vary, when you're interpreting your dream. So, be sure to look at your dream symbols with different symbolic points of view, while assessing your feeling, thoughts, action, and storyline as well as any type of revelatory/prophetic message within the dream; in addition too, comparing them to the real events in your waking life until the meaning clicks in your spirit and you feel that all of the dreams pieces have come together!

241

Then Joseph said to them, "Do not interpretations belong to God? Tell me your dreams."
Gen 40:8b"

Prophetic Dream Mysteries

And I, Daniel, fainted and was sick for days: afterward I arose and went about the king's business. I was astonished by the vision, but no one understood it.

As Christians, there may be some of you that walk in the gift of prophecy and if you operate in this gifting, please let me assure you that there will be times in your walk with the Holy Spirit that you'll have prophetic dreams that you cannot fully understand or interpret at the time you have the dream. And like me, no matter how good you are in interpretation and no matter how hard you may try to understand the dream and its message, please know that you will not understand the dream or know the full meaning of it until circumstances in your life change. It's then and only then that the dreams meaning will unfold to you and this is when it's Gods appointed time for you to finally understand the dreams message. Recently, God gave me a very interesting prophetic dream and at the time of the dream I felt that I had a general idea of what God was trying to say to me, but after interpreting the last scene of the dream, I could not figure out how it could have applied to my life during the time of the dream. So, I wrote it down and after a couple of weeks and some things took place in my life, I then fully understood what the dreams message was. And I now fully realize that God through His great love gave me the dream ahead of time, so I could experience His deep love and commitment to me during my time of struggle. In hindsight, I now know that I did not need the message at the time of the dream, but I did need this message later during the time of my intense struggle, which is why I did not understand the true meaning of the dream and its encouragement until two weeks later. I call this dream mystery, Hercules and me!

242

Dream: Hercules and Me: (Prophetic Dream Mystery)

I dreamt that I was in the isle of a grocery store and as I pushed the empty cart I was about to turn left to head into another isle to look for some food, and when I looked up from a distance I saw Hercules **(Kevin Sorbo)** and I knew that I had caught his eye. He had others around him that wanted his attention, but as he looked at me I could tell he was smitten with me and quite taken with my beauty. In a split second when I realized our eyes had locked, in my humility I immediately looked down and away from him as I thought to myself, there's no way he could possibly be attracted to me? I didn't feel like I was someone that he could like or that I was someone who would be appealing to him. I thought him liking me was too good to be really happening! Then I saw him looking at me again and this time his look towards me had intensified and it appeared as if he had made up his mind that I was the woman for him and then I saw him coming to pursue me.

Next scene, I see Hercules and me in the front seat of a car, while he's driving and I'm sitting far from him and close to my car door on the right side; he's taking me out to a restaurant because he wants to feed me. In the dream, I know I'm married. And in my mind, even though I'm with him and letting him take me out to eat, I know it's not a date.

In the last scene, he wants to be with me and I said to him "<u>but I'm married.</u>" Next, I'm somehow able to see inside of my jeep, from a bird's eye view and Hercules is alone and driving my jeep and for some reason he feels very strong about getting my jeep home where it belongs. For some reason he thinks it's his responsibility and feels a very strong commitment to me to make sure my jeep gets to my house, so it can be parked into its rightful place. So, I watched him as he drove my jeep down the road and at this point, I felt sorry for Hercules because I knew that my jeep was not very dependable and that it may break down on him at any point

243

and then he would be stuck! I knew that even though my vehicle had been good to me and it had always managed to get me where I needed to be. I knew it was old and that it ran a little rough and that it had a few things wrong with it that needed to be fixed. But, in the dream Hercules doesn't seem to care about that, and he's extremely determined to get this jeep home in its rightful parking place where it belongs! It's like he's on a mission to do this for me. So, as I watched him quickly hurry down the road, I knew that he cared more about my jeep getting home, than I did!

Background:

Before I share the interpretation of the dream with you, let me give you a little background concerning this dream. In my 18 years of walking with the Lord, I have loved Him and served Him with all my heart, but I have also, been extremely mad at Him twice. I had the Hercules and me dream two weeks before my last ought with God. I was very upset with God because he had asked me to do something for Him that I absolutely, positively, and emphatically did not want to do! What was it you ask? Well, the details are private; but, I will tell you this much. God asked me to minister and to serve someone and this request went against the very core and fiber of my being. I thought it was extremely unfair of Him to ask me accommodate this person considering what I knew about them. For the record, God never told me I had to go minister to them, but He said "**It would please me if you would do it.**" So, I thought, how in the heck is a person supposed to say no to a line like that? To me, the person God wanted me to regularly minister too, was such a drainer. In my eyes, for God to burden me with them in addition to all the other things I was trying to do for Him seemed extremely unreasonable, unfair and bias, and I felt that He preferred them over me. I thought to myself, how can He put this on me?

244

Then, I said to God, I think about you all day long, I serve you all day long and I always put you first in everything I do. I've been hot for you since the day you healed my broken heart and now you want me to minister to this person and carry their load, when their just being too spiritually lazy to carry it for themselves. I got very mad at God and I fussed Him out and told Him exactly what I thought about Him and His request in this situation. And after I told Him how I felt, I wasn't sorry either. I mean I was fuming mad! I stayed mad for two whole days and during that time and I did not want to hear anything from God, because in my heart and mind I was still just trying to process His unreasonable request. And I didn't need Him putting anymore fuel onto my fire! During this time, I was so mad at Him, but I was also mad and very disappointed in myself because it hurt me deeply to know that I had talked to the Lord like I did. I was very upset at myself because I loved Him so much. And afterwards, every time I thought of the way I talked to Him, I cried and cried because I felt like such a wretched and unworthy fool. I felt like Peter the traitor for flipping out on Him and fussing Him out like I did! After this happened and I calmed down a bit, I kept telling God, I don't know how you deal with any of us down here on earth? It's a mystery to me, why you don't just bring an angry fist down on us and kill us all! Then I thought wow, if I as a loving daughter am struggling with serving you in this manner, being someone who loves you like crazy and serves you like crazy. Eats, sleeps and thinks about God all day long, like I do. Then how in the heck am I, or any of us humans going to be able to make it up and into heaven? Because, it obvious to me that "The heart is deceitful above all things, and desperately wicked; who can know it"? (Jeremiah 17:9 NKJV) So, I thank God for John 3:16, which says, "For God loved the world so much that he gave his one and only Son, so that everyone who believes in Him will not perish but have eternal life."

My Interpretation: Symbols: (review chapter 5)

1. Hercules is symbolic of Jesus

I'm sure many of you remember the television series called Hercules, starring Kevin Sorbo. I hear your wheels spinning, ha, ha, tee hee. But, this is my dream and it's only a dream and in this case the Holy Spirit picked Hercules to play the role of Jesus based on the way I viewed Kevin Sorbo and the modern day Hercules television series. To me, Jesus and Hercules are similar in these ways, they both were the son of a god. Jesus of course was and is the Son of the one and only true God and Hercules was the son of Zeus the fake mythological, Roman god. In my eyes Hercules and Jesus were alike because of the similar roles they played. In addition to being sons of God/god, both were strong, caring, and good in the sense that they opposed evil as they journey throughout the earth to rescue helpless people from the evil that attacked them.

2. "In the market." In the market for some food = I'm in the market for some spiritual food (visions)

3. Heading for a Restaurant

Hercules wants to take me to a restaurant to get some food = Jesus thinks I'm worth the investment and wants to get me some spiritual food.

Since, I was emotionally abused in the area of my self worth when I was younger, I feel when a man takes a woman to a restaurant and he's willing to spend his hard earned money on her that this means that she is valued. So, to me a man taking a woman to a restaurant **means she is "worth the investment!"**

4. My Jeep = is symbolic for me

Since, I fleshed out at God, I felt I, like my jeep was not a dependable or reliable, "vehicle" (like the jeep) to get Him (Hercules/Jesus) and the mission He entrusted with me, to

246

where it needed to be. Specifically, in the admirable area of being a prophet for the Lord, which is a very important and visible role.

The Action or Storyline of the dream

1. Hercules, as Jesus thinks I'm pretty and is overwhelmed with my beauty.

2. Hercules, as Jesus looks at me and He has made up His mind, as if I'm the one for Him. He's chosen me.

3. Hercules, as Jesus wants me and passionately pursues me out of His intense love for me.

4. Hercules is determined not to leave me (the un-dependable jeep that needs some work done) where I am, but he is determined to make sure that I get home (heaven) because it is my rightful place to "park it" or to rest.

So now that I've told you the dream and the meanings of my dream symbols, as well as some background concerning the reason God gave me the dream; now I will pull it all together and spell it out for you in its entirety. Walk with me, as I bring the subject, storyline, and symbols together in its interpretation and how it related to my personal struggle. The story line of my dream starts off, with me being in the market for some food. Remember, earlier I told you that after I got mad at God that I had not had any visions for two whole days? Well, the visions I receive from the Lord are spiritual food too me. And for me, two days is a long time for me to go without any visions. So, just like in the dream, I was in the market for some visions because after two days of not having any heavenly food, I was now "in the market" for some! The action of dream shows that me being in the market, means that at the time of me understanding the dream, I was now in the proper mind set to receive some visions. Now, I'm ready to hear from God and in the market to hear from Him and then Jesus sees me and thinks I'm pretty even though I found it difficult to believe that He could

247

be attracted to someone like me. This is very significant to me because, in real life I felt so ugly and unworthy for fleshing out at God and I really didn't think He should even consider using me after a stunt like that. But, through the dream and by the story it's telling, the Holy Spirit is encouraging me that not only am I still very beautiful to Him, but God has made up His mind that I'm the one He wants and He see's my worth. In the dream Hercules (**Jesus**) is determined to pursue me and still use me as His vehicle (**prophet**). And even though, I may have my faults (**things that need to be worked on and fixed**) **Jesus** is determined to NOT leave me where I am, but He is committed and determined to drive me to my home (**prophetic office and symbolic of me getting to heaven**), which is my rightful place to be as a true child of God.

At the time of this dream, I had the general idea that God may be trying to warn me of an up and coming male pursuit, by showing me that a hot guy was going to be hot for me, even though I was married. But, now, I see that the dream was showing me that I was proclaiming to be married, so God could make the point that He's not talking about a natural man and woman type of love affair and that it's a God kind of love affair. I could have **only understood** this dreams interpretation in its fullness, **after** I got mad and fussed God out. This is when the dream came back to me and then I interpreted it. It was at this point that I completely under-stood why the Holy Spirit had given me this dream in advance. When, I got the revelation of what God was saying to me, I was so blessed and comforted by the prophetic message of this dream because the Lord was so loving and kind to send me this prophetic word of encouragement long before I made a fool of myself! It may not seem like a big deal to you, but it was a big deal for me because I fear the Lord and I don't ever want to be disrespectful to the Lord. However, I thank God for His forgiveness and it was so awesome to feel His love and comfort towards me, concerning this very difficult struggle in my life. I hope and pray that I have explained my dream well enough to do it justice. As well as show you, it was a prophetic message that

248

was not able to be fully interpreted until the appointed time, which was the **exact time,** I so desperately needed to hear His voice.

In addition to my Hercules and me dream, God sent me an identical confirming message of how beautiful I was to Him! Here is a night vision dream that my husband's co-worker had about me! In her dream, she said. "<u>I saw you (Vonda) in my dream; you were so beautiful and gorgeous. You were glowing and your skin was like porcelain and your eyes were like glowing jade.</u>"

It was only one to two days after my Hercules and me dream that God gave this night vision dream to a woman my husband works with. When Clae told me the dream God gave her about me it brought me great comfort because God was using her to confirm my beauty in the spirit realm and in the things of the Lord. This was the exact message I need to hear and it was right on time! God was so good to confirm His opinion of me and my beauty in His eyes.

So, be diligent to write down all your dreams, so you can review them and receive Gods messages to you in the proper season. These types of prophetic dream mysteries are rarer than other prophetic dreams and are impossible to interpret in their fullness until time reveals the answer, or the Holy Spirit gives you the interpretation in a Word of Wisdom.

The main reason I wanted to use this particular dream for an example is because, like me maybe at one time or another you too have been mad at God, and for some reason maybe you've felt unworthy of His forgiveness or unworthy to continue in a relationship with Him. Like me, is there something you may have done that you were ashamed of? Something so horrible that you feel is hard to forgive? Maybe you've done something and you feel humiliated and unworthy to partake in a relationship with Him. Well, I want you to know that the same message that God gave me in this dream is the same exact way that He feels about you too!

249

Like me, God looks on you from afar and He is passionately in love with you and wants to pursue a committed relationship with you and continue to use you for His Glory! The word of God says He loves us so much He leaves the 99 lambs to pursue the one lamb who is confused or the one who may have wandered off into a muddy ditch of sin. Just like Jesus spoke to me in my dream about my relationship with Him, I want you to know that He feels the same way about you. Even though you may feel humiliated ugly or unworthy, right now God thinks you're beautiful and fearfully and wonderfully made. If you're a Christian, please know that Christ is committed to you as a husband, the word husband means a house band or one who bands the house together; and Jesus your savior wants to feed, nurture, care, and love you, no matter what things may need to be fixed within you. And in spite of your faults, Christ is determined to be with you and to do His part to see that you get to walk in your calling; and He is committed to do His part to see you into Heaven, which is your rightful inheritance if, you will allow Him to sit in the driver seat of your life by allowing Him to Lord over your life. Please believe me, when I say that no matter what you have done, there is nothing to big, ugly or sinful that He will not forgive. Jesus longs for you to come unto Him and He is there waiting for you with open arms to forgive you. Just simply, repent and ask Him to forgive you and then forgive yourself. Please be encouraged, you are so extremely valuable to Him. Please don't null and void His forgiveness in your life by thinking that you are unlovable. God is rich in mercy, loving kindness and forgiveness and we are the reason He came to earth, suffered and died on the cross. So don't wait another minute to accept His complete forgiveness for your situation and get back in relationship with Him. He's there waiting for you with an open heart and the hope that you will once again be His friend.

Chapter 13

Misapplications & Misinterpretations

I would now like to take the time to share with you some of my personal experiences, as well as some of my thoughts on how a true prophet of the Lord can make a simple human error and misapply or misinterpret a vision or dream. It is possible and does happen at times to the best of us. In the past on the television and over the internet I have heard many Christians call true and well meaning prophets of the Lord, FALSE PROPHETS. Simply because they made an honest mistake, while sharing the heart of God. The word of God says, for we know in part and we prophesy in part (1 Corinthians 13:9.) Below, I will share some of my very own personal examples of misapplication.

Misapplication: Wisdom or Knowing Dream
(Prophetic revelation) May 18, 2010 Tuesday morning.

Word of Wisdom dream: I Vonda dreamt, I knew it was dark and I was sleeping and Clae (my hubby) put his hand on my left shoulder to wake me and then he said "its 9:18." He was not trying to tell me, I've slept too long but, it was as if he was gently trying to awaken me.

My Interpretation: (A phrase or sentence of revelation)
In real life Clae is a prophet and at times he speaks words from the Lord, concerning issues in our marriage. So, in the dream when Clae said its 9:18, it was because God was using my husband as a prophet to speak or declare a prophetic time into my life, concerning an area that I was "in the dark." God was using Clae to reveal a certain time to me concerning something I had been praying for, and God is enlightening me by giving me a specific date through Clae's revelatory statement in the dream. The interpretation is a MONTH and DAY not a TIME of DAY.

251

The time 9:18 is symbolic for 9/18 or SEPTEMBER 18th. However, I'm not sure of the year because God did not reveal the year to me in the wisdom dream. At the time of this dream there were a couple of things I had been asking God about and when they would happen? For one, I've been wondering about, when Clae and I would be moving to Texas? Also, I've been wondering about when I would start my TV show.

In real life, Clae is my husband and scripturally speaking he is also the **priest of our home.** In the past God has used him as a **prophet** to speak to me prophetically, as well as prophetically share with some men on his job. In this **"Wisdom dream,"** I believe God is using him to speak a prophetic revelation to me. In this dream, the reason I'm in the dark is because in real life I'm really in the dark about the exact time God will move us to Texas or the exact time He will let me be on my TV show. And the reason I'm asleep in the dream is because this represents an area in real life that I'm not CONSCIOUS too. Meaning, in real life when we are asleep we are not privy to the things that are happening around us. So, in this sense like when one is sleeping, I'm not conscious to the "exact time" I will get to walk into the promises God has made me. However, my sleeping is a correct symbolic representation of my current state. Recently, I've been praying hard about when we would be moving to Texas and I believe God is telling me that we will be moving to Texas, September 18th; now, the exact year I'm not sure! But, hopefully it will be this year in 2010.

Well, 9/18/ 2010 -2011 has come and gone and we did not move to Texas and in hindsight I have now discovered and have come to realize that I have **misapplied** the prophetic date to the wrong subject matter. However, I was correct in the interpretation part, but it was not the date for us to move; but it was predicting the date and time of my long awaited television show!

252

Even though I applied 9/18 to the wrong prayer request concerning when we would move; it is important to note that my interpretation of the time was correct in the fact that it represented a date! So, as you can see, I interpreted it correctly, but I applied it to the wrong area of my life. God was giving me a starting date for, when I would start recording for "Heart Hope," and not telling us the date to move; below is another example of misapplication.

Misinterpretation: An Honest Mistake

Now, I will share with you an honest mistake I made with the best intentions and heart to do the will of God concerning my friends "Word from the Lord." Because my friend is mature in the Lord, she was very gracious with me and didn't throw any stones. But, instead she really shared her heart, with me so we could both get to the meat of what the Holy Spirit was truly trying to relay to her through the visions He gave me. You can rest assured that no man is perfect and as humans we are all, at anytime capable of possibly misinterpreting a "Word from the Lord"; <u>specifically</u> when dealing with the symbolic language of dreams and visions and even people with the best track records are subject to error.

Recently, I was thinking of this friend of mine who is a prophet of the Lord and ministers to others within the body of Christ through her online prophetic radio show. I hadn't heard from her for a couple of months and as I laid in bed thinking about her, God gave me 2 visions concerning her. So, as I meditated on one of the main symbols of the second vision, I believed it to mean one thing and it did mean that one thing. But, I found out that I was off point in the specific category of its meaning, which gave the symbol a double meaning. Even though, the following interpretation example is in reference to these two visions I had. The principle is still relevant and applicable in dream interpretation.

253

Vision 1: A Dark Force

In this vision I saw a bedroom with its door open and the lights off. The bed was made and the room appeared to be clean, tidy and in order. But, inside the room to the right directly behind the door and near the wall, I saw a very strong dark force that was pushing in a downwards motion towards the floor. Even though, I could not see the force actually pushing against anyone or anything, I could see the texture and movement of the force. The best way I can describe it is, if you can imagine a hole in the ocean floor and the water is just gushing down through the hole; it was that type of texture and motion even though it had a wind appearance and not water. Except, in this vision there was no hole, but the dark force was the shape of a round hole that looked like a rushing wind pushing downwards with great force.

Dark force Interpretation:

Because I know this person and we have talked of many things together, I knew that in the first vision God was trying to show me that a dark spiritual force was coming against her and trying to keep or push something down in her life. God was showing me her bedroom because I know that it is where she spends time in prayer, and receives a lot of her revelations from the Holy Spirit. Based on my symbolism and the way God speaks to me, He showed me that her bedroom was clean, tidy and in order. And through this symbolic picture, He's relaying to me that her spiritual life is in order. Then I saw the second vision, which entailed broccoli.

254

Vision 2: The Broccoli

In this vision, I wasn't actually sitting there; but the view I had, was a bird's eye view. I saw myself sitting across the table from my prophet friend in a restaurant; our table was near a large storefront window that had the sun shining in it. And as I looked across the table at my girlfriend, I saw that she had a lot of raw broccoli that was not on her plate, but it was actually sitting on the table to the right of her plate and pushed over some leaving a gap between the plate and the broccoli. In the vision, as she ate the broccoli, I saw her squint up her nose in a little, in distaste as she nibbled on one of the broccoli heads. She ate it even though, it was not too tasty to the pallet. In the vision, I knew that she didn't want to share her broccoli with others.

Below are 2 interpretation outlooks.

Broccoli Interpretation:

Often when God speaks to me in dreams or visions, He will use food to symbolize the Word of God. For example, a steak will represent a hard, mature word, which symbolizes the meat of the Bible. And to me, cakes, pies or pastries usually represent the sweet prophetic or rhema words of the Spirit.

In this case the broccoli represented a hard, but good for you type of prophetic word. Because, a week before this vision I had just had a salad with some fresh broccoli spears in it and even though I had a little ranch dressing on my salad, it was not enough dressing to make the broccoli in the salad very enjoyable. So, as I swallowed the broccoli from within the salad, I found it very "hard to swallow." So, God was using my past recent experience with the broccoli in my salad to relay a relevant message to me through this vision.

So, when God showed me the vision of my friend nibbling on the broccoli, but not wanting to share it with others; I interpreted it to be that the broccoli was symbolic to me as a word from the Lord that she would eat, but others may find it "hard to swallow." In the vision I could clearly see, even though she wasn't thoroughly enjoying the raw broccoli, she didn't mind nibbling on it; moreover, she had pushed the broccoli, which was symbolic for the "hard to swallow" prophetic food, off to the side and the story line of this vision showed that she didn't want to share her broccoli with others.

There have been times in the past that I've shared some of my experience in the prophetic, and my experience in radio production with her. And she's always very gracious with me, whenever I feel the need to share with her prophetically or when I feel the need to share technical insights concerning the fine tuning of her radio show. She's always been very receptive to advice and correction and she has a very beautiful heart, towards wanting to hear what God desires to speak into her life; good or bad. She really desires to be on track with God in all areas of her life.

So knowing this about my friend, I called her and told her what God had showed me. She confirmed my first vision about the oppression in the spirit realm. As it turned out, not long before I called her, God had shown her a similar vision to mine that the oppression was there or could be on its way. At the time, she had overlooked the vision God gave her, while chalking it up to being tired that particular night. So, after we established that God was trying to show her something, I then proceeded to ask her, if there were any hard words of correction that God had given her to share, with others that she wasn't willing to share them with them? Or, if God had told her to correct anyone that she did not want to correct? And she said no, absolutely not! So, I told her that if, it had not happened already to be on the lookout because it may be something that will try to come to pass in the future. I told her that there may come a time in the future that she may find herself in that position and that she should just be aware that it's not God trying to keep her from sharing; but it's a dark force that is trying to push down concerning sharing the insights of God. I told her that God does want her to share these insights when the time comes.

So, as we continued to talk we tossed around some ideas about how it could apply to her life and during this time she shared with me that there were some "hard to swallow" prophetic words that God had given her about America and the end times that she had set off to the side. Specifically, prophetic words that she has not wanted to share with others on her prophetic radio show because she felt that these words were not to be made public at that time.

So, after I got off of the phone with her I began to meditate on what she said and I could start to see how it could fit, with what God was trying to show me. And to myself, I thought yes, she may be onto something here! So, I wrote her an e-mail note and let her know that I thought she was correct in her specific meaning and that even though the prophetic insights seemed "hard to swallow" that God wanted her to share them with others on her radio show and that she should take this to the Lord and see if, He confirms this to her.

Broccoli: First and Second Meaning

In my vision, God was using the broccoli as a symbol for His prophetic, end time words (word of God) that were hard to swallow (hard, like meat), in which, I originally identified as corrective words; but, He also wanted to let me know that the body of Christ needs to eat the hard prophetic greens, even the ones that are hard to swallow. God wants the body of Christ to have a balanced intake including the healthy veggies of His rhema Word. Not just the milk, meat and the pastries.

257

So, I originally identified the broccoli with a hard to swallow **word of correction** that needed to be released. And although I was right about the "hard to swallow words" part, I was wrong about it being in the category of **correction**. My friend did have words that she needed to release, however it was hard to swallow prophetic words of revelation concerning the "End Times" and not prophetic words of correction for believers. So, in this case the broccoli appeared to have two meanings and I was mistaken on the application area.

Misinterpreting: Steve is Symbolic of 4 Entities
(See pages 81-84 on symbolism)

Let me share another example with you of how at times it can be very easy to misinterpret a dream. Often, when I dream a man named Steve is in my dreams. Steve was a client of mine who is a lawyer and he helped out in so many areas of my life, when I owned my own business. He was a tremendous blessing to me and such a wonderful gift from God! Let me explain, when my salon needed to be relocated, twice he assisted me in negotiating contracts with build outs and when I turned my salon in to a beauty school he went to bat for me and got me out of an old lease and helped me to get a couple of months free rent at the new location. Since the beauty school was a Christian beauty school he answered my every concern about the things I could or could not do, within the guild lines of the law concerning many things. He was my client, friend and counselor. And after all was said and done and I made some poor financial decisions, when I had to close my business he was right there with the legal knowledge and help to deliver me from underneath most of my debt! God gave me favor with Steve and moved on his heart to kind of watch over me. Moreover, he did it all for **free** and out of the goodness in his heart! So, as you can see Steve is many things to me! He's my friend, counselor, mediator, lawyer, deliverer and over all too me he was Mr. Wonderful!

Since, in my spiritual life the Holy Spirit is my Friend, and Wonderful Counselor, often God will choose Steve to play the role of **God** in my prophetic dreams because in the spirit realm the <u>Holy Spirit</u> is my Friend and my Wonderful Counselor. Moreover, since Steve was my lawyer, mediator and deliverer, often God will choose Steve to play the role of <u>Jesus</u> in my dreams because in the spirit realm, Jesus Christ is our Lawyer, Mediator, and Deliverer! Now, that I'm newly married I have another "Mr. Wonderful" which is my husband and there are times when God will use Steve to represent my **wonderful husband** in a vision or dream. And finally, then there are times, when Steve will not play any of the previous roles but, will simply play the role of <u>himself</u>; meaning, Steve is just representing Steve and not my husband or one of the God head.

So, as you can see when Steve shows up in my dreams, I really, really, really, really have to evaluate and take into consideration the whole dream and compare the dream with the spiritual and natural realities in my waking life in order to interpret the "Steve symbol" correctly! Because, he is symbolic of **4 different entities**, if I do not apply the correct interpretation to him I can very easily misinterpret the vision or dreams meaning. Like Steve, there are a few other symbols I have that have several meanings too. So, when you are interpreting your dream, be willing to look at your dream symbols with different symbolic points of view, while considering your feeling, thoughts, action, and storyline in the dream; in addition to any type of revelatory message within the dream. Meanwhile, comparing them to the real events in your waking life, until the meaning clicks in your spirit and you feel that all of the dreams pieces are coming together!

So, as you can see from the examples above that there will be times that these types of "<u>honest mistakes</u>" will happen and I don't believe that it makes someone a FALSE PROPHET, just because they misinterpreted or misapplied the interpretation to the wrong area in someone's life. Mistakes will happen at times and God is very gracious. He does **not** expect perfection! If, He did expect perfection from us then He would NOT have sent Jesus Christ to the cross. So, just like you lovingly allow your children to make mistakes, while learning to read books in their early school years, God lovingly works with us to learn to read, interpret and apply the symbolism in our dreams and visions.

God graciously walks with us and allows us time and experience to hear and apply His voice better and clearer as time goes by in our walk with Him. Believe me when I say that, our loving heavenly Father is **not** up in heaven just waiting to drop the hammer on us and call us a false prophet every time we make a simple and honest mistake in our walk with Him. I just **don't** believe our God is that way! So, embrace the fact that many times you will get it, and some of the times you will miss it! But, just keep trying to grow and serve the Lord whole heartedly and you will grow in the giftings more and more as you learn to hear His voice! Be encouraged and keep pressing on and I promise you it will be well worth it in the end!

Chapter 14
Devil Dreams ?

You may find this hard to believe, but the bottom line is that it's **NOT** possible for the devil to give you a dream! What people fail to understand is, just like breathing, seeing, thinking, talking, walking, and sleeping, one's ability to dream is a God given natural function of the human body and "aside from those who experience certain kinds of injury, it's a biological fact that everyone dreams" (RandomHistory.com). To make my point please consider this. As an individual you would never say, I can breathe, think, see, hear, feel, talk, walk, or sleep because of the devil. Acts 17:28 says, "for in him we live and move and have our being, as some of your own poets have said, "We are his offspring." So, the fact of the matter is, it is God who enables us to dream! Since, in fact the majority of our dreams are true reflections of our conscious or sub-conscious emotions of our waking life, the truth of the matter is, if you as a Christian or non Christian allow the devil to be in your life in the waking hours of your day. Then it is extremely likely that he and the evil he represents will show up in your dreams at night, while you are sleeping. This is because your dreams are reflecting your life's TRUTH and some foot hold that he is trying to or has gained access to in your life as a Christian; or these bad dreams occur because of the sinful and demonic nature you walk in as an unbeliever. Throughout the Bible, God uses the words dreams and visions interchangeably, so let's see what the Lord, Himself has to say about dreams being influenced by the heart of a dreamer and how they can reflect the character of a person.

Jude 1:7-8 KJV

Even as Sodom and Gomorrha, and the cities about them in like manner, giving themselves over to fornication, and going after strange flesh, are set forth for an example, suffering the vengeance of eternal fire. Likewise also these [filthy] dreamers defile the flesh, despise dominion, and speak evil of dignities.

261

According to the "Blue Letter Bible" an online resource; in Jude 1: 8 the Greek word for dream is, **Enypniazomai, which means......**

1) to dream (divinely suggested) dreams
2) metaph., to be beguiled with sensual images and carried away to an impious course of conduct.

- So, unbelievers or Christians who allow the devil access in their lives can have dreams that are from the profane nature of their sinful heart!

Jeremiah 23:16 says, Thus says the LORD of hosts: "Do not listen to the words of the prophets who prophesy to you. They make you worthless; they speak a **vision of their own heart**, not from the mouth of the LORD."

It's my opinion that the principle the Lord is trying to relay to us concerning this scripture is, that dependent on the heart of the man, there are times that people can have dreams that are from the profane nature of their own heart and not from the heart or nature of God. Jeremiah 23:25-26 says, "I have heard what the prophets have said who prophesy **lies** in My name, saying, "**I have dreamed, I have dreamed**"! How long will this be in the heart of the prophets who prophesy lies? **Indeed they are prophets of the deceit of their own heart**" (NKJV). So, check yourself and make sure your heart is right so you will not misread your dreams and interpret them as the words or desires of the Lord, when in fact they are the desires of your own heart.

I have literally interpreted hundreds of dreams within the past eight years and it's my experience that there are two types of so called "Devil Dreams." One being, you're dreaming a demonic type of dream because as a Christian or non Christian your life is demonic and the devil is "**active**" in your life or secondly, you're a Christian who has "**mislabeled**" your dream because you are, "put off" by the offensive symbols and lack the ability to interpret the dream objectively, in turn calling it a demonic dream.

262

For Example: Sexual Dream (See chapter 12 for 8 easy steps)

I Vonda, once had a dream that I was very intimately kissing a man named Roy and in the dream my right hand grabbed a hold of his penis and as I held onto it, I felt like I really had a handle on it! There was no sexual feeling in the dream.

I had this dream as a single woman who was living celibate and holy unto the Lord. At first, when I had this dream I was a little concerned. Because at first glance this dream looked very ungodly, until I investigated it further by using my interpretation skills. (Review 8 easy steps on page 219)

So, I asked myself, what was the <u>feeling</u> or <u>thought</u> in the dream?

My Answer: <u>In the dream I knew "I really had a handle on it!"</u> In the dream there was no feeling of sexual gratification or lust and in real life, Roy was one of my clients, who in **NO** way, was I attracted too!

<u>So, I asked myself</u>; In my life, what did I feel I really had a handle on?

My Answer: Evangelism

So, then as I started to look at and evaluate my symbols and I could see how Roy as a fisherman in real life, could be playing the role of me as a great and successful "<u>fisher of men</u>" (<u>evangelist</u>) for Christ.

<u>Here are my symbolic meanings:</u>

Roy = A Great Fisherman, Roy was a client of mine, I knew in real life. He worked on a fishing boat and he always caught large amounts of fish.

263

Kissing = Intimacy in flesh as well as intimacy in the Spirit.

Kissing meant this to me, because at the time of the dream my former pastor taught the singles in his church, the principle that when a man and a woman kissed it was like when God breathed into Adam; thus, imparting HIS Spirit into the natural man. So my pastor was trying to relay the point or belief that kissing is a spirit exchange or a spiritual intimacy as well as a natural intimacy.

Penis = Reproductive organ: In my mind, I simply associated a penis as a reproductive organ.

My Interpretation: Through this dream, God was encouraging and showing me that I really had a handle on reproducing (penis is a reproductive organ) in the kingdom and that I was really passionate and intimate, while releasing a spiritual impartation (kissing) concerning evangelizing the lost (Roy, symbolic of being a fisherman of men).

This was so true! At the time I was winning souls left and right into the kingdom of God. Evangelism was my main focus at work and I did it consistently, no matter the financial cost. So the dream was showing that I had embraced that fisherman (evangelical) calling on my life and this was a VERY encouraging night vision dream.

But, if I didn't understand symbolism, I could have "misinterpreted" the dream. And if, I had only taken the dream at face value, I would have missed this encouraging message through what the Holy Spirit was showing me in my spirit man through a dream.

Many Christians have had dreams that are similar in nature, and then "BIND UP" the dream in Jesus name because they believe it's from the devil. But, believe me this is NOT something that needed to be BOUND up in the name of Jesus! Get my drift?

Sex with T.D. Jakes

Recently, I interpreted a dream for a wonderful woman of God who dreamed she was in her bed having sex with T.D. Jakes. In the dream, she felt it was very enjoyable and she wondered how she got herself in this position.

When she woke up and thought about the dream she immediately repented and asked the Lord to forgive her for having this dream. But, a couple of days later, when she told me about the dream I told her that most likely the dream did not mean what she thought it meant. I then proceeded to explore the dream and I asked her, what is your impression of T.D. Jakes? She said, he is a very powerful and anointed preacher! And then me, (Vonda) already knowing her answer would be a big fat YES! I then said to her, is there any part of you that is a very anointed and powerful preacher? And she said YES, like him I too am a very anointed and powerful preacher!

See, at the time she had the dream she had just started a new online radio show and like T.D. Jakes she was operating under a powerful preaching anointing! This dream was only symbolic of how much she was "loving" and "enjoying" being intimate with the powerful preaching (T.D. Jakes) part of her!

Within the context of sin, sex can have many ungodly meanings. But, within a godly context when a man and a woman have sex it means they have come together in a committed union. Feelings are being gratified and they're expressing their love for one another or the two are becoming one and it is a deep expression of love towards the other person. In her dream T.D. Jakes was merely symbolic for a part of her and this dream was absolutely nothing that she needed to repent about! It was a reflection dream of the emotions she was having and expressing towards her powerful yet, new preaching role as a powerful minister of God!

Recently, a friend of mine called me about a bothersome dream she had.

Dream: Sex with my best friend
In the dream my best guy friend was having sex with
me and I did not like it. I was not attracted to him at
all and I felt like I was just being screwed!

I helped my friend with her dream and as we walked through her interpretation she came to realize that her best friend in the dream was merely symbolic of a new guy that she had befriended on the internet. This new guy in her life had a lot of the same spiritual qualities as her real best friend. So the dream was using her real life best friend to play the part of the new guy she had befriended several months prior to the dream. Even though she was not attracted to the new guy and was just into him as a brother in the Lord, she was really spending a lot of time with him on the internet. They would talk about God and share prophetic insights that God had given to each of them as well as things they were experiencing in God.

Well to make a long story short as I helped her to understand her dream she shared with me that the new, so called "best friend" that she was sharing her heart with was taking the prophetic revelations that God had given her and he went and started making YouTube videos about her revelations and was claiming them as his own prophetic insight! So, in real life she was getting "screwed over" by him!

As you can see this dream is a reflection of her feelings and like all reflection dreams this dream was giving her a symbolic picture and storyline of the recent events that she had previously experienced, with this so called new best friend! This dream is showing her a picture scene with symbols and actions, which paralleled the offensive behavior of her new best friend! This is not a dream that should be ignored. This was a very serious offense to God and because her new friend looked up to her and was only 2 years old in

Christ, I told her she needed to confronted him, so he could be given the chance to repent and ask for forgiveness. Because some things should not be overlooked!

Gabriel's Message: (Prophetic dream with a prophetic word)
Here is a dream that one dreamer wrote to me and even though, she was not sure she thought the devil might have given her this dream.

Hi Vonda,
I had a short dream less than a month ago and just kind of tried to forget about it, but then today it came back to my mind and I thought maybe I should find someone to interpret it. So, I thought I'd let you tell me what you think. First, I'd like to say that I don't know if this was a dream from God or if Satan is just trying to mess with me. I know I have a lot of growing in the Lord still to do and I'm new to all this. Anyway, here it goes.

In the dream I had taken my son Gabriel to the doctor for some sort of procedure. I knew in my head that it wasn't supposed to be a big ordeal, just an outpatient procedure and I don't remember exactly what it was for, but they were going to cut into his chest. The nurse handed me a razor and told me to shave a small area where the incision would be. As I started to gently shave a small area, images of his heart popped into my head and then I heard a voice say "Martyr." Then the dream ended. Thank you and God bless you! Laura

Here is the dream again with the symbolic meanings in parentheses.

In the dream I had taken my son Gabriel (<u>symbolic for the innocent part of her in Christ and also the name represents the angel who delivered messages</u>) to the doctor (<u>Jesus our great Physician</u>) for some sort of procedure. I knew in my head that it wasn't supposed to be a big ordeal, just an outpatient procedure and I don't remember exactly what it was for, but they were going to cut into his chest

267

(open heart surgery.) The nurse (Dr.'s helper, symbolic of the Holy Spirit) handed me a razor and told me to shave (prepare the flesh) a small area where the incision would be. As I started to gently shave a small area, images of his heart popped into my head (Gabriel's spirit message from Gods heart into her head) and then I heard a voice say "Martyr." ("One who makes great sacrifices or suffers much in order to further a belief, cause or principle; online resource, American Heritage Dictionary"). Then the dream ended.

My Interpretation: (Watch Video Interpretation on "Heart Hope")
http://www.youtube.com/user/godsgirltv

So, in the dream the Holy Spirit had Laura taking her son, which was symbolic of the new born Spirit part of her, to the Dr's. In real life a nurse aids the Dr.; so this is a parallel to how the Holy Spirit aids the work of Jesus by living on the inside of us. One of the names for the Holy Spirit is the Comforter or Helper. In the dream Laura was asked to help the nurse (Holy Spirit) to prepare the flesh (carnal man) so the open heart surgery could be done. The dream shows that God wanted Laura to circumcise her flesh and prepare her heart to receive the message that the Spirit of God was trying to tell her. The action of the dream shows that the "Martyr" message needed to get from the heart of God and into the head of Laura.

God was saying, Laura I need you to prepare your heart and receive what the Spirit of the Lord wants to relay to your head, mind and reason. The heart of God told her that she needed to be a martyr for Him. Meaning she needed to be willing to lay down some things in her life and make the sacrifices and suffer even to the point of death (killing the flesh) for the kingdom of God. I'm happy to say that Laura gladly received the message from the Holy Spirit and decided to heed His prophetic Word in her life. This was a prophetic message from the heart of God for her to receive into her heart, soul and mind and this was definitely a message that she did not need to miss!

268

Demons In The Closet: Reflection Dream (video Interpretation on YouTube

Below is a reflection dream, that to most Christians would appear to be a "demonic dream" and they would most likely wake up rebuking the devil and pleading the blood of Jesus, in a panic! Let me share the dream and then I will share the interpretation with you after you've read the dreamers situation and the dream.

Hello Vonda, I will try to be brief as I know you receive a lot of requests. I'm currently married to my husband and both of us are in our second marriage. We met in 2005 and were married the following year. I have two daughters 12 & 14 from my previous marriage and he has 2 sons; one biological son 17 and the other is his first wife's son 21 from a previous marriage. My husband has never told me exactly when he was saved; but I have been saved, since I was 19 (back-slidden after my separation from my first marriage). Neither of us has ever been in the ministry but I feel a calling, of sorts (I mean, we are ALL called but, I do feel the Lord wants to use me - I am just not sure for what). We both recently graduated with a Bible Diploma at Liberty University; I took the classes primarily out of curiosity and seeking God. Not knowing how, if at all, I would use the Diploma in the future. My husband has always professed to be a Christian and has gone to church and studied God's word but on two separate occasions, I have found out that my husband has been having sex with numerous MEN that he has been finding online. Both of the times I caught and confronted him, he has sworn that God has delivered him. I have had dreams throughout the years that I know have come from God. I do believe the Lord can redeem anyone and who am I to judge a heart? However, my Spirit has been in turmoil since the last occurrence in January of 2011 and I do not know whether to stay with him or not? The last dream I had was pretty short; I pray you will have a word for me.

I simply dreamt that I was in my house and there were demonic spirits in the closet that I didn't know how to get rid of, in the closet. So I was going to move out!

Does this dream mean the Lord wants me to leave? Bye, and Thank you!

Dreams that reveal demonic activity should always be evaluated and interpreted, within the context of the dreamer's life. This dream is a perfect example of how a person can dream **metaphorically**. Because this woman's husband was gay and living "**in the closet**," the dream is showing her a picture that's a reflection of her marital struggle by, showing dream pictures of the demons **in the closet**, of their home.

In this dream, the demons were not symbolic, but were literal representations of her husband's literal demonic spirits of sexual perversion that he had welcomed into his life. So, this dream is a direct result of her knowing that her husband was in the closet and that he was still trying to hide his homosexuality. Her dream shows that she does not know what to do to get these demons out of her house; so she wants to move out. In real life, she did want to move out, but her husband kept trying to convince her that divorcing him would be a sin. Everything, in this dream is an EXACT reflection of her personal struggles with her husband's perverted sexuality and sin.

So, her question to me was? Does this mean to say the Lord wants me to leave?

I shared with the dreamer that this dream leaves off with her having the **feelings** that she wants to move out! The dreams **story line** supports the fact that this dream is in reference to the demons in his life because in real life, he's the one that is "**in the closet**". So now that we have interpreted the dream and we can see that this is just a "Reflection dream" that parallels her real life drama; it's important to note that we cannot add or take away from the story line of this dream. Meaning, we can't say the dream shows her actually moving out, when it doesn't. And even if the dream did show her moving her things out we would seriously need to consider the possibility that she could be reflecting her very strong desire to want to move out and that this moving out scene could be in the dream, since her marriage has been perverted for quite some time. This dream shows no revelation, prophetic insight or additional message; so we need to measure the dreamer's real life dilemma and then do, act or respond based on what the word of God says, concerning divorce.

I hear some of you thinking to yourselves; doesn't God hate divorce? Yes, that is true and God does hate divorce, but he never said that we couldn't do it! And the truth of the matter is that, since this dream is an exact reflection of her life's TRUTH, then we know that she can rebuke those demons all she wants and get absolutely no results. Because her husband is the head of the home and his authority is superior to hers in this situation. The Lord will not override her husband's free will and she cannot override her husband's free will, when it comes to choosing homosexuality over righteousness, or any other sin for that matter. This man has been caught and confronted twice within a few years time span, so, his actions clearly show that he did not want to change! So, let's see when Jesus says it's permissible to divorce.

Matthew 18:8-9
Jesus replied, "Moses **permitted you to divorce** your wives **because your hearts were hard**. But it was not this way from the beginning. I tell you that anyone who divorces his wife, except for **marital unfaithfulness**, and marries another woman commits adultery." Paul says, in 1 Corinthians 5.9-13 "I have written you in my letter **not to associate with sexually immoral people not at all** meaning the people of this world who are immoral, or the greedy and swindlers or idolaters. In that case you would have to leave this world.

But now I am writing you that you must **not associate with anyone who calls himself a brother but is sexually immoral** or greedy, an idolater or a slanderer, a drunkard or a swindler. With such **a man do not even eat**. What business is it of mine to judge those outside the church? Are you not to judge those inside? God will judge those outside. "**Expel** the wicked man from among you."

So, when you have a reflection dream, after you have interpret it correctly, use the Word of God as your guide before you act or make any life decisions based on the on the interpretation of the dream and the truths that were mirrored, within its reflection. In this case the dreamer was not able to rightly divide the word for herself, so with the scriptural counsel of her pastoral leadership, me and the still small voice of the Holy Spirit within her; she has taken the proper steps to divorce her husband and now has a new and wonderful fresh start! Praise God for His tender mercies are new every morning.

So, not every dream that **appears** demonic is demonic, as you can see at first glance these dreams looked bad. However, once these seemingly demonic types of dreams were interpreted they both proved to contain very valuable messages from within the heart of God to encourage the dreamers'. So, as the old saying goes "never judge a book by its cover;" I say never take a dream at face value because there is usually more to it than meets the eye! So my friends, if this applies to you pleazzzzzzzzze **stop** binding up every dream you've had, just because you don't know how to read the symbols! Just because you can't read the dream doesn't mean God's not trying to speak through it. So, take some time and meditate on your dream and see, if the Holy Spirit could possibly be trying to speak to you!

Sexual: Reflection Dream (Background Information)
Now, I will give you an example of how a person who is saved, sanctified, Holy Ghost filled and sold out for Jesus, can have a sexual reflection dream; at times these dreams can occur because of the enemy's temptations, inward struggles or personal desires concerning one's daily circumstances and spiritual battles. Jesus was tempted in the wilderness, so we know that temptations will come and that it is not a sin to be tempted but, it is a sin to give into that temptation. So, the important thing to remember here is when you have a dream like this, your response to the dream is what is important! Below, I will share one of my personal dream experiences.

I Vonda, had been loving and living holy in the Lord for about ten years and while working on my job I started to struggle with a monthly "he's the wrong guy" temptation. Please let me explain, I like many people, all my life have wanted to be loved and married so bad. And as a holy, sanctified, and single woman in the Lord I struggled with a specific temptation for thirteen long years. During this time in my life I was starving for love and affection because I had come out of an emotionally abusive relationship and in all my time loving the Lord, I had seen no glimpse of anyone that even remotely looked like the godly husband I so deeply desired. I always joked, and reasoned within my own heart as I thought about how when Adam and Eve were in the garden they had each other. And besides the forbidden tree they at least had other trees to eat from to satisfy their flesh! Well unlike them my flesh was starving and I had not even one single "love tree" to eat from.

So, for years there was this one guy, who I was very attracted to and he was attracted to me. In my heart I would have loved to have been with him and I really got the impression that he would have loved to have been with me. I really liked this guy and I thought he was great husband material and he was exactly my type; except for one small detail. He wasn't saved! In my heart I desired him so bad and because of my feelings, I had to warfare against these thoughts and desires weekly. I did not want to sin against God in my heart or in the natural, because based on God's guidelines in His Word I knew that he was not the one for me. However, this did not change the fact that he was absolutely "*fine as wine in the summertime*". Because of my work based relationship with him we were friends for over ten years, as I regularly continued to cut his locks. Because of this I was sexually and spiritually tested with every month that passed by. This torture went on for thirteen very long years and all because he needed a stupid haircut and because I needed the stupid income! I'm telling you the absolute truth, when I say that I did everything within my power and God's power to fight against it and endure this temptation! How did I do this you ask?

Well, for one I never gave in and said yes to him and secondly, I quoted and stood on the Word of God for years and years. And during those years, when my heart was struggling against my flesh, I regularly asked for God to forgive me for the feelings and desires I had in my flesh and heart concerning this man. I really believed that I could have married him if, I wanted to settle for the Ishmael and not wait for the Isaac, but I really did want to please God. And so, I chose to wait for God's blessing. I never let this man know my intense struggles concerning him, but I kept it to myself. I did this so the enemy would not be able to use this man against me more in this specific temptation causing this person to pursue me harder. I didn't want this guy to use the information of knowing my weakness to his advantage and turn up the heat! So, I said all that to say this, during this time I had the following dream.

> I dreamt that the lights were low and he and I were naked and in the shower together; it was very romantic as we passionately kissed and enjoyed each other.

My Interpretation: This dream was showing me a picture of the sexual, romantic, and passionate feelings I had for him, and how I truly was attracted and desired to make out with

274

him in my real life. In my dream I was actually experiencing his love and I was showing him my love in return. We were being intimate sexually and sexually loving on each other. This was exactly, how I felt for him in real life, so there is nothing symbolic about this dream!

So even though, in real life I never **actually** gave into the desires of my flesh and sinned with this guy, this dream was a mirroring or reflection of what my heart and flesh truly desired; thus making it a sin. Then to top it all off, in real life after many years this dude gets married and my trial became even worse. Because, there I was left struggling with all of these emotions and feelings, after he had met someone and married; thus turning my feelings from a fornication struggle into adultery struggle.

Matthew 5:27-28
You have heard that it was said, "Do not commit adultery. But I tell you that anyone who looks at a woman lustfully has already committed adultery with her in his heart."

Mark 9:47
And if your eye causes you to sin, pluck it out. It is better for you to enter the kingdom of God with one eye than to have two eyes and be thrown into hell.

So, as you can see, it is possible to have a sexual reflection dream that reflects the sinful desires of your mind, heart, soul and flesh even though you're being obedient and love God with all your heart! During those days of my intense struggle as a Christian, it was my job to stay before the Lord and warfare, while saying no to the temptations of this world. Because this man was not saved the enemy was able to use him and his fleshly nature to consistently tempt me; however, God did not allow me to go through any more then I could possibly bear! As Christians it's our job to guard our own hearts through the power of God's Word and the blood of Jesus. I thank God that His strength is made perfect in my weakness and that He is my Righteousness during the times, when I try to do what is right but still miss the mark because of my flesh. God really helped me to stand faithful to my covenant with Him. So, this is an example of how the enemy through life's circumstances can show up in our dreams, while we sleep, but yet still be a reflection dream.

In Leviticus 15:16 and Deuteronomy 23:10 please know that these scriptures appear to hold the man responsible, if not for dreaming, but for the character of the dream. So, as first Peter 5:8 says, "be sober, be vigilant; because your adversary the devil walks about like a roaring lion, seeking whom he may devour." So, my friends "above all else, guard your heart, for it is the wellspring of life." Proverbs 4:23

Sexual Demonic Encounters

There have been well documented, Christian and non Christian accounts of people who have been sexually attacked by demonic spirits in their sleep. However, it is my opinion that some people can and do invite these demons into their bedroom based on the ungodly lifestyle they choose to live. Some time ago, I remember seeing and hearing about Anna Nicole Smith as she delightfully and publicly shared "**A ghost would crawl up my leg and have sex with me.**" It was my observation, while she was saying this that she seemed to enjoy her sexual encounters with her so called love ghost. Let's explore what the Bible says about demons and sex.

Genesis 6:4 NLT

In those days, and for some time after, giant Nephilites lived on the earth, for whenever the sons of God had **intercourse with women**; they gave birth to children who became the heroes and famous warriors of ancient times.

Numbers 13:33

"We saw the Nephilim there (**the descendants of Anak come from the Nephilim**). We seemed like grasshoppers in our own eyes, and we looked the same to them."

276

The Word of God shares in Numbers 13:33 that the Nephilim were a particular race of Giants in the Old Testament and Genesis 6:4 says they had intercourse with the women of the earth. Unger's bible dictionary says that the Nephilim, "were considered by many, giant demigods, the unnatural off spring of the "daughters of men" (mortal women) in cohabitation with the sons of God (angels) This was an unnatural union that violated created orders of being and was so abnormal that it necessitated the world-wide judgment of the Flood.

Today, RandomHistory.com defines evil spirits that sexually attack people in their sleep as; "female demons known as succubi (sub; under cubare; to lie) and their male counterparts incubi (to lie upon, related to "incubate") are spirits that sexually molest human dreamers for evil purposes."

Personally, I have heard **many** stories, concerning how these evil spirits try to approach some people. Often these spirits will take on the familiar form (familiar spirits), or mimic sexual overtures of a person that the "<u>sleeping individual</u>" knows or loves.

For example, while the person is sleeping these spirits will act or trick the victim into thinking that it is their husband, wife, boyfriend or girlfriend that is the one who is gratifying them in their sleeping state; but soon wake up and turn over in bed only to find out that their spouse is dead asleep or that there's **no one** in the bed with them. It's at that point that the sleeping individual will get alarmed and discover that it was a spiritual attack and not a natural incident. Then there are times when the sleeping person does not care but allows the evils spirit to bring them much pleasure and chooses to embrace this evil in their life.

Regardless, of the Christian or non Christian victim it's obvious that this still happens in the world today. However, if you're a Christian who lives a holy life, please know that you **do not** have to tolerate these sexual attacks or any other type of attacks in your sleep state. Know that you do have the authority to kick theses spirits out of your life through the blood of Jesus, His Word and your covenant with Him. His Word is your only weapon! For the word of God says, **and they were casting out many demons and were anointing with oil many sick people and healing them.** (Mark 6:13 NASB)

I'm sorry to say, if you're a non believer you **do not** have any authority to use the name of Christ Jesus. However, it is **NOT** His will for you to be attacked or oppressed in any way shape or form. God, longs for you to come into relationship with Him and to help you in all areas of your life. So, if you would like to have a relationship with Jesus and desire for Him to save you from your sins as well as the devil's attacks. Please know that, if you choose Him as your Savior you will then have the right to use His authority and many other wonderful benefits that come with being in relationship with Him. Jesus Christ as your savior is the only weapon that will make the devil and his demons let you go! It is by the blood of Christ that Christians have the power in and through His name to accomplish these things. So, please, if you don't know Christ, but would like to know Him, call on Him and He will rescue you from the "Evil One" that continually hurts you. When you put your trust in Christ Jesus, it's through your new found relationship with Him that you will discover His wonderful grace concerning any struggle in your life. He is the victor over all evil!

Troubling Dreams

Job 7:11-16 NLT

"Therefore I will not keep silent; I will speak out in the anguish of my spirit, I will complain in <u>the bitterness of my soul</u>. Am I the sea, or the monster of the deep, that you put me under guard? When I think my bed will comfort me and my couch will ease my complaint, even then <u>you frighten me with dreams and terrify me with visions,</u> so that I prefer strangling and death, rather than this body of mine. I despise my life; I would not live forever. Let me alone; my days have no meaning.

Most Christians believe when they have a bad or troubling dream that it's from the devil and not of God, so they rebuke the dream and rebuke it until their rebuker is worn out! The belief that all bad dreams come from the devil is a fallacy within the body of Christ and it's my experience and opinion that there are two reasons a person can have bad or troubling dreams. One reason is because we may have led troubled lives in the past by the things we have experienced and over time we have suppressed the memories from our past. Things like emotional abuse, brokenness, disappointments, sadness, rejection, fear, anxiety, rape, molestation, addictions, anger, stress, poverty, tragedy or trauma; and over time since, we have never been healed from the past hurts these feelings have been suppressed. And as a result, many years later the wounded person is still experiencing old or bad memories pertaining to their sufferings, while they re-live their brokenness through their night dreams. But, please believe me when I tell you that the devil did not give you these dreams, but these dreams are "Reflection Dreams" that are indeed, terrible reflections of your previous bad, troubling, or evil experiences. Hence, the dream is mimicking your tragic past events in a current dream picture, while using specific and disturbing personal symbols, with identical feelings, and a similar horrific storyline that parallels the past traumas of your life. For a perfect case and point let me share Job's story with you.

279

Job 1:1-22 (NIV)

In the land of Uz there lived a man whose name was Job. This man was blameless and upright; he feared God and shunned evil. He had seven sons and three daughters and he owned seven thousand sheep, three thousand camels, five hundred yoke of oxen and five hundred donkeys, and had a large number of servants. He was the greatest man among all the people of the East. His sons used to take turns holding feasts in their homes, and they would invite their three sisters to eat and drink with them. One day the angels came to present themselves before the LORD, and Satan also came with them. The LORD said to Satan, "Where have you come from?" Satan answered the LORD, "From roaming through the earth and going back and forth in it." Then the LORD said to Satan, "Have you considered my servant Job? There is no one on earth like him; he is blameless and upright, a man who fears God and shuns evil." "Does Job fear God for nothing?" Satan replied. "Have you not put a hedge around him and his household and everything he has? You have blessed the work of his hands, so that his flocks and herds are spread throughout the land. But stretch out your hand and strike everything he has, and he will surely curse you to your face." **The LORD said to Satan, "Very well, then, everything he has is in your hands, but on the man himself do not lay a finger."** Then Satan went out from the presence of the LORD. One day when Job's sons and daughters were feasting and drinking wine at the oldest brother's house, a messenger came to Job and said, "The oxen were plowing and the donkeys were grazing nearby, **and the Sabeans attacked and carried them off. They put the servants to the sword,** and I am the only one who has escaped to tell you!" While he was still speaking, another messenger came and said, "**The fire of God fell from the sky and burned up the sheep and the servants,** and I am the only one who has escaped to tell you!" While he was still speaking, yet another messenger came and said, "Your sons and daughters were feasting and drinking wine at the oldest brother's house, **when suddenly a mighty wind swept in** from the desert and struck the four corners of the house. It collapsed on them and they are dead, and I am the only one who has escaped to tell you!" At this, Job got up and tore his robe and shaved his head. Then he fell to the ground in worship and said: "Naked I came from my mother's womb, and naked I will depart. The LORD gave and the LORD has taken away; may the name of the LORD be praised." In all this, Job did not sin by charging God with wrongdoing.

Most Christians are familiar with Job's story, but if you are not familiar with his story please read the whole book of Job so you can better identify with his feelings concerning this time in his life; as we can see, Job is a prime example of someone who suffered much in his life. It's no secret that Jobs terrible suffering was by the hand of **satan** and that his life had taken a turn for the worst as he experienced great devastation, through his emotional pain. It's my belief that his **scary and terrifying** dreams were a direct result from the **fear or dread** of his pain (Job 9:28 NASB) and bitterness within his soul, by the evil trauma caused to him by the enemy.

Job was a righteous man but, like him we at times experience intense pain, dread, and bitterness in our souls because of some type of suffering we have experienced through the hand of the enemy or because of our own self inflections. But, as we read the scripture below we can clearly see, Job **accuses God** of giving him these dreams.

Job 7:11-16 (NLT)

"Therefore I will not keep silent; I will **speak** out in the **anguish of my spirit**, I will complain in the **bitterness** of my **soul**. Am I the sea, or the monster of the deep, that you put me under guard? When I think my bed will comfort me and my couch will ease my complaint, even then **you frighten me with dreams and terrify me with visions**, so that I prefer strangling and death, rather than this body of mine. I despise my life; I would not live forever. Let me alone; my days have no meaning."

281

Do you see it? Job complains and he accuses God of giving him the dreams. But, the bottom line is that even though he is accusing God here, when it's all said and done, in Job 40:1, God responds to Jobs complaints. And then in chapter 42, Job says, "I take back everything I said, and I sit in dust and ashes to show my repentance." (Job 42:6 NLT) So, as we can see, Job willfully and humbly admits that he was wrong and that he didn't know what he was talking about!

Within the all of the chapters of Jobs complaining he never complained about having bad dreams until after he was suffering by the hand of Satan; thus supporting my point and case that emotional trauma in a person's life can cause them to have scary, terrible and terrifying dreams. In Matthew 12:34 Jesus said to the Pharisees; Brood of vipers! How can you, being evil, speak good things? For out of the abundance of the heart the mouth speaks, and Daniel 2:30 says, that God spoke to Nebuchadnezzar in a dream so he would know the thoughts of his heart. So, Job was speaking out of the sorrow, fear, dread and bitterness that were within his own heart and soul; hence, dreaming his bad, terrible or terrifying dreams because of the thoughts of his heart.

Like Job, bad dreams can occur in your life because of the horrific devastation that your soul has suffered in the past or in the present circumstances of your life. The Bible says that God restored Job and he was more blessed in the latter years then in his former years. So, if you're a Christian, please know beyond a shadow of a doubt that you're merciful, gracious, kind, gentle, good and loving God desires to restore you too! And for the non-Christian, God longs for you to accept His free gift of salvation so you can experience the fullness of His saving grace through the Lord Jesus Christ, which is the only way and hope for the restoration of your soul! (For salvation see chapter 1)

For the Word of God says, Psalms 23:1-6 (NKJV)

A Psalm of David. The LORD is my shepherd; I shall not want. He makes me to lie down in green pastures; He leads me beside the still waters. He **restores my soul**; He leads me in the paths of righteousness For His name's sake. Yea, though I walk through the valley of the shadow of death, I will fear no evil; For You are with me; Your rod and Your staff, they **comfort me**. You prepare a table before me in the presence of my enemies; You anoint my head with oil; My cup runs over. Surely goodness and mercy shall follow me All the days of my life; And I will dwell in the house of the Lord Forever.

Psalms 41:3 says, "The LORD nurses them when they are sick and **restores** them to **health**." (NLT)

Job 33:26 says, "He shall pray to God, and He will delight in him, He shall see His face with joy, For He **restores** to man His **righteousness**." (NKJV)

Jesus said in Luke 4:18-19 (NKJV)

"The Spirit of the LORD is upon Me, Because He has anointed Me To preach the gospel to the poor; He has sent Me to heal the brokenhearted, To proclaim liberty to the captives And recover of sight to the blind, To set at liberty those who are oppressed; To proclaim the acceptable year of the LORD."

Brothers and sisters, if your soul is broken, battered, and abused and you're having bad dreams, please take refuge in these scriptures and stand in faith for Christ to heal you and don't give up until your complete healing manifests, by the power of the Holy Spirit! It's not Gods will for you to be broken, but Jesus came to heal the broken hearted and to set the captives free. So be wise and "watch over your heart with all diligence, For from it flow the springs of life." (Proverbs 4:23 NASB)

283

And finally, the second reason Christians can have a bad or troubling dream, is because the Lord Himself, has given you a dream, which causes you to be troubled, afraid, terrified or causes you great suffering. Even though, this is contrary to popular opinion, it's still the truth! However, with the exception of Pilate's wife, usually these types of dreams are direct a result of the Holy Spirits **prophetic revelation,** concerning the occurrences in the dream, but nevertheless they do happen and here are some scriptures that highlight this principle.

Genesis 41:8 (NKJV)
Now it came to pass in the morning that his **spirit was troubled,** and he sent and called for all the magicians of Egypt and all its wise men. And Pharaoh told them his dreams, but there was no one who could interpret them for Pharaoh.

Daniel 2:3 (NLT)
He said, "I have had a dream that deeply **troubles me,** and I must know what it means."

"I saw a dream which made me **afraid,** and the thoughts on my bed and the visions of my head **troubled** me." (Daniel 4:5 NKJV)

In the first year of Belshazzar king of Babylon, Daniel had a **dream** and visions of his head while on his bed. Then he wrote down the dream, telling the main facts.(Daniel 7:1 NKJV)

"I, Daniel, was grieved in my spirit within my body, and the visions of my head **troubled** me." (Daniel 7:15)

"That was the end of the vision. I, Daniel, was **terrified** by my thoughts and my face was pale with fear, but I kept these things to myself." (Daniel 7:28 NLT)

284

Matt 27:19 (NASB)

While he was sitting on the judgment seat, his wife sent him *a message,* saying, "Have nothing to do with that righteous Man; for last night I **suffered** greatly in a **dream** because of Him."

Matt 27:19 (NLT)

Just then, as Pilate was sitting on the judgment seat, his wife sent him this message: "Leave that innocent man alone. I **suffered** through a **terrible nightmare** about him last night."

So, concerning Job, please take in to consideration that most likely he was experiencing terrible reflection dreams of the terrible attacks, from Satan, in his life; but, the scriptures also, show that Daniel and others did claim to receive very troubling prophetic dreams from God. So, for a balanced view please note that troubling dreams can come from two sources; the soul and God. Therefore, please take both sources into account, if you find yourself experiencing a troubling dream. Please carefully consider the scriptures, my experience and the personal insights that I have shared, within the pages of this book, as you take the time to evaluate your dream; when and if your dream is evaluated properly you will then have a wonderful chance of receiving a meaningful and accurate interpretation! God bless you!

Chapter 15
Closing thoughts

Just as God has made and fulfilled wonderful promises to me, concerning several very significant areas of my life; please know that you too, can hear from the Lord in your dreams and live a spirit lead life of purpose, while walking into the exciting and abundant promises of God! If, you were an unbeliever, I pray this book brought you into a deep desire to know Christ as well as a desire to hear from the sovereign God of all creation. And if you're a Christian who knew the importance of dreams, but never fully knew how to interpret your dream, I pray this book as helped you and brought you into a deeper level of interpreting your dreams. If you're a Christian who knows a lot about dream interpretation, but has managed to glean some valuable insights from this book and the dream stories I've shared; then I'm thrilled that the information on these pages were able to help enlighten you further, within the realm of dream interpretation. My prayer is, no matter who you are or where you're at in your life, that God was glorified in this book and that you, truly are inspired and thirsty to hear what God has to say to you, in your dreams. So, as you follow the steps in this book, I know it will help you to gain a better understanding of how to interpret your dreams so God can reveal His promises to you concerning the known dreams as well as the unspoken secret dream desires of your heart for your life!

"Dream Quest" was only the equipping, but now you have to do the practice, because practice makes perfect! So, remember friends, just as diamonds are not formed overnight and usually are not found on the surface, so it is with obtaining the revelation within your dreams. Before you can obtain the jewels or treasures of what God is trying to say to you in your dreams, it will take some digging, time, meditation, patience, much practice and pain staking effort to correctly develop your dream interpretation skills. But, with the anointing of the Holy Spirit, you too can understand your dreams and of this you can be sure! So, let's not lose heart in doing good, for in due time we will reap if we do not grow weary. (Galatians 6:9) So, just stick with it because God and the revelations He wants to share with you are worth it! Below, I would be honored, if you would pray this short prayer over your life!

Dear Heavenly Father, I come to you and ask you that you anoint and enable every child of God to successfully apply the guidelines, within this book into their life. I pray that you would rise up within them and come upon them and quicken their minds to be able to remember these truths and quicken their hearts into understanding the dreams, feelings, symbols, action, and storyline with any prophetic word from you. We thank you for your word says that we can do all things through Christ Jesus who strengthens us! In Jesus name, amen.

Thank you for purchasing and reading "**Dream Quest: Dream Interpretation 8 Easy Steps**"; I pray it has been a blessing to you. <u>P.S.</u> If you purchased Dream Quest from www.Amazon.com would you please leave a review on their site.

<u>Contact Information:</u> For information concerning dream interpretation seminars conducted in your church or for in depth dream interpretation teaching courses in your bible college, contact Vonda Brewer at <u>hearthopetv@yahoo.com</u> and enter the phrase "Dream Teaching Inquiries," in the subject line. Finally, my **Dream Quest Online Webinar** course is for all the die hard dreamers who desire further teaching and personal aid in application through one on one personal Skype coaching from me. In addition, students will develop their own symbolic dictionary using my newly created Dream Quest workbook. For enrollment information, please e-mail me at <u>dreamquestonline@yahoo.com</u>

"Heart Hope" Christian prophetic videos can be watched at:
www.youtube.com/user/godsgirltv
"In Your Dreams" Christian dream interpretation radio shows can be listened to online at: www.blogtalkradio.com/gods-girl

Made in the USA
Lexington, KY
25 May 2016